pa

Regulating International Business

Regulating International Business

Beyond Liberalization

Edited by

Sol Picciotto
Professor of Law
Director of the Programme in International Law
and International Relations
Lancaster University

and

Ruth Mayne
Policy Adviser
Oxfam GB

 in association with

First published in Great Britain 1999 by
MACMILLAN PRESS LTD
Houndmills, Basingstoke, Hampshire RG21 6XS and London
Companies and representatives throughout the world

A catalogue record for this book is available from the British Library.

ISBN 0–333–77677–1 hardcover
ISBN 0–333–77678–X paperback

First published in the United States of America 1999 by
ST. MARTIN'S PRESS, INC.,
Scholarly and Reference Division,
175 Fifth Avenue, New York, N.Y. 10010

ISBN 0–312–22587–3

Library of Congress Cataloging-in-Publication Data
Regulating international business : beyond liberalization / edited by
Sol Picciotto and Ruth Mayne.
p.   cm.
Includes bibliographical references and index.
ISBN 0–312–22587–3
1. Trade regulation.   2. International business enterprises—Law
and legislation—United States.   3. Investments, Foreign—Law and
legislation.   4. Sustainable development—Law and legislation.
I. Picciotto, Sol.   II. Mayne, Ruth.
K3840.R435   1999
341.7'53—dc21   99–15309
                                                                      CIP

This book is printed on paper suitable for recycling and made from fully managed and
sustained forest sources.

10   9   8   7   6   5   4   3   2   1
08   07   06   05   04   03   02   01   00   99

Printed and bound in Great Britain by Antony Rowe Ltd, Chippenham, Wiltshire

Contents

---

*Includes as appendix: Sainsbury's Code of Practice for Socially Responsible Trading.

Preface

This book arose from the considerable amount of research and advocacy work in the debate stimulated by the proposed Multilateral Agreement on Investment (MAI). A number of academics and NGO staff members based in the UK formed the International Business Regulation Forum, and organized a seminar in London in March 1998, sponsored by Oxfam GB. Although the immediate focus was the MAI, the aim was to broaden the agenda to address wider concerns which should be dealt with in a multilateral framework for investment.

To many of its critics, the suspension of negotiations on the MAI in April 1998, and their virtual abandonment by the OECD in October 1998, was no surprise. The growing financial and economic crises, which had begun in Asia, reinforced the view that the MAI was one of the dying gasps of the laissez-faire neo-liberal agenda which had dominated the 1980s. The sweeping liberalization obligations envisaged in the MAI, covering every type of short-term and speculative transaction as well as longer-term direct investment, aimed to 'discipline' or restrict national state regulation, thus weakening state capacity. Its strong rights for investors, backed by binding arbitration, were not balanced by any responsibilities.

Increased global economic integration and interdependence needs to be underpinned by a strengthened international regulatory framework. Measures are needed to curb the excessive volatility of short-term capital flows, and while international direct investment by TNCs has been the motor of growth in some countries, it is not always beneficial and should not go unregulated. Indeed, TNCs themselves have helped create and foster the system of offshore centres and tax havens which has contributed so much to financial volatility, tax evasion and money laundering. A broader framework is needed, which should aim to strengthen international cooperative arrangements to combat avoidance and evasion of tax as well as other regulations. It should put sustainable development at its heart, should be bottom-up and aimed at building the regulatory capacity of governments, and create responsibilities as well as rights for investors and firms. The key principles of such a framework should be transparency and other mechanisms to enhance the accountability of business to citizens, especially the weak and disadvantaged. As the debate on investment regulation has shifted away from the OECD and to wider forums, these issues should come to the fore. This book aims to contribute to that debate.

vii

Many of the chapters in this book are based on papers given at the seminar in March 1998. We thank the speakers, as well as the authors of additional contributions, who responded to the tight deadlines required. Special thanks for organizational help with the seminar go to Michael Anderson, Julio Faundez, Peter Muchlinksi and Jake Werksman, as well as Anni Long and Dianna Melrose at Oxfam GB. We are also grateful to members of other NGOs involved in the continuing discussion of these issues, in particular Chee Yoke Ling and Martin Khor of Third World Network, Nick Mabey of the World Wide Fund for Nature, Barry Coates and Jessica Woodroffe of the World Development Movement, Jayanti Durai of Consumers International, Hilary Coulby, then of the Catholic Institute for International Relations, and Ronnie Hall and Joy Hyvarinen of Friends of the Earth. We also thank the government officials and other policy makers who participated in the dialogue on the MAI.

RUTH MAYNE
SOL PICCIOTTO

Notes on Contributors

Dominic Ayine is a graduate of the Universities of Legon in Ghana and Michigan at Ann Arbor; he has worked as an intern with FIELD (the Foundation for International Environmental Law and Development).

V. N. Balasubramanyam is Professor of Development Economics at Lancaster University; his publications include *The Economy of India*, *International Transfer of Technology to India*, and *Multinationals and the Third World*.

Dr Petrina Fridd is Project Manager for Socially Responsible Sourcing at Sainsbury plc, where she has worked since 1989.

Dr Stephany Griffith-Jones is a Fellow of the Institute of Development Studies, Sussex University; she has written widely on international finance and advised many governments and international organizations; her latest book *Global Capital Flows: Should They Be Regulated?* was published by Macmillan.

Bob Hepple, QC, is Master of Clare College, Cambridge, and Professor of Law, University of Cambridge; he is also a specialist and adviser to international organizations on labour law.

Neil Kearney is General Secretary of the Brussels-based International Textile, Garment and Leather-Workers' Federation, the main aim of which is elimination of exploitation, including child labour, in this sector.

Jenny Kimmis is Research Assistant at the Institute of Development Studies, Sussex University.

Dr Nick Mabey is Head of Economic Policy at the World Wide Fund for Nature (UK), covering investment and development issues, the economics of climate change, and economics and the environment.

Ruth Mayne is Policy Adviser in the Trade, Investments and Livelihoods Unit at Oxfam GB.

Peter Muchlinski is the Draper's Professor of Law at Queen Mary and Westfield College, University of London; he is the author of *Multinational Enterprises and the Law*, and a consultant to UNCTAD on investment issues.

Dr Robert O'Brien is an Associate Professor in the Department of Political Science and member of the Institute on Globalization and the Human Condition, McMaster University, Canada. He is the author of *Subsidy Regulation and State Transformation*.

Sol Picciotto is Professor of Law at Lancaster University, has taught at universities in Dar es Salaam and Warwick, and is the author of *International Business Taxation*.

Pedro Roffe is a staff member of UNCTAD and inter-regional adviser on its programme on a Possible Multilateral Framework for Investment (PMFI).

Jessica Sainsbury is Project Assistant for Socially Responsible Sourcing at Sainsbury plc, and author of *The New Inequality: Gender Relations in Thailand and the Philippines,* published by CIIR.

Dr Lawrence Tshuma is a Programme Legal Counsel at the International Development Law Institute in Rome, and has an LL M from the University of London and a PhD from Warwick University.

Jacob Werksman is Managing Director and Senior Lawyer at FIELD (the Foundation for International Environmental Law and Development), and has provided legal advice to WWF-International on the environmental implications of the MAI.

List of Abbreviations

APEC = Asia-Pacific Economic Coordination
BIAC = Business and Industry Advisory Council (of the OECD)
BIT = bilateral investment agreement
EU = European Union
FDI = foreign direct investment
GATT = General Agreement on Tariffs and Trade
GATS = General Agreement on Trade in Services
ICC = International Chamber of Commerce
ICSID = International Centre for the Settlement of Investment Disputes
IGO = international governmental organization
ILO = International Labour Organization
IMF = International Monetary Fund
INGO = international non-governmental organization
IOSCO = International Organization of Securities Commissions
LDC = less developed country
MAI = Multilateral Agreement on Investment
MERCOSUR = Mercado Commun del Sur
MOU = memorandum of understanding
NAFTA = North American Free Trade Area
NGO = non-governmental organization
OECD = Organization for Economic Cooperation and Development
TNC = transnational corporation
TRIMS = agreement on Trade-Related Investment Measures
TRIPS = agreement on Trade-Related Intellectual Property Rights
TUAC = Trade Union Advisory Council (of the OECD)
UNCTAD = United Nations Conference on Trade and Development
WTO = World Trade Organization

1 Introduction: What Rules for the World Economy?

Sol Picciotto

This book is a contribution to the debate about one of the most important public issues at the turn of the millennium: the institutions and rules which are to govern the world economy. This impinges directly on the kinds of livelihoods, welfare systems, social protections, goods and services, culture and environment which people all over the world might enjoy. Our focus is the regulation of international business and international investment flows, which has become the subject of increasing public debate and concern in recent years. This book explores positive new regulatory approaches aimed at poverty reduction and sustainable development.

Debate about the scope, form and content of such regulation revived during the 1990s, with the increasing awareness of the pace and impact of globalization. This culminated in the world-wide campaigns connected with the proposed Multilateral Agreement on Investment (MAI), which gathered momentum in 1997–8. Public concerns about the damaging effects of economic liberalization were confirmed by the global economic chain-reactions sparked off initially by the financial crises which began in Asia in July 1997. It has become evident that new thinking is needed if the devastating effects of the new globalism are to be tamed within an adequate framework of global governance.

INTERNATIONAL INTEGRATION: NEGATIVE OR POSITIVE?

The past two decades have seen a progressive removal of restrictions on the international flows of money and goods. Currencies have become convertible, and investors and speculators have become able to switch funds around the world at a moment's notice. Firms, especially the giant TNCs, have found it increasingly tempting to locate production facilities wherever they can find the most profitable conditions. Long-term investment still flows mainly between developed countries, and when it ventures elsewhere expects to be provided with skilled labour, a good infrastructure and a large market, but for many firms in many industries factors such as tax breaks, labour that is low-paid relative to its productivity, and poor protection of health, safety or the environment play a significant part. On the other hand, for most people freedom of movement in search of a better life or work has become more tightly controlled (Phizacklea, 1997). So if contemporary globalization has created stronger and more complex international linkages, its benefits have been very uneven. A bond-trader in New York, a coffee-grower in Uganda, a Bangalore software programmer, and an outworker stitching clothes on piece-work rates in Leicester or Bataan are all linked in very different ways to the rapid and unpredictable flows of the world economy. Not only are their gains and losses disparate, but perhaps more importantly, their power to control and cope with the risks of these flows is very different.

In many ways, the opening of markets and the greater international mobility of factors of production can bring opportunities and advantages. Consumers in developed countries benefit from being able to buy exotic produce or low-cost manufactured goods, just as workers in developing countries gain from the employment such trade generates. However, it is a dangerous myth to suppose that unalloyed benefits can come from free or unregulated world markets. This idea became prevalent with the laissez-faire neo-liberalism of the 1980s, which argued for the removal of state 'intervention' and the unleashing of untrammelled market forces as the key to economic growth and prosperity. Certainly, bureaucracies are often inefficient, and under-investment and other factors led to the deterioration of public-sector services, paving the way for privatization in many countries. However, theories which assume the efficiency of markets, and seek to confine the role of the state or the public sphere to remedying 'market failure', greatly underestimate the importance of normative standards and regulation in establishing the trust and confidence necessary to ensure that production and exchange can operate smoothly and to the benefit of society as a whole.

Liberalization and Regulation

The recent processes of globalization have been dominated by liberalization, or the removal of impediments to competition, both border barriers such as tariffs and exchange controls, as well as internal restrictions, such as directed credit and preferential purchasing. In many ways this has entailed deregulation, especially the reduction of state ownership (privatization) and of structural controls (such as distinctions between banks and other types of financial intermediaries). However, there has also been a significant counter-trend towards re-regulation, often as an international process, in the form of more elaborate legal frameworks for business.

The opening up of markets to competition, and of societies to outside influences, means that local standards, norms and regulatory arrangements are often challenged or undermined. Groups cemented by traditional customary practices come under pressure from outsiders, whether they are closed financial communities such as the City of London invaded by foreign banks, forest peoples in Sarawak disrupted by logging companies, or *avocats* in Paris threatened by Wall Street business lawyers. In such cases the impact of external economic forces is mediated by changes in regulation, although often only following a crisis or conflict. Thus, the redefinition of the City of London as a global financial centre entailed a series of regulatory reforms, initially sparked off when an influx of credit mainly through foreign bank branches triggered the secondary bank crisis of 1974 (Moran, 1984, 1991), a pattern very similar to that of the Asian financial crisis of 1997. The activities of foreign logging companies in Sarawak have been facilitated by legislative amendments made by the state government, making it harder for native peoples to maintain their customary land rights (WRM-FM, 1998: 26). The penetration of American-style business law practices in many countries around the world, disturbing traditional legal cultures, has been accommodated by changes to professional practice rules (Dezalay, 1992; Garapon, 1995).

Thus, both the form and content of regulation are themselves an instrument of economic competition. In all societies formal rules enacted by the state influence social behaviour only indirectly, filtered through layers of formal and informal social institutions, and normative patterns and practices. Ordinary people are primarily influenced by the generally accepted standards of social behaviour prevalent in their own communities. Formal state law applies generally and compulsorily to everyone, but it operates by validating some social practices and delegitimizing others, empowering some people and disempowering others. Law attempts to mediate and accommodate social conflicts, by establishing generally applicable principles, often couched in universal terms (equality, freedom, reasonableness, and so on). These may remain hollow aspirations, and in practice may reinforce the economically powerful, if they are not given concrete content and backed by effective compliance mechanisms. Enforcement depends not only on legal procedures, access to which also often favours those with greater economic and social resources, but also on broader social factors, which create the cultural climate in which the abstract principles of the law become translated into the concrete norms and understandings which actually guide people's conduct. For example, laws against bribery operate very differently in different countries; a range of political, commercial and social factors will influence whether such a law is interpreted to prohibit, for example, 'grease payments', commission payments to middlemen, or favours by politicians in exchange for campaign contributions.

In fact everywhere, and above all in advanced capitalist countries, economic activities have become regulated in increasingly complex ways. General laws and other regulations cover everything from corporate governance, finance and competition, to employment terms, health and safety at work, and environmental and consumer protection. More specific regulatory arrangements apply to particular industries, ranging from approval procedures or labelling requirements for food or pharmaceutical products, to qualification standards for professionals and skilled service providers.

The State and Global Governance

Significantly, the importance of regulation and of 'governance' more generally became increasingly recognized during the 1990s, notably by the World Bank. The 'Washington consensus' of the 1980s stressed deregulation and the slimming down of the state, but a counter-current emerging from the resistance to structural adjustment in Africa and debates about the success of state-led development in Asia culminated in the 1997 World Development Report, *The State in a Changing World*. This accepted a broad role for the state, and stressed the importance of reinvigorating state capacity, conceding that the shift to the minimalist state of the 1980s 'sometimes tended to overshoot the mark' (p. 24), and urging that '[e]very country must look to build and adapt its institutions, not dismantle them' (p. 75). However, perhaps because its constitution forbids it from political involvement, the Bank uses the term 'governance' which embodies a technicist and apparently apolitical view of the role of the state and the design of institutions (Faundez, 1997; Tshuma, 1999). Furthermore, critics cannot fail to point out that the dismantling of many state institutions, and the weakening of important state capacity and infrastructure, resulted partly from the 'structural adjustment' policies advocated by the Bank and the IMF during the 1980s.

Although the modified Washington consensus now includes the importance of the state and regulation, and discusses a range of options and strategies, it is advocating a 'market-friendly state'. The role of such a state is essentially defined in terms of what is needed to establish and maintain markets, and is only justified if it can be shown capable of remedying 'market failures'. But how are we to ensure that the market, or rather the systems of production and exchange, are people-friendly? The concept of the market-friendly state side-steps important political and ethical questions about who benefits from any particular pattern of state-market interaction, and what social values it promotes. The concept of 'regulation' indeed is thought by some to exclude direct state involvement in economic activity, and to be limited to establishing the ground-rules, or setting the framework for the activities of private economic actors. In doing so, however, it mediates between individuals and groups which have very different interests, and are often very unequal in their economic power. Regulation entails allocating costs and benefits, and it is not enough to ask whether 'efficiency' is increased in abstract economic terms; it is necessary also to consider who bears the costs and who gains the benefits, and whether human welfare is enhanced in terms less easily quantifiable than by an increase in consumption of goods. The concept of 'regulation' indeed is thought by some to exclude direct state involvement in economic activity, and to be limited to establishing the ground-rules, or setting the framework for the activities of private economic actors. In doing so, however, it mediates between individuals and groups which have very different interests, and are often very unequal in their economic power.

The notion of a 'market-friendly state' tends to slip back into that of a laissez-faire, minimalist state, which is confined to protecting private property and enforcing contracts. In fact, the state *creates* property rights, and defines their limits, so that even this illusory minimalist state is far from a neutral arbiter abstaining from 'intervention' in the market. This has been seen in recent years, for example, in the processes of privatization, under which the various terms of asset-transfer in different countries have created opportunities for financiers, managers and all types of speculators and entrepreneurs.

Indeed the state, and the public sphere more generally, are essential to the management of the social conditions of production and exchange, of which the apparently private sphere of the 'market' is only an aspect. Hence, the contemporary debates and conflicts over the reorganization of state-market relations, on a world-wide scale, involve political and ethical, as well as economic efficiency and technical legal concerns. Recent experience has shown that globalization based simply on liberalization can increase economic insecurity and generate social tensions, exacerbate the damage to the environment, and destabilize the financial system causing economic recession. The challenge is to design international institutions and rules which can help to ensure that the increasing international contacts, flows and opportunities empower ordinary people and enable them to improve their lives, strengthen the safeguards against environmental degradation, and facilitate orderly financial intermediation.

Too often, the spectre of competition is used as a reason to reduce standards for social and environmental protection and financial prudence. Regulatory requirements can be seen, certainly in the short run, merely as imposing costs and reducing competitiveness, which generates pressures for deregulation and a 'race to the bottom'. This is not inevitable: increased international contacts and closer integration can lead to a diffusion of best practices, and improvements in social and environmental conditions can attract people and investments and improve productivity, leading to a regulatory 'race to the top'. There is certainly a strong element of competition between regulatory systems, and an increased awareness of the need to adapt regulation in response to the international mobility of some economic factors. However, this competition is not played out in terms of abstract economic exchanges, but within specific institutional structures, mediated by political and social practices, and influenced by ideological perceptions. Thus, the stress by politicians and others on the need to be competitive is often more important than actual changes in regulation.

GLOBAL BUSINESS AND REGULATORY NETWORKS

Transnational Corporate and Contractual Networks

The new patterns of globalization generated by post-industrial capitalism have been characterized by Manuel Castells as based on a 'network society' (Castells, 1998). A key element in these processes are international business networks, dominated by TNCs. The TNCs became the focus of political attention after their emergence in the 1960s and 1970s as the dominant private institutions in the world economy. The pace of internationalization of business accelerated during the 1980s and 1990s, with new trends towards internationalization in finance, services and retail sectors and in medium-sized and even smaller firms. By 1996 there were an estimated 44 000 TNCs with some 280 000 foreign affiliates, although the top 25 firms controlled over half of the outward investment stock (UNCTAD, 1997: 1, 28). These giant corporate groups dominate international economic flows: notably, about one-third of inter-state trade consists of internal flows between affiliates of such groups (UNCTAD, 1997: 18).

However, business networks go well beyond corporate groups: a high degree of control is also exercised through contractual links in supply and delivery chains. Thus, technology licensing and business-format franchising enable firms such as Coca-Cola, Benetton and McDonalds to control large numbers of outlets which are owned and financed by small entrepreneurs (Felstead, 1993). Conversely, large retailers and firms making brand-name consumer goods source their production from hundreds or thousands of small businesses or even artisanal producers, who themselves may sub-contract to smaller workshops and even outworkers. Although the units in these supply and delivery chains are independently owned, the quantity and quality of their products are tightly supervised.

Thus, a high proportion of international economic flows is controlled by major firms which dominate business networks, and can take a longer-term strategic view of trade and investment. The central position of these firms in the global economy puts them at the heart of the issues of business standards, explored by many of the chapters in this book. Much depends on whether they take advantage of inconsistencies and loopholes in international arrangements, in order to give regulatory competition a downward push, or whether accountability mechanisms can be devised to ensure that they adopt and act as a transmission-belt for high business standards. Certainly, the firms themselves can and should actively promulgate and police standards for themselves and their suppliers, as shown by Fridd and Sainsbury in Chapter 12. However, as Hepple points out in Chapter 10, the worst abuses often take place outside the formal corporate sector. Thus, a broader national and international regulatory system is necessary, to ensure that improved standards are generally disseminated (see Chapter 13 by Ruth Mayne).

This does not necessarily mean detailed state requirements and enforcement: the important role of formal law is often to strengthen the *mechanisms of accountability*. Thus, several of our contributors (Hepple, Mayne and Kearney) stress that among what have been described as the core labour standards, the key ones are the right of association and free collective bargaining. It is neither economically nor morally defensible for workers in developed countries to begrudge the transfer of production to lower-paid workers in developing countries; but it can be an act of international solidarity for them to insist that the workers in those countries should have the right to form and join independent trade unions. Equally, Ayine and Werksman point to the obstacles that hinder transnational legal accountability of TNCs. Since these firms gain competitive advantage from their ability to manage dispersed activities in an integrated way, they should not be allowed to shelter behind the fictions of separate legal personality and jurisdictional limits to avoid their global responsibilities.

Untamed Financial Flows

A more recent and very different phenomenon has been the resurgence during the 1990s of large-scale, short-term international capital flows. Since the 1930s, capital markets and financial intermediation have been largely national, and the postwar regime supervised by the IMF aimed to liberalize only current account payments. However, the ability of TNCs to manage their internal cross-border payments undermined the distinction between current and capital accounts, and the emergence of the Eurocurrency markets and of the system of 'offshore' finance dominated by TNCs and their banks created a vast pool of 'hot money' and inevitably led to currency floating. During the 1980s the developed countries ended exchange controls and began to reform their rules to make it easier for domestic banks and savings institutions (such as unit trusts and investment funds) to lend and invest abroad. By the early 1990s, financial liberalization became more general, and the rapid-growth countries of East Asia and Latin America, as well as former communist countries offering apparently promising investment opportunities, became identified as 'emerging markets'. However, the resulting boom in short-term portfolio capital flows was very uneven (many countries in Africa and elsewhere had little inflow, or even net outflows) and extremely volatile. Peaking at $104bn in 1993, portfolio capital flows to emerging markets fell to less than a quarter of that level in 1995 due to the Mexican *peso* crisis, but rebounded to $50bn in 1996 (IMF, 1998: 12–13).

The financial crisis sparked off in Asia in 1997 led to an even more dramatic reversal, with drastic economic and social repercussions. The spreading contagion of financial volatility led to proposals through the IMF and elsewhere for 'strengthening the architecture of the international financial system'; but as Stephany Griffith-Jones points out in Chapter 9, these were aimed essentially at increasing the availability of information (transparency) and tightening supervision, intending to facilitate continued liberalization. She stresses that the inherent volatility of such short-term flows requires more serious consideration of regulatory requirements that can act as a brake on both inflows and outflows. Although some of these can, in principle, be introduced unilaterally by states, the competition to attract capital is such that some coordination is necessary. Certainly, collective action would be needed to introduce measures such as a tax on foreign exchange transactions, first proposed in 1972 by Nobel laureate James Tobin, which has been widely supported (ul-Haq *et al.*, 1996; Porter, 1996).

Yet powerful voices in New York, London and Washington still press for the facilitation of unrestricted international capital flows. Unrestricted capital flows were a basic principle of the MAI, and were also proposed (though rejected on this occasion) as a condition of the $18bn US contribution to the new IMF facility in October 1998. The continued enthusiasm of key decision makers and institutions for the concept of a free global capital market has been attributed by Jagdish Bhagwati to the influence of a 'power élite' based on the Wall Street/Washington nexus, dominated by individuals linked to the large investment banks (Bhagwati, 1998). Indeed, the capacity to switch an enormous volume of finance between countries at a moment's notice is available to relatively few individuals and institutions (perhaps 60 or 70 large globally organized financial firms), while a few hundred banks and other investment houses act as the channels for the enormous and growing volume of private savings, all seeking above-average returns. It seems no longer acceptable that they should be allowed to continue these activities with a minimum of regulatory supervision, while expecting to be bailed out by states at enormous expense when their operations create a crisis.

The experience of 1997–8, when many countries which had liberalized capital flows suffered economic disaster, while others such as China and India which had retained controls fared much better, revived the case for capital controls. It also cast a large shadow over the project to extend the IMF's aims and jurisdiction to liberalization of capital flows, which, combined with the MAI and the liberalization of financial services under the WTO, would have created a single global capital market under the aegis of the IMF (Wade and Veneroso, 1998).

Global Regulation

A counterpoint to global business networks has been the growth of global regulatory networks (Picciotto, 1996; Braithwaite and Drahos, 1999). These entail not only new forms of regulatory cooperation and coordination between states, but also at sub-state level between a wide range of administrative and public authorities, as well as various forms of private governance. The result is a spaghetti bowl or spider's web of intertwined organizations and arrangements, which evade the traditional categories of private and public, national and international law. The classic liberal international system which emerged during the nineteenth century was seen as a community of equal, sovereign states, loosely coordinated by consensual rules and agreements. This envisaged a hierarchy of legitimacy hinging on governments, which voluntarily entered into public obligations externally with other states, and internally laid down rules binding the private transactions of individual legal persons.

Today, the emerging forms of global governance are characterized by the fragmentation of the public sphere into a complex and multi-layered network of interacting institutions and bodies. Consequently, national systems of accountability and legitimacy have been weakened, as public power has been transferred to bureaucratic, technical and professional bodies at supra-state and sub-state levels. However, there has also been an important resurgence of a social internationalism, sometimes described as the growth of an 'international civil society', which has begun to re-infuse global governance with some of the life-blood of accountability. In some ways globalization opens up opportunities for new forms of international solidarity, political empowerment and direct popular sovereignty (Braithwaite and Drahos, 1999).

It may be helpful here to outline the skeletal anatomy of the new global governance.

Organizations

Firstly, the distinction between international governmental and non-government organizations (IGOs and INGOs) has become blurred, in many ways. Participation in the work of IGOs has been broadened out, not only by giving some NGOs consultative status, but also by including representatives of private interests and organizations in official delegations. A new kind of professionalized politics has grown up around the *caravanserei* of major international meetings, in which the power of corporate leaders and lobbyists to enter the inner sanctums has been counterpointed by the increased skill of NGOs in combining well-researched analysis, grass-roots involvement and knowledge, and often spectacular political action. The effect has certainly been to politicize the activities of international economic organizations in recent years, as discussed by O'Brien in Chapter 14. Furthermore, a growing number of international organizations have a varied membership, which may include officials from governments, quasi-governmental public bodies, and even representatives of private associations or firms. For example, the Codex Alimentarius Commission, set up as a subsidiary body of the Food and Agriculture Organization (FAO) and the World Health Organization (WHO) to set food standards, accepts food industry representatives on its committees and in national delegations, to the point where it has been widely accused of being industry-dominated. Finally, many INGOs, although they are private associations, perform quasi-public and regulatory functions: for example, business associations such as the ICC set standards for key international contractual arrangements, and operate important international arbitration systems. The work of the International Accounting Standards Committee in agreeing harmonized accounting standards has been a highly political process, and one which is central to the development of adequate corporate transparency.

Beyond the formal organizations, there has been a mushroom growth of bodies whose status is often informal or uncertain, involving specialists with specific regulatory functions. They are often created *ad hoc*, as a result of particular political initiatives, bringing together the countries, organizations or individuals considered to be key to the issue in question. They may have only an informal constitution and a small secretariat, or none at all, and may be attached more or less loosely to an existing, more formal body. For example, the Port State Control Committee, set up by maritime authorities which are members of the Paris Memorandum of Understanding (MOU) on Port State Control, coordinates its programme of ship inspection (applying standards laid down by the International Maritime Organization and the International Labour Organization), operating a computerized system of deficiency reporting and a black-list of defective vessels (http://www.parismou.org); it covers ports in the European region, but has stimulated the formation of similar organizations in other regions. Similarly, the Financial Action Task Force (FATF), set up by the Group of Seven industrialized countries (G7) to combat money-laundering, has been attached to the OECD, although not formally part of it.

This process of formation of *ad hoc* groupings is to some extent the result of tactical manoeuvring by powerful bodies or states, which seek to ensure that an issue will be dealt with in a forum which they regard as suitable for their purposes. Perhaps the most successful example in recent years was the move of the USA, urged by its high-tech industries, to include the issue of intellectual property protection in the GATT's Uruguay Round negotiations, thus side-stepping the unanimity requirements for amendment of the multilateral treaties which come under the responsibility of the World Intellectual Property Organization (WIPO), and the developing countries' domination of UNCTAD. However, the move to negotiate the MAI under the auspices of the OECD, with which some of this book's chapters are concerned, was unsuccessful, as it excluded many developing countries of special interest to investors, while agreement even between the OECD countries proved elusive.

A degree of coordination between related state regulatory arrangements is provided by regional and global trade-liberalization organizations. The epitomy of this is the EU which, having started with a relatively strong institutional foundation underpinning a common market, has evolved into what could be described as a major node or point of intersection for many regulatory networks. Other regional organizations, such as NAFTA and APEC, have a much less institutionalized basis, but also act as nodal points. At the global level, the WTO has become a broad umbrella organization covering issues going well beyond trade, although there is increasing opposition to extending its remit further and diluting its free-trade mission. The WTO has also been slow to develop its coordination with other related organizations, especially those within the UN system, although this forms part of its charter.

A more comprehensive approach was suggested in the Report of the Commission on Global Governance (1995), which proposed the establishment of an Economic Security Council in the UN, the main role of which would be to improve coordination of the activities of these various disparate regulatory networks. This was seen as part of a broader reform of intergovernmental organizations (including greater involvement of NGOs) with an appeal for a commitment to common 'neighbourhood values' (respect for life, liberty, justice and equity, mutual respect, caring and integrity), and for the articulation of a 'global civic ethic'. The Commission also suggested that a useful source of revenue for often financially hard-pressed international organizations would be the Tobin tax, mentioned above (Commission, 1995: 219).

Law: International, Supranational and Transnational

A corollary of the fragmentation of the global public sphere into multi-layered networks has been the emergence of more complex patterns of law, across as well as between states. Formally, treaties and other international agreements are part of public international law, which binds only states. Even general multilateral treaties, such as the package of agreements under the WTO, do not create global law that is directly binding on individuals or firms. However, the WTO has established a strong mechanism for setting disputes, to which states may refer complaints, often on behalf of business lobbies. In many ways this procedure is an advance, since it restrains unilateral protectionist action (a powerful weapon for states with large markets), and requires rule-based justifications. The availability of the sanction of denial of market access remains the underlying strength of the WTO's procedures; its weaknesses are the priority it (necessarily) gives to free trade compared to other values, reinforced by the inadequate resources of developing countries to bring or defend cases, and the lack of formal standing for either INGOs or NGOs representing social concerns (see Ayine and Werksman, Chapter 7). By comparison, other international economic obligations on states are backed by less direct sanctions, but long-term reciprocal advantage and the threat of reputational damage are enough to ensure that most states most of the time pay at least lip-service to their undertakings. The bigger danger is the threat of non-participation or withdrawal, especially by an important state. Notably, the USA has frequently used its non-participation to hobble new initiatives, or ensure they are modified to suit US interests, for example its refusal to ratify the UN Convention on the Law of the Sea until the deep-sea mining provisions were effectively amended.

Various techniques have been developed, however, to give direct applicability to internationally agreed rules so that they can immediately create rights and (less often) duties for firms and individuals. Under the constitutional law of some countries (for example, the USA) an international treaty is considered part of national law, and can therefore in some circumstances create law directly applying to individual legal persons. This is limited to those treaty provisions which may be regarded as 'self-executing', which means rules which are intended and capable of being applied as law without further legislation. Thus, for example, bilateral tax treaties generally give immediate benefits to international investors in the form of reduction of withholding tax rates. In countries such as the UK, where treaties do not automatically have this force, the same effect is produced by legislation: in the case of tax treaties, a general provision in the tax code enables each bilateral treaty to be given direct effect as subsidiary legislation.

Where rights, or indeed obligations, are created in this way for individual legal persons by international legal agreements, they can be said to be 'supranational'. In principle, rights created by treaty can be over-ridden by subsequent national legislation, provided the intention to do so is explicit. In practice, once a state is locked in to a binding multilateral convention, or a network of bilateral treaties, reconciling changes to national laws with international obligations can involve many difficulties. For example, several states complained that some of the changes in the major US tax reform of 1986 entailed breaches of their tax treaties with the US, leading to complex renegotiations and several legislative amendments. A major criticism of the MAI is that states would be locked in to its liberalization and investment protection obligations, which would potentially over-ride a wide range of national laws, leading to uncertainty rather than a stable climate for investors (see Chapter 5). Since the MAI envisaged direct access to international arbitration by investors, it would make these arbitrators the judges of the validity of any national laws which might be considered contrary to the MAI's principles.

The most developed system of supranational law is that of the EU, membership of which carries an obligation to implement EU law. Each member state has therefore entrenched EU law internally, so that it over-rides inconsistent national laws even if passed later. This is reinforced by the role of the European Court of Justice (ECJ), which has actively developed the doctrines of supranationality and direct effect. The ECJ's activism has been made relatively acceptable politically by balancing the rights of business with some individual social rights (notably, equal pay for women); but nevertheless many consider that European integration has rested too heavily on judicial activism and too little on institutions with more democratic accountability.

The impact on the national-international law divide of increased international economic and social integration has been greatest in relation to the concept of jurisdiction. Already in the 1950s some US academics identified the concept of 'transnational law', referring to the multiplicity of laws that might apply to internationally organized businesses and transactions (Jessup, 1956; see Picciotto, 1995: 195). The notion that economic and business activities which cross national boundaries, or have contacts in several countries, might be subject to several national legal systems, has posed great problems for state-based concepts of international law. Although principles of private international law have long existed to deal with potential conflicts of private law (for example, which legal system should apply to a contract in international trade), it is harder for a state to cede to another's regulatory law, which involves state policy and entails sanctions.

Understandably, host countries which were recipients of foreign investment began to resent the application to local business activities of the laws of the 'home' countries of the foreign investors. Also unsurprisingly, as the main home country of FDI in the post-war years, the USA increasingly generated hostility for applying 'long-arm' laws to the foreign activities of US-owned businesses. A major arena of conflict was the application of US anti-trust laws to break up many of the international cartels which had dominated many industries in the first half of this century. US regulations also commonly disregarded the separate legal personality of foreign subsidiaries, by applying to companies, wherever incorporated, which were owned or controlled by US persons. Accusations of 'extraterritoriality' were especially vociferous when US laws were applied even to agreements between non-US firms outside the US, on the grounds of their 'effects' on the US economy, its consumers and even exporters. The greater propensity of the US to apply economic sanctions in pursuit of foreign policy goals led to conflicts with its allies over the application of export embargoes, which prohibited US-owned foreign subsidiaries from supplying banned items to destinations under the embargo such as the USSR or Libya. These sometimes extended even to foreign firms which had licensed technology of US origin, or which had dealings with nationalized property, notably in Cuba. In principle, the territorial basis of state jurisdiction should mean that such extensive claims to prescriptive jurisdiction would be hard to enforce without the cooperation of other states. Today, however, any major firm which wishes to have a meaningful presence in the global economy cannot easily afford to disregard the requirements of US law, unless it is willing to forgo access to US markets. Increasingly, the same can be said of EU law. Such conflicts have led to the enactment of 'blocking statutes' and retaliatory legislation, as well as attempts to agree limits to the assertion of jurisdiction and to develop regulatory cooperation, for example in competition law (see Roffe, Chapter 8 of this volume, and Picciotto, 1983).

In contrast to the expansive tendencies of US regulatory law, US courts have shown increasing reluctance to allow access to private litigants seeking to take advantage of the more highly developed US laws of liability (for example in negligence), in order to sue US parent companies for injuries suffered abroad. This was seen most starkly in the Bhopal litigation (discussed by Ayine and Werksman in Chapter 7), when the New York courts held that they were not a 'convenient forum' to hear the claims of Indian victims of the gas plant disaster at the Indian subsidiary of Union Carbide Corporation. This argument becomes harder to maintain if the parent company can be shown to have a direct responsibility for the activities concerned (as was alleged, for example, in the *Cape Industries* case, discussed in Chapter 7), but direct knowledge or involvement by the parent (through directors or senior employees) may be hard to prove. Only rarely have courts accepted that the fact that a TNC operates under centralized management should create a presumption of parent-company liability under home-country law (Blumberg, 1993).

MOUs, Codes and Guidelines

The main response to the pressures that globalization has created on the formal separation between national and international law has been the growth of new forms of so-called 'soft law' in the international arena. Firstly, arrangements for administrative cooperation between regulatory bodies have increasingly become semi-formalized, often through MOUs (Memorandums of Understanding). Since these are not negotiated through central governments, they are not considered binding on states. However, by establishing procedures and conditions for direct cooperation among public authorities and administrative bodies with immediate responsibility for particular areas of regulation, they can be of great practical significance. Cooperation is obviously crucial for effective enforcement of economic regulatory requirements, not only to deal with activities affecting more than one jurisdiction, but also to combat regulatory avoidance which makes use of convenient intermediary jurisdictions to route transactions. Regulatory authorities need to ensure that they have adequate powers under national law to provide appropriate assistance, which may not always be easy to obtain. Legislatures may be willing to give agencies the power to exchange with their foreign counterparts relevant information which they may have acquired as part of their own enforcement activities, although this is increasingly being made subject to guarantees that confidentiality be safeguarded. They are more reluctant to grant powers to investigate on behalf of foreign authorities, to assist in enforcing laws benefiting the other state, or based on principles or policies which they do not recognize. This in turn leads to pressures to establish equivalent regulatory standards.

Clearly, to establish a single global code comprehensively covering the complete range of business responsibilities would be an impossible undertaking. Viewed retrospectively, it is hard to believe that so much effort was expended in attempting to agree a UN Code of Conduct for TNCs, and easy to understand why the attempt eventually failed. It was not fruitless, however, in that the debates spawned more specific initiatives, some of which achieved some success.[1] As Pedro Roffe points out in Chapter 8, the UN did agree the Set of Principles on Restrictive Business Practices (RBP Principles), although discussions on the Transfer of Technology Code were stalemated by a difference of perspectives. Indeed, early on in the process two general codes were agreed: the ILO Tripartite Declaration of Principles concerning Multinational Enterprises and Social Policy (1977), and the OECD's Guidelines, appended to the Declaration on Multinational Enterprises adopted in 1976. Codes with a more specific focus include the WHO Code of Marketing of Breastmilk Substitutes, and the various banking supervisory standards developed by the Basle Committee on Banking Supervision (BCBS, 1997), which were tied in to a comprehensive set of Core Principles put out in 1997.

Such codes have been criticized as ineffective, and this is generally ascribed to their 'non-binding' status. Certainly, they are often explicitly said to be voluntary and not legally enforceable (for example, OECD Guidelines, Introduction, para. 6). However, the negotiation of binding international agreements is a complex and generally very protracted process, often resulting in rules which are expressed in very general and often ambiguous or anodyne terms. Furthermore, such 'binding' rules would depend on state implementation for their effectiveness. Enactment of 'binding' rules into national law can be very patchy, as can be seen for example in relation to ILO Conventions (discussed in Chapter 10 by Hepple).

A more valid reason for the non-effectiveness of non-binding codes is the weakness of their mechanisms for monitoring and inducing compliance. Usually they envisage only some kind of general review procedure, and they normally exclude the possibility of complaints about the behaviour of specific firms (for example, RBP Principles, para. F5). Under pressure from its Trade Union Advisory Committee (TUAC), the OECD's Committee for International Investment and Multinational Enterprise (CIIME) has on some occasions considered specific cases arising under the OECD Guidelines (mainly in the period 1975–85) with a view to providing 'clarifications'. However, the trade unions themselves took the view that responsibility for enforcement lay at national level, and generally refrained from conducting international campaigns targeting specific firms (Blanpain, 1979: 52; Blanpain, 1983).

By comparison, campaigns by pressure groups and NGOs around specific issues, and sometimes aimed at the behaviour or activities of specific firms, have had more success, at least in spotlighting and dramatizing particular problems. Perhaps the best known has been the long campaign focusing on the baby-milk issue (discussed by Mayne in Chapter 13), but others include pesticides, pharmaceutical drugs and toxic waste dumping. The issues of child labour, and of exploitative working conditions more generally, have also been the focus of recent campaigns, again sometimes targeting individual companies (see Chapter 11). These campaigns can perhaps be criticized for prioritizing the concerns of consumers or workers in developed countries, and singling out specific companies on a relatively arbitrary basis, so that they do not necessarily result in lasting and generalized improvements for the people intended to be their beneficiaries. These pitfalls indicate the importance of ensuring that standards should not be unilaterally formulated and imposed, but developed and applied in an internationally coordinated manner. In particular, efforts to raise social and environmental protection standards, especially in developing countries, should be sensitive to local conditions, and should be accompanied by appropriate assistance programmes (illustrated by the Sialkot project discussed by Mayne in Chapter 13). This again emphasizes that international regulation should aim to empower people, especially the weak, and strengthen mechanisms of accountability.

STRENGTHENING GLOBAL REGULATION

The international regulatory networks described in the previous section have resulted in complex and multi-layered interactions between laws, codes and guidelines, operating locally, nationally, transnationally, regionally and internationally (Jacobs, 1994). The challenge of globalization is to design and manage these interactions so as to enhance rather than diminish regulatory effectiveness. As it has become clear that global

Table 1.1 Global Business Standards

Subject-Matter	Organization, Form & Date	Compliance Arrangements
Taxation and Finance		
Convention on Mutual Assistance in Tax Matters	Council of Europe/OECD Treaty 1988, 8 members 1998	bilateral reciprocity
Harmful Tax Practices	OECD Recommendations & Guidelines, 1998	review and reports by Forum
Core Principles for Effective Banking Supervision	Basle Committee on Banking Supervision, code 1997	review by Committee
Forty Recommendations on Money-Laundering	Financial Action Task Force, 1990 revised 1996	self-assessment and peer review
Corporate Behaviour and Fair Competition		
Restrictive Business Practices Set of Principles	UNCTAD, UN General Assembly resolution 1980	bilateral consultations, studies by Expert Group
Draft Agreement on Illicit Payments	UN, proposal for treaty sent to General Assembly 1979	national + mutual assistance
Bribery of Foreign Public Officials	OECD treaty, signed 1997	Working Group monitoring
Corporate Governance	proposed OECD Guidelines, under discussion	none: 'reference point' for national & corporate practice
Consumer Protection		
Guidelines for Consumer Protection	UN General Assembly resolution 1985	none
Marketing of Breastmilk Substitutes	WHO Code, 1981	informal NGO actions

Social & Employment Standards

Fundamental Principles and Rights at Work	ILO Declaration, adopted 1998	annual country review and report to ILO Governing Body
Principles on MNEs and Social Policy	ILO Tripartite Declaration, adopted 1987	Committee interpretation
Labour Standards	ILO Conventions and Recommendations, various dates	self-assessment + complaints
Development Objectives and Action Programme	Declaration of Copenhagen Summit 1995	UN system, esp. UNDP
Principles of Good Practice Social Policy	proposal to World Bank Development Committee spring 1999	to be agreed

Environmental Protection

Rio Declaration	UN Conference on Environment & Development, 1992	UN, esp. UN Environment Programme + NGO activism
Agenda 21	UN Conference on Environment & Development, 1992	UN, esp. UN Environment Programme + NGO activism

Human Rights

Universal Declaration on Human Rights	UN Declaration 1948; general international law	Commission investigates & reports
Covenant on Civil & Political Rights	UN treaty, agreed 1966, into effect 1976	states report to Committee; opt-in for inter-state complaints
Covenant on Economic, Social & Cultural Rights	UN treaty; agreed 1966, into effect 1976	states report to Committee, UN Ecosoc. liaises with UN system

General

Guidelines for MNEs	OECD App. to Declaration & Decisions, 1976, revd. 1991	Committee review and interpretation

economic integration is not just a matter of removal of restrictions on market forces, officials and academics have begun to give greater attention to the improvement of regulatory coordination and 'rapprochement' (OECD, 1994). However, this has mainly focused on technical questions, and has only hesitantly begun to tackle the broader issues of how to design arrangements and institutions which balance business rights and responsibilities, strengthen accountability and state capacity, and empower the disadvantaged. Efforts at improving the effectiveness of international regulation should combine principles of accountability with an understanding of the dynamics of the links between the various layers and types of regulation generated by the new globalism (Braithwaite and Drahos, 1999).

Accountability

First, there is the question of accountability of international regulatory processes. There is no shortage of examples of the 'democratic deficit' caused when intergovernmental bodies operate in secret, or consult selectively, often mainly with business interests. Agreements reached in this way are often subject to little or no scrutiny by national parliaments, since they entail bargains that cannot be unpackaged; but the conflicts around 'fast track' negotiating authority in the US and the Commission's negotiating mandates in the EU demonstrate the perils. In recent years, as O'Brien shows in Chapter 14, international economic organizations have learned the importance of ensuring wider consultations and involvement, and the OECD's experience with the MAI will perhaps prove a salutory turning-point. However, this opens up much more difficult questions about how to design international structures and procedures which are more genuinely responsive to a broad range of public opinion.

An important element must be greater transparency. This is a principle which has increasingly been put forward as an international obligation on states, in respect of their national economic regulations – it features in many of the WTO agreements, and was included also in the MAI. International bodies have been slower to accept this obligation for themselves, although it has now been made much easier, and indeed forced upon them, by the facilities offered by the Internet. But the opening up of international space for debate of itself will be insufficient, unless it takes account of the great inequalities of access which privilege the powerful and silence the disadvantaged. This places an immense responsibility on the intellectuals and professionals who now play the central roles in global networks. They must try to foster principles and procedures to evaluate arguments, taking due account of vested interests and partial positions, including their own.

Global-Local Regulatory Linkages

The second major effectiveness issue lies in managing the interaction between vertical layers of regulation (local, national, regional, international). As discussed in the previous section, the fragmentation of the public sphere has created greater complexity in the forms of interaction between these levels. This question is often considered mechanistically, failing to take into account the greatest virtue – and vice – of the law, and of regulation more broadly: its great flexibility. The application of rules is not a mechanical but a social process, which depends in particular on interpretation. Rules are always expressed at a certain level of abstraction, and their application to specific contexts allows a degree of flexibility of interpretation. Indeed, this feature is a major reason why regulation has become a central feature of the current phase of globalization, since it offers the possibility of mediating between the pressures for global homogeneity and those for local diversity and difference.

However, the indeterminacy of abstract legal rules, especially those expressed in universal terms, also tends to undermine effective enforcement, especially in an international context where national interpretations may vary greatly. For example, both the recent OECD anti-bribery convention and the proposed UN draft require the criminalization of 'undue' payments to an official for performing public duties; this leaves considerable room for interpretation in deciding on the acceptability of the common practice of paying commissions to 'middlemen'. So even a binding international standard may remain an empty aspiration unless it is supported by effective international procedures for monitoring practical implementation at the national and local levels, but these are often lacking or weak. Where they exist, they generally rely on self-assessments by each government or regulator, which do not always receive close scrutiny by the international body to which they are submitted. An alternative is a process of 'peer review', adopted for example by the Financial Action Task Force, which enables closer examination of actual practice on the ground by an experienced regulator from another country. National regulators of all kinds are now increasingly aware of the need to improve cross-border cooperation, and although they are sometimes suspicious of the role of international bodies, arrangements for mutual recognition and assistance in enforcement are proliferating. However, the practical impact of all these procedures crucially depends on their transparency, and their responsiveness to pressures of public opinion.

Codes appear to provide a more direct link than do treaties between internationally agreed standards and practical compliance by firms. Thus, an industry or company code, such as Sainsbury's Principles and Code of Practice explained in and appended to Chapter 12, may provide a direct link between local practices of contract suppliers and internationally agreed principles; indeed, consumer pressures may mean that high standards in Sainsbury's home market are transmitted via the code to the suppliers, providing a positive impetus or social spread-effect in the supplying country. It is noteworthy that while some regulations, such as product standards, will be regarded as binding contractual conditions, the social standards in the code are more negotiable, although they are to be monitored by the same inspection system. Clearly the company considers it important to ensure that standards are not imposed inappropriately or without sensitivity to local conditions. On the other hand, Kearney argues forcefully in Chapter 11 that firms may adopt codes merely to deflect social and political pressures, and Mayne in Chapter 12 argues that corporate codes should complement not replace state regulation. Once again, the key to practical effectiveness is whether such codes improve accountability by helping to empower those whose social conditions they aim to improve.

Enhancing Multilateralism

Effective international regulation also requires improved horizontal coordination, not only between states but also between and across international organizations and arrangements. As discussed in the previous section, linkages between such bodies have increasingly developed, but in an *ad hoc* way, in response to tactical and often power-political considerations. Liberalization and the new wave of globalization have led to an awareness of the need for improved coordination between related international regimes. Thus, the formation of the WTO has created formal links between the multilateral trade system and other related regimes (Picciotto, 1998). Most of these may be described as negative linkages, creating a presumption that national rules are compatible with GATT market-access obligations if they comply with internationally agreed standards, for example technical or health standards for goods and products. The TRIPs agreement goes further, and establishes a positive linkage, by requiring WTO members to implement its detailed minimum standards for intellectual property protection, including the main provisions of international intellectual property treaties.

The liberalization of currency and capital controls, followed by the financial market crises and volatility since 1994, finally led in 1998 to talk of 'strengthening the architecture of the global financial system'. This included the concept of 'a system of multilateral surveillance of national financial, supervisory and regulatory systems [which] could encompass surveillance of such areas as banking and securities supervision, corporate governance, accounting and disclosure, and bankruptcy' (G7, 1998: para. 17). However, there has been little indication of how this might be accomplished, apart from some mention of 'greater cooperation and an improved relationship' among existing institutions such as the IMF, the World Bank and the Basle Committee. The failure to address this need to improve regulatory coordination was perhaps the central flaw in the MAI, due to its origins in the laissez-faire neo-liberalism of the 1980s. Thus, as discussed in detail in Chapter 5, the MAI's obligations would have acted as 'disciplines' on national state regulation. As it became clear that this would bring into question many regulatory regimes (for example, intellectual property, taxation, monetary and financial regulation), this resulted in various exclusions and 'carve-outs'. Thus, far from providing a framework of rules offering a stable and secure basis for international investment, the MAI would have fostered uncertainty about the validity of many existing national rules, and actually undermined efforts to improve international coordination in some important areas.

The failure of the MAI demonstrated the need for a new approach to a global regulatory framework for international business. This would need to link the rights of business to fulfilment of responsibilities, and aim to strengthen state-level regulation through flexible linkages to internationally agreed standards. A high priority should be to link liberalization and investment protection provisions, such as those envisaged in the MAI, to equally strong multilateral arrangements to strengthen international fiscal and financial regulatory cooperation. These already exist in embryo (see Table 1.1), but they are greatly weakened by the reluctance of states to participate in them, or to enforce them rigorously, due to the fear of losing out in the competition to attract finance. In fact, long-term capital is most likely to be attracted to states with educated and skilled workers and a sound infrastructure (as pointed out in Chapter 2), but the capacity to develop these been undermined everywhere by a fiscal 'race to the bottom'. A major element in the decline of the legitimacy of income taxes has been the availability of facilities for international tax avoidance and evasion. Developed states, through the OECD, have slowly begun to develop the means of combatting this (OECD, 1998), but they are finding it hard to maintain sufficient consensus among themselves, let alone extend the initiative to other countries. The unwillingness to make decisive moves to block some of the main international tax loopholes is mainly due to fears that financial markets would use the 'offshore' system to go further underground. Much the same argument is made about some aspects of financial market regulation.

The problems posed by international avoidance of tax and financial regulations would be more easily overcome by accepting the principle that the advantages of an investment protection agreement should be open only to states which also accept the rules for cooperation in tax enforcement and elimination of harmful tax practices, and to investments coming from such participating states. Also included in such a package deal should be participation in systems for regulation of financial markets and prudential supervision of financial firms, as well as money-laundering and financial fraud. The arrangements which have been developed at the international level so far are far from perfect, but their inclusion in a broader multilateral framework would facilitate their acceptance and make it easier to strengthen them. This would reverse the presumption of the MAI, which would have encouraged the continued use of offshore centres and havens for tax and regulatory avoidance, by offering protection to investments even if routed through such jurisdictions.

A wide range of internationally agreed standards for business could also be included within such a framework, such as agreements to combat bribery and illicit payments, corporate governance and disclosure requirements, and marketing rules for products such as drugs, tobacco or baby food. These need not form part of the basic package which states would be required to accept, but could be linked to it in various ways. For example, a firm's rights under investment protection rules could be conditional on its compliance with relevant business standards; thus, it could not complain of cancellation of a hospital supply contract if it could be shown to have breached rules on marketing of pharmaceuticals or baby food. Principles of environmental protection, and minimum social and employment standards, could also be associated within the framework, by creating a presumption that an investor is responsible for ensuring compliance with such standards by the businesses involved with the investments. Such linkages need not require the inclusion of all these arrangements under the same institutional umbrella. However, the time is surely ripe for some rethinking of the roles and relationships of the international financial and economic institutions, and the lack of an organization responsible for regulating international investment and business standards is clearly a gap which needs to be filled.

Above all, what is needed is a recognition that globalization is not merely a matter of unrestricted market forces. It requires a strengthening of international standards and cooperative arrangements, to provide a strong basis of mutual confidence. Without such a strong foundation of positive standards, paper guarantees against discrimination or expropriation, or unfair treatment of any kind, would in any case be ineffectual or illusory.

NOTE

1. An excellent collection of the relevant documents has been provided by UNCTAD in the three-volume *International Investment Instruments: a Compendium* (1996).

REFERENCES

BCBS (1997) *Compendium of Documents Produced by the Basle Committee on Banking Supervision*, 3 volumes. Bank for International Settlements, Basle.

Bhagwati, Jagdish (1998) 'The Capital Myth: the Difference between Trade in Widgets and Dollars', *Foreign Affairs*, vol. 77(3), 7–12.

Blanpain, R. (1979) *The OECD Guidelines for Multinational Enterprises and Labour Relations 1976–79: Experience and Review.* Kluwer, Deventer.

Blanpain, R. (1983) *The OECD Guidelines for Multinational Enterprises and Labour Relations 1979–82: Experience and Mid-Term Report.* Kluwer, Deventer.

Blumberg, Philip (1993) *The Multinational Challenge to Corporate Law.* Oxford University Press, New York.

Braithwaite, John and Drahos, Peter (1999) *Global Business Regulation* (forthcoming).

Castells, Manuel (1998) *The Rise of the Network Society.* Blackwell, Oxford.

Commission on Global Governance (1995) *Our Global Neighbourhood.* Oxford University Press, Oxford.

Dezalay, Yves (1992) *Marchands de Droit.* Fayard, Paris.

Faundez, Julio (1997) *Good Government and Law: Legal and Institutional Reform in Developing Countries.* Macmillan, Basingstoke.

Felstead, A. (1993) *The Corporate Paradox: Power and Control in the Business Franchise.* Routledge, London.

Garapon, A. (1995) 'French Legal Culture and the Shock of Globalization', *Social and Legal Studies*, vol. 4, 493–506.

G7 (Group of 7) (1998) *Strengthening the Architecture of the Global Financial System.* Report of the G7 Finance Ministers to G7 Heads of State or Government for their Meeting in Birmingham, May 1998. Department of Foreign and Commonwealth Affairs, London.

IMF (1998) *International Capital Markets. Development, Prospects, and Key Policy Issues.* International Monetary Fund, Washington DC.

Jacobs, S. H. (1994) 'Regulatory Co-operation for an Interdependent World: Issues for Government' in *Regulatory Cooperation for an Interdependent World*. OECD, Paris.

Jessup, Philip C. (1956) *Transnational Law*. Yale University Press, New Haven.

Moran, M. (1984) *The Politics of Banking: the Strange Case of Competition and Credit Control*. Macmillan, Basingstoke.

Moran, M. (1991) *The Politics of the Financial Services Revolution: the USA, the UK, Japan*. Macmillan, Basingstoke.

OECD (1994) *Regulatory Cooperation for an Interdependent World*. OECD, Paris.

OECD (1998) *Harmful Tax Practices: an Emerging Global Issue*. OECD, Paris.

Phizacklea, A. (1997) 'Globalization and Migration: a Feminist Perspective' in K. Koser and H. Lutz (eds) *The New Migration in Europe: Social Construction and Social Realities*, 21–38. Macmillan, Basingstoke.

Picciotto, Sol (1983) 'Jurisdictional Conflicts, International Law, and the International State System', *International Journal of the Sociology of Law*, vol. 11, 11.

Picciotto, Sol (1995) 'International Law in a Changing World' in G. P. Wilson, (ed.) *Frontiers of Legal Scholarship*. Wiley, Chichester.

Picciotto, Sol (1996) 'The Regulatory Criss-Cross: Interaction between Jurisdictions and the Construction of Global Regulatory Networks' in W. Bratton, J. McCahery, S. Picciotto and C. Scott (eds) *International Regulatory Competition and Co-ordination*. Clarendon Press, Oxford.

Porter, T. (1996) 'Capital Mobility and Currency Markets: Can They Be Tamed?', *International Journal,* vol. LI, 669–89.

Tshuma, Lawrence (1999) 'The Political Economy of the World Bank's Legal Framework for Development', *Social and Legal Studies*, vol. 8.

Ul-Haq, M., Kaul, I. and Grunberg, I. (eds) (1996) *The Tobin Tax: Coping with Financial Volatility*. Oxford University Press, Oxford.

Wade, Robert and Veneroso, Frank (1998) 'The Gathering World Slump and the Battle over Capital Controls', *New Left Review*, no. 231, 13–42.

WRM-FM (1998) *High Stakes: the Need to Control Transnational Logging Companies – a Malaysian Case-Study*. World Rainforest Movement and Forests Monitor Ltd, Montevideo and London.

Part I
International Investment
Protection and Liberalization

2 Foreign Direct Investment to Developing Countries
V. N. Balasubramanyam

One of the premises of the case for a Multilateral Agreement on Investment (MAI) is that it would promote increased flows of foreign direct investment (FDI) to developing countries. As the Fitzgerald Report puts it, 'for developing countries, membership (of the MAI) would bolster the confidence of not only foreign but also domestic investors by ensuring that the policy regime is unlikely to shift in the future due to cost of withdrawal of a multilateral agreement of this type' (Fitzgerald, 1998). This may be so. But does FDI necessarily promote development objectives everywhere and anywhere? Is FDI a tested and tried instrument of development? Is the ability of FDI to promote development constrained or enhanced by the rules and regulations on its entry and operations widely used by developing countries? These and other issues have been the focus of much debate and discussion. Indeed, there may be no other area of economic inquiry where so much has been written and yet we know so little.

This chapter aims to review what little we know about the relationship between FDI and development, to provide a background for the discussion on the MAI in later chapters. It is not intended to be a complete survey of the vast literature on FDI in developing countries, but a commentary on basic propositions which emerge from it. The chapter begins with an overview of the volume and dimensions of FDI in developing countries, continues by establishing the main basic propositions emerging from the literature on FDI, and then reviews these propositions in the context of the debate on the relationship between FDI and development. The final section pulls together the main conclusions.

THE STATISTICAL DIMENSIONS

Size, Growth and Destination of FDI

The total stock of FDI in the global economy at the end of 1996 was estimated at $3.2 trillion. Annual average flows of FDI accelerated from $55 billion over the period 1981–6 to $243 billion during the years 1991–6. Indeed, the annual average rate of growth of FDI at around 12 per cent during the period 1991–6 exceeded the rate of growth of world exports, estimated at 7 per cent. These figures on FDI, published by UNCTAD and based on data supplied by states, are generally used to estimate the importance and growth of international production by transnational corporations (TNCs), which essentially involves managing business assets or operations under a system of common corporate control. Although they are helpful in giving broad orders of magnitude, they should be used with caution given the difficulties of adjusting for currency fluctuations and changes in price levels (UNCTAD, 1997: 23–5). FDI data count as a capital inflow any contribution made by a foreign owner of more than a specified minimum (in IMF data, 10 per cent) of the equity of a local firm; this can include the capitalized value of inputs such as know-how, intellectual property rights or capital goods, as well as the local firm's reinvested

Table 2.1   Stock of Inward Foreign Direct Investment: Share of Principal Countries, 1980–96

	1980	1985	1990	1995	1996
Total world $bn	479.2	745.2	1726.2	2865.8	3233.2
Developed countries $bn	372.9	537.7	1370.6	2042.1	2269.3
(%)	77.8	72.2	79.4	71.3	70.2
Of which (%)					
US	22.2	34.3	28.8	27.4	28.4
UK	16.9	11.9	15.9	15.4	15.2
France	6.1	6.2	6.3	7.2	7.4
Germany	9.8	6.9	8.1	8.2	7.5
EU	49.6	42.1	51.9	54.6	53.7
Japan	0.9	0.8	0.7	0.9	0.8
Developing countries $bn	106.2	207.3	352.7	789.7	917.6
(%)	22.2	27.8	20.4	27.6	28.4
Of which (%)					
Malaysia	5.6	4.1	4.0	4.7	4.6
Taiwan	2.3	1.4	2.8	2.0	1.9
Hong Kong	1.6	1.7	3.8	2.8	2.6
Singapore	5.8	6.3	8.1	7.3	7.3
Thailand	0.9	1.0	2.3	2.2	2.1
Korea	1.0	0.9	1.6	1.3	1.4
Indonesia	9.7	12.1	11.0	14.3	6.3
China	0.1	1.6	4.0	16.1	18.4
India	1.1	0.5	0.5	0.7	0.9
Mexico	7.6	9.1	9.2	8.1	7.8
Brazil	16.5	12.4	10.5	12.5	11.8
Chile	0.9	1.1	2.9	2.0	2.0
Argentina	5.0	3.2	2.5	3.1	3.1

Source: United Nations, *World Investment Report 1997*.

earnings. On the other hand, such data do not normally include increases in asset values financed from other sources, such as funds raised in the local capital market, which may be very large: in the case of US TNCs they are at least equivalent to the value of inputs from the parent company (UNCTAD, 1997: 25–7). It should also be borne in mind that between 30 per cent and 70 per cent of the estimated value of FDI flows are accounted for by cross-border mergers and acquisitions: in 1996 they were 47 per cent of the estimated $350bn of FDI (UNCTAD, 1997: 9).

The total stock of FDI in developing countries at the end of 1996 stood at $918 billion and accounted for 28 per cent of the world stock (Table 2.1). Annual flows of FDI to developing countries from the OECD countries increased substantially from around $20 billion in 1987 to $129 billion by the end of 1996. Latin America and Asia were the principal recipients of these flows. Some three-quarters of the total flows of FDI were received by only ten developing countries. The least developed countries accounted for less than 1 per cent of the total flows (Table 2.2).

Table 2.2 Inflows of Foreign Direct Investment: 1985–96

	1985–90	*1994*	*1995*	*1996*
Total world $bn	141.9	238.7	316.5	349.2
Developed countries $bn	116.7	142.4	205.9	208.2
Of which (%)				
US	41.6	35.0	29.5	40.6
UK	16.3	7.2	10.7	14.5
France	6.2	11.7	11.5	10.0
Germany	2.0	0.6	4.3	1.9
EU	45.2	50.8	53.9	47.7
Japan	0.3	0.6	0.02	0.1
Developing countries $bn	24.7	90.5	96.3	128.7
Of which (%)				
Latin America	32.8	29.8	26.4	30.0
Brazil	5.3	3.4	5.1	7.4
Mexico	10.5	12.2	7.3	5.8
South & East Asia	50.2	61.5	67.7	63.1
Malaysia	4.5	4.8	4.3	4.1
Taiwan	3.6	1.5	1.7	1.1
Hong Kong	6.5	2.2	2.2	1.9
Singapore	12.1	6.1	7.2	7.3
Thailand	4.0	1.4	2.1	1.9
Korea	2.9	0.9	1.9	1.8
Indonesia	2.2	2.3	4.5	6.2
China	10.9	37.3	37.3	32.9
Least developed countries $bn	0.4	0.4	0.3	0.5

Source: United Nations, *World Investment Report 1997*.

Dimensions of FDI in Developing Countries

As a proportion of total capital stock in developing countries as a whole, FDI accounts for 8 per cent. In some of the Latin American and Asian countries, however, the ratio is substantially higher: in 1995 FDI inflows accounted for over 25 per cent of total gross fixed capital formation in Singapore, China, Bolivia and Peru (Table 2.3), but this differs substantially between countries. The sectoral distribution of FDI in developing countries shows a shift away from primary (raw materials/agriculture) and secondary (manufacturing) sectors towards the tertiary sector (services). The secondary sector, which accounted for nearly 56 per cent of the total stock of FDI in 1975, now accounts for less than 50 per cent. In contrast,

Table 2.3   Inward Stock of FDI as a Percentage of Gross Fixed Capital Formation (percentages)

	1985–90	*1993*	*1994*	*1995*
Total world	5.4	4.4	4.5	5.2
Developed countries	5.5	3.7	3.5	4.4
US	5.3	4.9	4.8	5.9
UK	13.7	11.0	6.8	13.2
France	10.3	9.0	6.9	8.6
Germany	1.6	0.4	0.2	1.7
EU	9.1	5.9	5.0	6.8
Japan	0.2	0.2	0.1	n.a.
Developing countries	8.0	6.6	8.0	8.2
Latin America	11.3	7.2	10.3	11.0
Argentina	13.0	31.0	4.8	11.7
Bolivia	25.0	14.9	17.6	47.7
Brazil	3.1	1.3	3.0	4.7
Mexico	16.9	6.0	14.3	17.1
Peru	15.5	8.7	37.3	24.7
South & East Asia	9.7	7.5	8.3	9.0
Malaysia	43.7	22.5	16.1	17.9
Taiwan	5.1	1.8	2.5	2.7
Hong Kong	12.2	7.1	8.2	8.4
Singapore	59.3	23.0	23.0	24.6
Thailand	10.2	3.4	2.3	2.9
Korea	1.9	0.5	0.6	1.1
Indonesia	7.6	3.8	3.7	6.5
China	14.5	20.0	24.5	25.7
Least developed countries	2.3	2.1	1.3	1.3

Source: United Nations, *World Development Report 1997*.

the share of the tertiary sector increased from 24 per cent in 1975 to 30 per cent during the early 1990s.

Foreign-owned affiliates account for a sizeable proportion of exports in some developing countries, particularly in East Asia: for example they provide more than 50 per cent of the manufactured exports and (more than 40 per cent of total exports) from Malaysia, and over 40 per cent of total exports from Indonesia (UNCTAD, 1998). Exports of foreign affiliates in developing countries as a whole increased from $242 billion in 1982 to $585 billion in 1994 (Table 2.4). It is, however, noteworthy that the share of affiliates in the exports of developing countries has remained stationary at around 32 per cent although the number of affiliates increased substantially over the period. In terms of geographical distribution of exports of affiliates, there has been a considerable shift away from Latin America towards Asia. Each of the two continents accounted for around 45 per cent of exports of foreign affiliates in developing countries in 1982, but by the end of the year 1994, the share of Asia increased dramatically to nearly 74 per cent while that of Latin America declined to 24 per cent (Table 2.4).

The record of FDI on job creation in developing countries is much less impressive than its record on exports. Available data for 1992 shows that around 41 per cent (or 12 million) of the 29 million jobs accounted for by the foreign affiliates of TNCs the world over were located in developing countries (Table 2.5). This represents a mere 2 per cent of the economically active population in these countries, although in some developing countries TNCs account for more than a quarter of total employment in the manufacturing sector. It is worth noting, however, that while the direct

Table 2.4   Exports of Foreign Affiliates, 1982–94

Region	Exports of foreign affiliates	
	1982	*1994*
Total world ($bn)	732.0	1850.0
Developed countries ($bn)	491.0	1255.0
(% of total)	67.0	68.4
Developing countries ($bn)	242.0	585.0
(% of total)	33.0	31.6
Of which: (% of LDCs)		
Africa	9.5	2.5
Latin America	45.0	23.8
Asia	45.5	73.7

Source: United Nations, *World Development Report 1997*.

Table 2.5 Estimated Employment in Transnational Corporations
(millions of employees)

	1975	1985	1990	1992
Total employment	40	65	70	73
Parent companies at home	n.a.	43	44	44
Foreign affiliates	n.a.	22	26	29
Developed countries	n.a.	15	17	17
Developing countries	n.a.	7	9	12

Source: United Nations *World Investment Report 1994*.

employment effects of FDI in developing countries may be small, the indirect employment effects could be more substantial. These include jobs in subcontractor firms which form TNCs' often extensive supply chains (although these are often of poor quality and worse paid than jobs within TNCs), as well as those generated by forward and backward linkages and multiplier effects resulting from income growth.

BASIC PROPOSITIONS

Determinants

Some three-quarters of FDI is received by a select group of ten developing countries. These are countries which possess one or more of the features and endowments sought by TNCs. These include natural resources, large domestic markets, endowments of relatively cheap but efficient labour, a developed infrastructure, macroeconomic stability, liberal trade regimes and institutional arrangements, such as export processing zones, designed to promote exports. The extant empirical literature identifies these features as the major determinants of FDI. The following basic propositions on the determinants of FDI in developing countries emerge from the literature.

Countries which pursue export-oriented trade policies as opposed to foreign trade regimes designed to promote import-substituting industrialization tend to receive larger volumes of FDI. In its strict version, the proposition is that foreign firms favour locations which are free of policy-induced product and factor market distortions (Bhagwati, 1985). They prefer to exploit the inherent comparative advantage in the production of goods and services which host countries possess, rather than profit from short-term and uncertain inducements in the form of protection from import competition provided by tariffs and quotas. However, countries such as some of the smaller Latin American countries and those in Africa which have adopted liberal trade policies have still failed to attract substantial investment inflows. This suggests that the allied factors of cheap and efficient labour, macroeconomic stability and availability of infrastructure facilities are equally important. These combined prime determinants of FDI have been statistically tested and found to be robust (Balasubramanyam and Salisu, 1991).

Where these advantages sought by TNCs are not available, various sorts of incentives including tax concessions, tax holidays and investment subsidies offered by host countries may not prove effective in attracting FDI. Competition between developing countries on the basis of incentives may not increase the total volume of FDI. As Guisinger (1992) notes, 'once the appropriate volume of investment is attained, further incentives aimed at increasing one country's share may prove to be collectively futile'.

The perceived political stability of host countries is a factor which influences the investment decisions of foreign firms. Opinion on the relative importance of political as opposed to economic stability as determinants of FDI is divided. Some studies assign primacy to economic as opposed to political factors (Root and Ahmad, 1979; Levis, 1979), others suggest that economic and political factors are equally important determinants (Schneider and Frey, 1985, Balasubramanyam and Salisu, 1991). Studies based on interviews with managers of foreign-owned firms suggest that it is the stability of policies over time rather than the stability of governments and political regimes which weigh heavily in the FDI decision process of foreign firms.

Opinion on the relationship between foreign aid and FDI is also divided. Some empirical studies report a positive relationship between private and public capital flows (Schneider and Frey, 1985). Here the explanation is that aid donors may exercise political leverage on aid recipients to provide a favourable climate for the operations of their TNCs. But a study by Balasubramanyam and Salisu (1991) reports a statistically significant negative relationship between aid flows and FDI flows for a sample of 38 developing countries over the period 1970–80. The explanation for the finding here is that countries exhibiting a relatively poor economic performance tend to receive relatively large amounts of aid, but their poor economic performance also deters them from receiving large volumes of FDI.

Impact

During the 1960s and 1970s, views on the impact of FDI on the economic welfare of developing countries ranged between extremes. Some left-wing critics charged FDI with many a sin, including fostering economic colonialism and dependency, exploitation of the international division of labour, and importation of inappropriate cultural patterns and technologies into developing countries. For its generally right-wing advocates, FDI was a potent instrument of development, with a unique ability to transfer capital, know-how and technology to developing countries. The policy makers in these countries, for their part, entertained an ambivalent attitude towards FDI, wooing it for the riches it was supposed to offer and at the same time railing against TNCs for their supposed pernicious activities. There were attempts here and there at statistical verification of the contribution of FDI to the development process, but most of them were inconclusive. The literature on FDI during this period mostly consisted of either a long list of benefits FDI could confer on developing countries, aptly dubbed the 'laundry list approach' by Paul Streeten, or a polemical diatribe on the neo-colonialist nature of the TNC and FDI.

By the middle of the 1980s, developing countries were much more sanguine about the contribution of FDI to the growth process. The debt crisis following the Mexican default of 1982 compelled most developing countries to rely increasingly on non-bank sources for their requirements of external capital. Also, by then Japan, France, Germany and the Scandinavian countries had emerged as substantial exporters of capital and opened up new sources of FDI, in addition to the US and the UK. Parallelling the change in attitude of the developing countries, there were some more objective academic attempts at assessing the contribution of FDI to development. This literature has yielded some useful data, summarized in the following propositions.

The contribution of FDI to the growth of the national product tends to be relatively higher in countries which have instituted export-oriented as opposed to import-substitution and protectionist trade regimes. Indeed, the tariff-jumping variety of FDI imposes a series of social costs on the host countries.

1. FDI in protected industries promotes the production of goods and services in which the host countries may not possess a comparative advantage.
2. Foreign firms tend to profit from the tariff protection and earn profits over and above that which they would have made in a competitive market environment.
3. In the absence of competition from imports, and in many cases from domestic firms too, foreign firms rest content with tried and tested technologies and methods of production which may be inappropriate to the factor endowments and needs of the host countries.

FDI in a competitive trade regime, however, assists the host country in exploiting its comparative advantage and promotes the growth of the social product.

These propositions have been elegantly demonstrated with the aid of theoretical models (Bhagwati, 1973; Brecher and Allejandro, 1977) and they have also received considerable statistical support. FDI has been shown to have a statistically significant impact on the growth of the real product in a sample of developing countries which had pursued liberal trade policies over the period 1970–85. In contrast, in the case of countries which had pursued the import-substituting strategy, FDI appears to have had very little impact on growth (Balasubramanyam *et al.,* 1996; de Mello, 1996). In the case of India, statistical studies show that several of the foreign firms in the chemicals and machinery sectors of the economy would not have withstood competition from imports in the absence of protection. In other words, protection had enabled them to make handsome profits but the economy could have imported the products produced by these firms at a price much lower than that charged by the protected foreign firms (Lal, 1975).

FDI has an appreciable impact on growth in countries which have attained a threshold level of development (Blomstrom *et al.*, 1996). The more developed of the developing countries are able to provide foreign firms with the sort of growth-promoting factors they seek and this explains their efficacy in promoting growth in these countries. This proposition also endorses the suggestion that foreign firms seek locations with well-developed infrastructure facilities and efficient workforces.

FDI has an appreciable impact on growth in countries which have accumulated substantial volumes of human capital (Balasubramanyam *et al.,* 1995). This proposition follows on the previous one and emphasizes that it is the human capital endowments of recipient countries which are one of the main ingredients which FDI utilizes in promoting growth.

Productive efficiency tends to be high in those sectors of manufacturing activity with relatively high levels of FDI. This proposition is based on statistical evidence relating to the manufacturing sectors in Mexico, Brazil and Uruguay (Blomstrom, 1986; Bielschowsky, 1994; Kokko *et al.*, 1996). The case studies on which the proposition is based suggest that there could be technology spillovers from foreign-owned firms to the locally owned firms.

Productivity levels of local firms converge to the levels achieved by foreign-owned firms in sectors with a strong foreign presence. This proposition too is based on statistical evidence from Mexico. The productive efficiency of foreign-owned firms tends to be high in the face of competition from locally owned firms. Spillovers of technology from foreign to local firms are unlikely to occur in industries and sectors where the technology gap between the former and the latter is large.

Evidence on the contribution of foreign firms to the growth of exports from developing countries is mixed. In countries such as Malaysia which have established a number of export processing zones, FDI has been instrumental in promoting exports of labour-intensive products such as electronic goods and clothing. In most other East Asian countries, perhaps with the exception of Singapore, locally owned firms have been as active in promoting exports as foreign-owned firms.

The contribution of foreign-owned firms to direct employment creation in developing countries is not noticeably high, except for firms located in the export processing zones in countries such as China and Malaysia. It is estimated that in 1992 TNCs accounted for a total number of 73 million jobs the world over. Around 60 per cent of these jobs were located in the home countries of the TNCs. Of the other 29 million jobs accounted for by TNCs, around 12 million were in developing countries, which is the equivalent of less than 2 per cent of the economically active population in developing countries. It is noteworthy that China alone accounted for 50 per cent of the jobs within TNCs in developing countries. These estimates do not include the number of jobs indirectly accounted for by TNCs, which are reported to be substantial, although as mentioned above, may be of lesser quality.

Evidence on the contribution to development of export processing zones, which are to be found in almost every developing country and are heavily populated by foreign firms, is mixed. In some countries, when their costs and revenues are all evaluated at world prices, the social rate of return to investment is found to be very low or negative (Balasubramanyam, 1988). In others, such as China and Korea, the social rate of return to investment is positive and they are reported to make a substantial contribution to employment.

Foreign-owned firms in general use a relatively high proportion of imported inputs in the production process. Many host countries (including OECD members) have used local content requirements and trade-balancing obligations to reduce this import propensity, although such requirements are to be phased out under the WTO's agreement on trade-related investment measures (TRIMs). Some TRIMs have been shown to introduce distortions and reduce consumer welfare (Greenaway, 1991), but there is also evidence that, carefully used, they can encourage foreign firms to accept the costs of searching for local suppliers, and thus enhance economic welfare (Balasubramanyam, 1991).

ASSESSMENT

Growth

What do all these propositions add up to? The most striking feature of FDI is that not only does it mainly take place between developed countries, but even in developing countries the bulk of it goes to only ten countries, most of which are middle-income countries. These are also the countries which are endowed with relatively high volumes of human capital and a good infrastructure. FDI appears to find its way to 'him that hath'. This should be of little surprise, as the TNC which is the major purveyor of FDI is a profit-maximizing entity: its mandate from its owners and shareholders is not to engage in altruistic development activities but to maximize profits. It can best deliver this in locations which provide an investment climate conducive to its operations. It could, however, be argued that the very act of FDI generates and promotes labour skills, technological change and investments in infrastructure. However, whether FDI promotes growth or growth promotes FDI is a much-discussed proposition in the literature. To the extent that FDI is attracted to countries which possess one or more of the growth ingredients, it may be concluded that growth promotes or attracts FDI rather than the other way round.

The other propositions concerning the impact of FDI suggest the same. FDI appears to be an effective instrument of growth in countries which have achieved a threshold of growth and human capital. The inference to be drawn from this is that FDI further trains the available human capital; it does not add to the existing stock of educated and skilled workers. If this is the case, the claim that the MAI would somehow promote inflows of FDI into the poorer of the developing countries or the least developing countries rings hollow. It would be illogical to believe that profit-maximizing firms would invest in countries with relatively low endowments of human capital, inadequate infrastructure and limited domestic markets. Acceptance by these countries of a binding multilateral agreement would have no effect in this respect.

The necessary condition for attracting FDI appears to be the possession of growth-promoting ingredients. Poorer countries with their low levels of income and savings are hardly in a position to afford the volume of investments required to make substantial improvements to human capital and infrastructure facilities. Certainly, increased foreign aid could enable these countries to equip themselves with the human capital and infrastructure facilities attractive to foreign firms. The Fitzgerald Report acknowledges the need for assistance from the OECD countries to the poor countries if they are to embrace the MAI. The report is, however, concerned with the existing external debt overhanging the poor countries, and their lack of legal and negotiating experience. It is in these areas it enjoins the OECD countries to assist the poor countries. Admittedly, poor countries might need such assistance if they were to be credible signatories of the MAI, but assistance which enables them to equip themselves with the sort of institutions and growth ingredients attractive to foreign firms would be much more important.

Would the OECD countries offer increased aid to the poor developing countries without demanding a *quid pro quo*? Their demands, as embodied in the MAI, would be for unhindered access to the poor countries for their TNCs, investors and speculators. There is some – though not conclusive – evidence, as stated earlier, that countries which are favourably disposed to FDI and TNCs from the rich countries receive substantial amounts of aid. But many developing countries which regard the MAI as no more than a neo-colonial design on the part of the rich countries to limit their economic sovereignty are likely to look upon foreign aid coupled with the MAI as a poisoned chalice.

Trade and FDI

The propositions concerning trade and FDI are also of interest in the context of the MAI and developing countries. The proposition that countries with liberal foreign trade regimes receive relatively large volumes of FDI is now well established. However, liberalization of the trade regime alone may not attract large volumes of FDI, but has to be accompanied by a favourable economic environment, which can be fostered by investments in infrastructure and promotion of labour skills. Moreover, efficient utilization of FDI requires coordination of trade policy with the policy framework governing FDI. In the absence of a coherent trade and FDI policy host countries may unwittingly give away income to TNCs, to levels incommensurate with the latter's contribution to the social product. India's programme of liberalization instituted in 1991 is a case in point. Whilst the programme has reduced tariffs and quotas on a variety of capital goods and intermediates, most consumer goods imports are prohibited or subject to steep tariffs. But restrictions on inflows of FDI into the consumer goods sector have been lifted, allowing foreign firms a protected market for consumer goods unhindered by import competition. The social costs of FDI in protected sectors referred to earlier have been rehearsed time and again in the literature. Such lack of coordination between trade and FDI policies may arise for a number of reasons. In the Indian case it is explained by the valiant attempts of policy-makers at attracting increased volumes of FDI while at the same time appeasing local business and sectional interests, which argue that imports of luxury goods should be restricted and that domestic firms producing consumer goods should be protected.

More generally, such lack of coordination between trade and FDI policies may arise if the different agencies are involved in formulating the two policies. At the global level, if the WTO is the body charged with formulating trade policy and the OECD formulates FDI policy, coordination between the two may turn out to be problematical. Indeed, one of the objections of developing countries to the MAI is that they would be unable to seek a *quid pro quo* for acceding to the MAI in the form of increased market access for their manufactured exports, if the MAI is formulated and administered by the OECD which has no mandate to regulate trade. This point has merit for a number of reasons.

1. Most developing countries are not members of the OECD, which any case does not provide a forum for negotiations on trade, which is the preserve of the WTO.
2. There is no evidence that FDI necessarily generates and promotes exports save in the case of a select few developing countries. Although technology spillovers and other externalities arising from the operations of foreign-owned firms do assist the promotion of exports, it is generally locally owned firms which are the prime movers of exports. Ways and means of gaining negotiated access to the markets of the developed countries are, therefore, essential for developing countries.
3. The growth in regionalism in the West has posed severe obstacles to the exports of developing countries, especially for the Asian countries. Again, the MAI would not provide an appropriate basis for bargaining over this important issue.

Import Intensity of Foreign Firms

The other trade-related proposition which has a bearing on the MAI is the observed relatively high import intensity of foreign-owned firms. One aspect of this is the much discussed issue of the transfer pricing practices of TNCs. It is difficult to ascertain the extent to which the high import propensity of foreign-owned firms reflects abusive transfer pricing practices. But it cannot be denied that such practices do contribute to their high import propensity. An adequate framework for investment should therefore include provisions for the regulation of transfer pricing practices, and this is a notable omission from the MAI.

On the other hand, the MAI would greatly strengthen the requirement, already established in the TRIMS agreement, to phase out performance and local content requirements. These have been used by most developing countries to try to counteract the often negative balance-of-payments and trade impacts due to the high import propensity of some FDI. Foreign firms including the Japanese firms argue they would source supplies from local sources if only they were available . Also many TNCs have successfully promoted local suppliers of inputs: in some cases these are subsidiaries of the TNCs; in others they are locally owned but have access to markets and technical help from the TNCs. Even so, local content requirements, judiciously used, may influence the foreign firms to bear the search and development costs involved in establishing local suppliers of components and parts (Balasubramanyam, 1991).

It is noteworthy here that there is no suggestion in the empirical literature on FDI that performance requirements imposed by host governments have either deterred inflows of FDI or impaired their efficiency. Admittedly, both IBM and Coca-Cola withdrew from India during the early 1970s rather than comply with the requirement that they should shed a certain proportion of equity in favour of local investors. But their withdrawal was in response to equity sharing requirements and not performance requirements. Most TNCs seem to comply with requirements concerning employment of local nationals and local content requirements. Performance requirements are often required as a condition of the granting of incentives, to ensure that firms which are recipients of incentives do contribute to development objectives in some measure. By allowing only these incentive-conditional performance requirements, the MAI could disadvantage poorer countries, which are less able to offer attractive incentives.

It should, however, be noted that such regulations may impose social costs on host countries if they are instituted indiscriminately without heed to the stage of development of host countries. Here again the strong suggestion is that FDI contributes to development objectives in countries which are able to provide it with the sort of environment and ingredients it requires for efficient operations.

Indeed, the one strong message in the empirical literature is that, in the presence of an appropriate policies and investment climate, FDI could be a potent instrument of development. Not only can it supply money capital, but more importantly it is also a channel for the transfer of technology and know-how from the rich to the poor countries. Nevertheless, it is not a panacea for the development problem. As stated earlier, efficient utilization of FDI requires a threshold of human capital, well-developed infrastructure facilities, a competitive market environment, a stable economic policy and allegiance to a liberal foreign trade regime. It is only a select few developing countries which can boast all of these advantages. Admittedly, China is now the recipient of large volumes of FDI, but China has registered a growth rate in excess of 10 per cent in recent years, she is relatively well endowed with human capital and has attempted to follow economic policies designed to maintain economic stability. But not all developing countries can measure up to the exacting demands made by foreign firms. Those which do not possess these attributes, and offer either various sorts of incentives or protection from competition as a sort of a compensation for the attributes they lack, only succeed in transferring incomes from their citizens to foreign firms.

One attribute of host countries which is essential for the efficient utilization of FDI is competition in product markets from locally owned firms. Such competition compels foreign firms to engage in product marketing innovations and cost-cutting exercises, and such research and development is beneficial to host countries. It is also competition which provides for the generation of externalities, much talked about as a major gain to host countries from the operation of foreign firms. In the face of competition, foreign firms would invest in labour training and new product innovations, and competing locally owned firms might successfully copy such innovations and entice skilled labour without having to pay for such training. Recent press reports from India suggest such competition for trained labour has emerged in the soft drinks sector, which includes both Pepsi and Coca-Cola and locally owned producers of soft drinks.

In sum, the literature on the impact of FDI suggests that whilst it does contribute to growth, technological development and employment, the conditions required for its efficient utilization are fairly stringent. It is not a recipe for development which each and every developing country can hope to adopt. It can augment existing human resources, it can provide new technologies, it can supply money capital, but it cannot ensure the efficient utilization of all these ingredients. In the absence of co-operant factors and an economic environment conducive to their operation, foreign firms may augment their private profits but do little for the growth of the social product of their host countries.

CONCLUSIONS

The main conclusions of this chapter can be briefly summarized.

1. FDI is attracted to a select number of developing countries which possess the advantages and economic environment sought by foreign

firms. Other countries which do not possess such endowments have attracted relatively low volumes of FDI, but they have paid a price for attempting to attract it, from both the costs of fiscal incentives and the low social rates of return from foreign investments.

2. FDI can be a potent instrument of development, but only in the presence of a threshold of human capital, well-developed infrastructure facilities and a stable economic climate. However, these are features exhibited by the more developed of the developing countries, and for this reason the paper has argued that FDI is a rich country's good. Until and unless developing countries are able to reach a threshold level of development, they may neither attract large volumes of FDI nor efficiently utilize that which they do attract.

3. Trade and FDI are intertwined. Efficient utilization of FDI requires coordination of trade and FDI policies. International agreements relating to FDI should recognize this interdependence between trade and FDI, and such agreements should be negotiated in fora which have a mandate to deal with both trade and investment issues.

4. There is no evidence to suggest that judiciously formulated performance requirements impair efficient operations of foreign firms.

Additionally, the chapter has argued that the premise underlying the MAI – that a legal framework giving foreign investors guaranteed rights of access to and strong protection of their rights in developing countries will serve to increase FDI flows to developing countries and also promote it efficient utilization – is false. An agreement enforceable by law will no doubt be reassuring to potential investors, but a binding agreement alone is unlikely to lure foreign firms to the relatively poor developing countries. Indeed, a great danger of the MAI is that it may further widen the gap between those countries which already have the advantages which TNCs seek, and the poorer countries which do not. The sort of advantages and economic environment foreign firms seek in these countries would have to be developed with considerable amounts of investment. Resources required for such investments have to be provided, whether through foreign aid and/or increased access to markets in developed countries for the labour-intensive exports of developing countries. FDI is a catalyst of development, not its prime mover. A catalyst will work only in the presence of other elements which can stimulate the process of development. Future attempts at formulating a multilateral framework for international investment should recognize this basic fact.

REFERENCES

Balasubramanyam, V. N. (1988) 'Export Processing Zones in Developing Countries' in D. Greenaway, (ed.) *Economic Development and International Trade.* Macmillan, Basingstoke.

Balasubramanyam, V. N. (1991) 'Putting TRIMs to Good Use', *World Development*, vol. 19, 1215–24.

Balasubramanyam, V. N. and Salisu, M. A. (1991) 'Export Promotion, Import Substitution and Direct Foreign Investment in Less Developed Countries' in A. Koekkoek and L. B. M. Mennes (eds) *International Trade and Global Environment; Essays in Honour of Jagdish Bhagwati.* Routledge, London.

Balasubramanyam, V. N., Salisu, M. A. and Sapsford, D. (1995) *Foreign Direct Investment and Growth.* Discussion Paper, Department of Economics, Lancaster University.

Balasubramanyam, V. N., Salisu, M. A. and Sapsford, D. (1996) 'Foreign Direct Investment and Growth in EP and IS Countries', *Economic Journal*, vol. 106, no. 434, 92–105.

Bhagwati, J. (1973) 'The Theory of Immiserizing Growth' in A. K. Swoboda and M. B. Connolly (eds) *International Trade and Money.* Allen & Unwin, London.

Bhagwati, J. (1985) 'Investing Abroad.' Esmee Fairbairn Lecture, Lancaster University.

Bhagwati, J. (1995) 'Trade Liberalization and "Fair Trade" Demands: Addressing the Environmental and Labour Standards Issues', *The World Economy*, vol. 18, 745–59.

Bielschowsky, R. (1994) 'Two Studies on Transnational Corporations in the Brazilian Manufacturing Sector: the 1980s and Early 1990s'. Division of Production, Productivity and Management Discussion Paper, no. 18, ECLAC.

Blomstrom, M. (1986) 'Foreign Investment and Productive Efficiency: the Case of Mexico.' *Journal of Industrial Economics*, vol. 35, 97–110.

Blomstrom, M., Lipsey, R. E. and Zejan, M. (1994) 'What Explains Growth in Developing Countries'. NBER Discussion Paper no. 1924.

Brecher, R. and Alejandro, C. (1977) 'Tariffs, Foreign Capital and Immiserising Growth', *Journal of International Economics*, vol. 7, 317–22.

Brittan, L. (1995) 'How to Make Trade Liberalization Popular', *The World Economy*, vol. 18, 761–7.

De Mello, L. R. (1996) 'Foreign Direct Investment, International Knowledge Transfers and Endogenous Growth: Time Series Evidence'. Department of Economics, University of Kent, UK, mimeo.

Fitzgerald, E. V. K. (1998) *The Development Implications of the Multilateral Agreement on Investment.* Department for International Development, London.

Greenaway, D. (1991) 'Why Are We Negotiating on Trims' in D. Greenaway, R. C. Hine, A. P. O'Brien and R. M. Thornton (eds) *Global Protectionism.* Macmillan, Basingstoke.

Guisinger, S. (1992) 'Rhetoric and Reality in International Business: a Note on the Effectiveness of Incentives', *Transnational Corporations*, vol. 1, 111–23.

Kokko, A., Tansini, R. and Zejan, M. C. (1996) 'Local Technological Capability and Productivity Spillovers from FDI in the Uruguayan Manufacturing Sector', *Journal of Development Studies*, vol. 32, 602–11.

Lal, D. (1975) *Appraising Foreign Investment In Developing Countries.* Heinemann, London.

Levis, M. (1979) 'Does Political Instability in Developing Countries Affect Foreign Investment Flow? an Empirical Examination', *Management International Review*, vol. 19, 59–68.

Root, F. R. and Ahmad, A. A. (1979) 'Empirical Determinants of Manufacturing Direct Foreign Investment in Developing Countries', *Economic Development and Cultural Change,* vol. 27, 751–67.

Schneider, F. and Frey, B. S. (1985) 'Economic and Political Determinants of Foreign Direct Investment', *World Development,* vol. 13, 161–75.

UNCTAD (1997) *World Investment Report 1997.* United Nations, Geneva.

3 A Brief History of Business Regulation

Peter Muchlinski

Recent calls for new approaches to international business rules have been created by the rapid post-war growth of international business through the activities of transnational corporations (TNCs). This has resulted in the need for a regulatory order which can both promote TNC activities and, where necessary, control them in the public interest. However, it is often overlooked that demands for international business regulation are far older than might be imagined. International business is not entirely new, and many of the issues discussed in this book were not unknown to previous generations.

The aim of this chapter[1] is to introduce the debate on investment regulation with a brief overview of the major developments in the history of international business regulation as it extends to foreign direct investment by TNCs. It does not deal with regulation of short-term capital flows, which is covered elsewhere in this book. The story to be told is one of attempts by international organizations to build an international regime of investor protection against a backdrop of reluctance by states to qualify their sovereign rights to control the entry, establishment and operations of foreign investors. The resulting tension between these interests has led to many failures of proposed investor protection treaties, though there have been some enduring institutional developments. It has also led to attempts at striking a balance between the protection of investors' rights and the rights of states to regulate them, most notably in voluntary codes of conduct.

This chapter will begin with a brief discussion of the concept of international minimum standards of treatment for aliens and their property, which, for reasons outlined below, represents the starting point for much of the historical evidence that follows. It will then catalogue the major events in the story of attempts to create an agreed international code or treaty for the regulation of foreign investor/host state relations, dividing the evidence into two sections: first, attempts to conclude a binding international investor protection convention, and, secondly, attempts to reconcile the interests of investors in protection and the interests of states in controlling investors in the national interest. This is necessary, as the first trend involves a policy of preferential treatment for foreign investors, while the latter can be seen as a reaction to such one-sided approaches. Both trends have co-existed chronologically, demonstrating that preferential treatment for foreign investors in law has never been a policy based on consensus. The chapter will end with some comments on the current state of the FDI regulation/protection debate.

INTERNATIONAL MINIMUM STANDARDS FOR ALIENS AND THEIR PROPERTY

During the nineteenth century the major Western European powers and the United States developed agreed international minimum standards for the treatment of aliens and their property. In particular, they considered that the property of foreigners should not be taken without due process of law and without prompt, full and effective compensation. Furthermore, contracts between host states and private foreign investors were to be accorded the utmost respect, requiring the preservation of the bargain even where its terms proved disadvantageous to the host state.

As Lipson points out, these principles emerged out of the 'orderly climate of European diplomacy after the Congress of Vienna', and were 'elaborated and sustained by the expansive foreign policies of the Great Powers, particularly Great Britain' (Lipson, 1985: 38). As such they represented the consensus of the great capitalist and imperialist powers of the nineteenth century.

However, these principles did not go unchallenged. They were opposed, first, by the Latin American states that gained their independence during the nineteenth century. In particular, the Calvo doctrine, named after the Argentine jurist Carlos Calvo, sought to redress what was perceived as an unjust intrusion into the domestic affairs of those states by the home countries of foreign investors. In response to regular instances of armed and/or diplomatic interventions by these states on behalf of investors who claimed damage to their property and commercial interests, the Calvo doctrine asserts, first, that aliens should not be granted better than strict national treatment (treatment no different from that accorded to local nationals in the same situation) by the host state; and, secondly, that foreign states shall not enforce their citizens' private claims by violating the territorial sovereignty of host states either through diplomatic or armed intervention (Wiesner, 1992: 437).[2]

The second line of challenge came from the ideology of socialism, which denied the validity of private property rights, whether held by

nationals or foreigners, and which resulted in the first major nationalizations of foreign-owned property following the Russian Revolution in
1917 (Lipson, 1985: 66–70). The third major challenge came after the
Second World War from the newly independent former colonial states of
Asia and Africa (Lipson, 1985: ch. 4). In unison with the much older but
economically less developed states of Latin America, these countries
sought redress for past and, in their view, continuing economic exploitation from the Northern former colonial powers. This was to be achieved
through active state involvement in the economy, including the use of
expropriation as a weapon of sovereign power. This was expressed in the
principles for a New International Economic Order put forward in 1974.
This view legitimated the expropriation of foreign-owned property for
'appropriate' rather than 'full' compensation, the termination of
unfavourable contracts with foreigners and increased state control over the
activities of foreign investors (Muchlinski, 1995: 503; United Nations,
1974: Article 2).

The result of these challenges to traditional norms of international law
was to generate uncertainty as to the content of customary international
law in the field of foreign investment. Indeed in the *Barcelona Traction*
case (ICJ, 1970: 46–7, paras. 89–90), the International Court of Justice
maintained that there was no single accepted body of international law that
laid down universally recognized standards for the treatment of foreign
investors by host states. The Court saw the reason for this as lying in 'an
intense conflict of systems and interests' between states, from which no
generally accepted rules of international law in the field could emerge.
Such standards as did apply were the product of bilateral agreements
between states and, therefore, could not bind other states.

On the other hand, it should be stressed that all states, whether capital
exporting or importing, have accepted as a general principle of public
international law the right to control the entry, establishment and presence
of foreigners. Only where the receiving state has entered into treaty commitments that guarantee rights of entry and establishment is this general
principle modified. Thus the debate on international minimum standards
has tended to emphasize the post-entry treatment of foreign investors
rather than the pre-entry issues of market access and rights of establishment. Such pre-entry issues have, in the past, been included in bilateral
friendship, commerce and navigation treaties and in regional economic
integration agreements. However, it is only recently that such matters have
taken a central place in multilateral negotiations, as is the case with the
Multilateral Agreement on Investment (MAI).

ATTEMPTS TO DEVELOP AN AGREED INTERNATIONAL
CODE FOR THE REGULATION OF FOREIGN INVESTOR/
HOST STATE RELATIONS

Against this background of normative uncertainty, numerous attempts
have been made over time to develop an agreed international code for the
regulation of foreign investor/host state relations. Such a code can be seen
as an international instrument that seeks to define with certainty the minimum standards of behaviour that states should follow in their treatment of
foreign investors and/or that investors should follow in the conduct of
their operations in host states. These attempts at codification will be
described by distinguishing between proposals that aimed purely at reinforcing investor protection standards without reference to the rights of
states to control investors, and those which sought to strike a balance
between investor and state interests.

Investor Protection Initiatives

Attempts to formulate a binding investor protection regime were made
periodically between the late 1920s and the early 1960s (Fatouros, 1961;
Miller, 1959; Snyder, 1961; Boyle, 1961). In 1929 the League of Nations
held a diplomatic conference for the purpose of concluding an international convention on the treatment of foreigners and foreign enterprises.[3]
This was followed in 1930 by the Hague Conference on the Codification
of International Law, which included the subject of the responsibility of
states for damage caused in their territory to the person or property of foreigners (Hackworth, 1930). Neither initiative met with success, due to the
refusal of Latin American, newly independent East European and other
ex-colonial states to accept the traditional international minimum standards of treatment insisted upon by the capital-exporting states.[4]

   After the Second World War, attempts at stimulating interest in a multilateral convention on foreign investment were made mainly by private sector bodies.[5] In 1949 the ICC issued a draft code for the 'Fair Treatment of
Foreign Investments' as a continuation of its campaign, launched in 1931,
for the conclusion of an international convention guaranteeing the protection of the private property rights of foreign investors. The ICC repeated
its call for such a treaty in 1957 (Miller, 1959: 372; Snyder, 1961: 480–1).
Also in 1957, the German Society to Advance the Protection of Foreign
Investments published a draft code entitled 'International Convention for
the Mutual Protection of Private Property Rights in Foreign Countries'.[6]
In early 1958, another privately inspired draft convention on foreign

investments came from a group of European international lawyers headed by Sir Hartley Shawcross (Brandon, 1959: 12–15). These two initiatives were combined into a single draft convention in 1959. The draft was concluded under the auspices of a new body of international lawyers and European business representatives, the International Association for the Promotion and Protection of Private Foreign Investment (Abs-Shawcross Draft, 1960). This convention was taken up by the then Organization for European Economic Cooperation (OEEC, now OECD), and led to the OECD Draft Convention on the Protection of Foreign Property (OECD, 1962). However, this draft convention failed to achieve sufficient support to be opened for signature, owing to the reluctance of the less developed members of the Organization (including Greece, Portugal and Turkey) to bind themselves to some of the proposed provisions, which leant heavily towards the interests of capital exporters (Snyder, 1963: 1112–13; UNCTC, 1988: 7, para. 20). Instead, the Council of the OECD, by a resolution adopted on 12 October 1967, commended the draft convention to member states as a model for investment protection treaties and as a basis for ensuring the observance of the principles of international law which it contained (UNCTC, 1988: 7, para. 20; Denza and Brooks, 1987: 910). Thus the OECD draft, while failing to contribute towards a general codification of the international law relating to foreign investments, has provided 'important guidelines for some of the more fundamental provisions on the treatment and protection of investments included in bilateral investment treaties.' (UNCTC, 1988: 7, para. 20).

Finally, the European League for Economic Cooperation, a body representing the views of industrial and banking interests (Fatouros, 1961: 88, n. 88), published a report in February 1958 on the initiative of the group's German national committee, suggesting that countries of the European Economic Community (EEC) draw up a common plan for the protection of foreign investments. This involved the conclusion of a 'solidarity convention' between the member states binding them to common action on the protection of foreign investments. This convention would be open to non-EEC capital-exporting states and would act as the first step towards the acceptance of a Charter of Fair Treatment for Foreign Investors.

These private initiatives all had as their objective the affirmation, by binding treaty, of what were described above as contested international standards for the protection of foreign investors. The pattern of action in the decades between the early 1930s and 1960s was little changed: private bodies representing business interests sought to reinforce disputed rules of international law by attempting to persuade international organizations to adopt conventions containing those norms, while the member states of those organizations could not agree whether those norms represented international *opinio juris* on the subject. The various attempts at codification in the interests of private foreign investors therefore failed.

This left the route of bilateral investment treaties (BITs) as the only means of institutionalizing norms of international law in the field of investor protection. The standards of protection contained in such treaties centre on fair and equitable treatment for investors, the non-discrimination standards of national treatment and 'most favoured nation' treatment, and the general duty to observe obligations entered into with the investor. In addition, BITs protect the investor's right to compensation for losses due to war or other armed conflict, national emergency or civil disturbance, or for expropriation, and assert the principle of free transfer of funds (Dolzer and Stevens, 1995).

More recently, three significant developments occurred during 1994: the NAFTA came into force, while the Energy Charter Treaty and the Uruguay Round Final Act were signed. All contain significant investor-protection provisions. The NAFTA offers an approach based mainly on US BIT practice, which is not generally reflected in the BIT practice of other states. In particular, it extends the notion of investor protection on the basis of non-discrimination standards to the pre-entry stage, thereby subjecting market access issues to review, and effectively giving a right of entry (Muchlinski, 1995: 239–45; Gestrin and Rugman, 1994, 1996). The Energy Charter treaty represents an experiment in multilateral standard setting for the protection and promotion of trade and investment in a specific sector – the energy industry – and a specific region – the former Soviet Union, the transitional states of Central and Eastern Europe and the EU. However, the US did not sign this treaty, essentially on the grounds that it did not contain pre-entry protection for foreign investors (Waelde, 1996). The Final Act of the Uruguay Round contains three agreements relevant to the protection of foreign investors: the GATS, which contains some limited rights of market access for providers of services, based on an 'opt-in' approach that allows the host state to specify which sectors of services industries will be open for foreign investors, as well as non-discrimination standards for the treatment of foreign investors; the TRIPS, which protects investors' proprietary rights in intellectual property held by them; and the TRIMS, which seeks to control certain types of performance requirements imposed upon foreign investors on entry where these involve trade restrictions, for example local content rules (Muchlinski, 1995: 250–60).

Finally, certain notable institutional developments should be mentioned that aim to further the protection of foreign investors. The earliest in point of time is the World Bank-sponsored Washington Convention on the

Settlement of Investment Disputes Between States and Nationals of Other States 1965 (World Bank, 1965). This was the first multilateral system for the delocalized settlement of investment disputes, offering conciliation or arbitration for disputes between a host contracting state and an investor from another contracting state before a tribunal established for that purpose, the International Centre for the Settlement of Investment Disputes (ICSID). Secondly, the World Bank has entered the sphere of investment-guarantee insurance through the principles found in the Multilateral Investment Guarantee Agency Convention 1985 (World Bank, 1985) (Muchlinski, 1995: 514–19).

Attempts to Reconcile Investor and State Interests

After the Second World War, a major attempt was made at a general multi-lateral treaty that included a code on the protection of foreign investment, as well as a right of states to regulate foreign investors, through the proposed Charter of the International Trade Organization signed at Havana, Cuba, on 24 March 1948. The Havana Charter contained a number of provisions relevant to the regulation of foreign investment, including the control of restrictive business practices (Article V: see Lockwood, 1947), protection of the security of foreign investments[7] and an assertion of the right of capital-importing states to control the conditions of entry and establishment of inward investment.[8] The inclusion of a right of capital-importing states to control the conditions of foreign investment, and the absence of any unequivocal provision for compensation in the case of expropriation, caused widespread opposition to the Havana Charter among business interests and contributed to its demise when the United States and other signatory states did not ratify it (Fatouros, 1961: 80; Lipson, 1985: 86–7).

A similar fate befell the Economic Agreement of Bogota, the second post-war multilateral attempt to deal *inter alia* with the regulation and protection of private foreign investment. This agreement, signed at the Ninth International Conference of American States on 2 May 1948, did not come into effect, as a result of fundamental disagreements between the capital-exporting and capital-importing states over the proper measure of compensation in cases of expropriation (Fatouros, 1961: 81; Snyder, 1961: 474).

By contrast, in the 1970s international organizations began to accept the legitimacy of claims by capital-importing states for greater control over the conditions of entry and establishment, and over the subsequent conduct of foreign investors within their territory. The balancing of the interests of private foreign investors and those of the host state, first attempted in the abortive Havana Charter, became the basis for the new codes of conduct for multinational enterprises first proposed in the early 1970s. In particular, the now-defunct UN Draft Code of Conduct for Transnational Corporations sought to provide such a balance. The initial emphasis of the UN Code was on the control of possible abuses of power by TNCs in both the political and economic spheres. However, from as early as 1980 the Code included a section on the protection and promotion of investment. It was gradually moved towards this position and away from a position emphasizing investor control during the negotiating process. However, the Draft Code failed to secure general agreement as a result of the resurgence of irreconcilable differences between capital-exporting and capital-importing states over the role of international law in the draft Code and the related issues of the proper rule as to compensation for expropriation and as to the conduct of disputes, as well as the precise meaning of references to 'national treatment' (Muchlinski, 1995: 592–7).

Despite the failure of the draft UN Code, other codes have been concluded. Within the UN family of specialized agencies there has been the 1977 ILO Tripartite Declaration of Principles Concerning Multinational Enterprises and Social Policy, which deals with basic labour standards and is addressed to TNCs and governments alike. Other codes have dealt with more specific issues, such as the Set of Principles on Restrictive Business Practices, approved by a UN General Assembly Resolution (UNGA 35/63, 5 December 1980), the Guidelines for Consumer Protection (UNGA 39/248, 9 April 1985), and the WHO's International Code of Marketing of Breastmilk Substitutes.[9] Outside the UN the most important codes of conduct are the OECD Declaration and Guidelines on Multinational Enterprises of 1976 and the 1992 World Bank Guidelines on the Treatment of Foreign Direct Investment. Both include provisions on the protection of foreign investors (of which TNCs are the most significant) with an emphasis on the 'national treatment' principle as modified by reference to rules of international law. Thus, both codes assert that a foreign investor is entitled to treatment no less favourable than that accorded to a domestic investor in the same line of business, subject to preferential treatment where this is required under the international minimum standards of treatment for aliens and their property.[10] On the other hand, the OECD Guidelines also include provisions on the behaviour of TNCs ranging from general attitudes towards host states to more specific matters concerning *inter alia* disclosure of information, employment practices, taxation and environmental matters. However, the OECD Guidelines are not legally binding and they cannot be used to bring cases against firms that are alleged to have behaved in breach of the Guidelines. Nevertheless, when the TUAC has raised issues about the behaviour of particular firms (mainly plant closures during the 1970s), it has been accepted that the CIIME can be approached for an interpretation of the Guidelines without being asked to pronounce on a particular dispute (Muchlinski, 1995: 578–92; Blanpain, 1983). Equally, the World Bank Guidelines are non-enforceable and so cannot be used by foreign investors to bring cases against host states. Finally, also of importance are the OECD Codes of Liberalization, which embody the OECD member countries' commitment to the progressive liberalization of capital movements and provision of services, including a right of establishment (OECD, 1961).

Conclusions on the Current State of the Debate

From the foregoing it is clear that the continuing tension between the protection and regulation of investors by states has raised a number of unresolved issues concerning multilateral investment rules: should these tend towards investor protection alone, or towards a balance between protection and regulation? should they be binding or voluntary? should foreign investors be offered privileged treatment based on international minimum standards or only strict national treatment, in other words, should foreign investors be entitled to better treatment than domestic investors? should other standards of treatment apply, for example, fair and equitable treatment, bearing in mind that this standard has been criticized for being vague and not necessarily sensitive to the needs of developing host states?

It has been argued in the 1990s by proponents of the so-called New World Economic Order that these debates have been overcome by events, in that the contemporary environment is more suited to the successful creation of a new multilateral regime for investor protection, as a result of shifts towards liberalization, privatization and the recognition of the utility of inward direct investment by TNCs as a source of capital and technology. As a product of this conviction, the draft MAI is based on earlier models of binding investor protection standards, with the novel and very important extension of non-discrimination standards to the pre-entry stage, while confining business responsibilities to already existing voluntary standards through the addition of the OECD guidelines to the MAI as a non-binding annex. This formulation has been criticized as displaying an imbalance between investor rights and responsibilities, and has prompted NGOs, unions, consumer groups and others to campaign for the introduction of tougher responsibilities for investors in the MAI and greater respect for the state regulation of foreign investors.

Arguably, the prospects for such responsibilities and state powers being enshrined in binding multilateral rules remain poor, although pressure continues for such developments. Alongside this, many of the recent efforts of campaigners and social activists have concentrated upon the use and development of voluntary codes, which appear, for the present, to offer the most effective way of achieving change in a negotiating environment that may be as yet unwilling to accept binding rules for international business. It is to the effects of such codes that the next two chapters turn.

NOTES

1.   This chapter draws heavily and expands upon Muchlinski, 1995: 573–5, and Muchlinski, 1996: 207–17.
2.   In more recent years Latin American states have tended to move away from the Calvo doctrine.
3.   See Cutler, 1933; Kuhn, 1930; Potter, 1930. For the proceedings of the conference see League of Nations, 1930; for the text of the draft convention under discussion see League of Nations, 1928.
4.   Lipson argues that the outcome of these initiatives

> is less surprising than the fact that they were held at all. That they were illustrates the decline of traditional norms and enforcement capacity during the interwar period. Major European states could no longer legitimate the old standards, and they could no longer substitute effective force for agreement. To revive the rules they needed sustained agreement among themselves and significant approval from a wide number of peripheral states ... If traditional norms were to be reestablished, truly international conferences were essential. Yet the outcome of those conferences paradoxically accelerated the decline of traditional norms.

> This was due to the equality of voting rights for all states, ignoring vast differences in wealth and power: Lipson, 1985: 75–6.

5.   Apart from these initiatives certain states also made proposals to international organisations for the adoption of a multilateral convention for the protection of foreign investments. Thus at the 14th Session of the UN Economic Commission for Asia and the Far East (ECAFE), in March 1958, the Prime Minister of Malaya suggested the conclusion of an international investment charter; also in 1958 both the German and Swiss governments submitted draft investment conventions to the Organization for European Economic Cooperation (now OECD). In 1957 discussions took place under the auspices of the Council of Europe for an investment convention between the member states of the Council and certain African states.
6.   For an analysis of this code see Miller, 1959. This code was inspired by the President of the Society, Dr Hermann Abs, a director of the Deutsche Bank, who proposed the adoption of a 'magna carta' of foreign investment at the

International Industrial Development Conference in October 1957: Brandon, 1959: 12.

7. Havana Charter Article 11(1)(b): '... no member shall take unreasonable or unjustified action within its territories injurious to the rights and interests of nationals of other Members in the enterprise, skills, capital, arts or technology which they have supplied.' Article 12(2)(a)(i): provision of reasonable security for existing and future investments; Art. 12(2)(a)(ii): the giving of due regard to the desirability of avoiding discrimination as between foreign investments; Article 12(2)(b): entry into consultation or negotiations with other governments to conclude bilateral or multilateral agreements relating to foreign investments.

8. Havana Charter Article 12(1)(c):

> ... without prejudice to existing international agreements to which members are parties, a Member has the right (i) to take any appropriate safeguards necessary to ensure that foreign investment is not used as a basis for interference in its internal affairs or national policies; (ii) to determine whether and to what extent and upon what terms it will allow future foreign investment; (iii) to prescribe and give effect on just terms to requirements as to the ownership of existing or future investments; (iv) to prescribe and give effect to other reasonable requirements as to the ownership of existing or future investments.

For a critical comment on this provision, see Woolsey, 1948: 126–8.

9. A useful source of such documents is provided by UNCTAD, 1996.
10. OECD, 1994a: 58, 'National Treatment'; World Bank, 1992, Guideline III. See further OECD, 1993, OECD, 1994b.

REFERENCES

Abs-Shawcross (1960) 'Draft Convention on the Protection of Foreign Property', *Journal of Public Law,* vol. 9, 116–18.

Barcelona Traction Case (1970) *Case Concerning the Barcelona Traction, Light and Power Company, Limited* (New Application: 1962) (Belgium v Spain), Second Phase, Judgement of 5 February 1970, ICJ International Court of Justice Reports 1970, 3.

Blanpain, R. (1983) *The OECD Guidelines for Multinational Enterprises and Labour Relations 1979–82: Experience and Mid-Term Report.* Kluwer, Deventer.

Boyle, D. A. V. (1961) 'Some Proposals for a World Investment Convention', *Journal of Business Law*, 18.

Brandon, M. (1959) 'An International Investment Code: Current Plans', *Journal of Business Law*, 7.

Cutler, J. W. (1933) 'The Treatment of Foreigners in Relation to the Draft Convention and Conference of 1929', *American Journal of International Law*, vol. 27, 225.

Denza, E. and Brooks, S. (1987) 'Investment Protection Treaties: United Kingdom Experience', *International and Comparative Law Quarterly*, vol. 36, 908.

Dolzer, R. and Stevens, M. (1995) *Bilateral Investment Treaties*. Martinus Nijhoff, The Hague.

Fatouros, A. A. (1961) 'An International Code to Protect Private Investment –
   Proposals and Perspectives', *University of Toronto Law Journal*, vol. 14, 77.
Gestrin, M. and Rugman, A. (1994) 'The North American Free Trade Agreement
   and Foreign Direct Investment', *Transnational Corporations*, vol. 3, 77.
Gestrin, M. and Rugman, A. (1996) 'The NAFTA Investment Provisions:
   Prototype for Multilateral Investment Rules?' in *Market Access After the
   Uruguay Round*. OECD, Paris, 63.
Hackworth, G. H. (1930) 'Responsibility of States for Damages Caused in Their
   Territory to the Person or Property of Foreigners', *American Journal of
   International Law*, vol. 24, 500.
Kuhn, A. K. (1930) 'The International Conference on the Treatment of
   Foreigners', *American Journal of International Law*, vol. 24, 570.
League of Nations (1928) Doc. C.174. M.53. 1928 II.
League of Nations (1930) Doc. C.97. M.23. 1930 II.
Lipson, C. (1985) *Standing Guard: Protecting Foreign Capital in the Nineteenth
   and Twentieth Centuries*. University of California Press, Berkeley.
Lockwood, J. E. (1947) 'Proposed International Legislation with Respect to
   Business Practices', *American Journal of International Law,* vol. 41, 616.
Miller, A. S. (1959) 'Protection of Private Foreign Investment by Multilateral
   Convention', *American Journal of International Law*, vol. 53, 371.
Muchlinski, P. T. (1995) *Multinational Enterprises and the Law.* Blackwell
   Publishers, Oxford.
Muchlinski, P. T. (1996) 'The Energy Charter Treaty: Towards a New International
   Order for Trade and Investment or a Case of History Repeating Itself?' in
   T. Waelde (ed.) *The Energy Charter Treaty.* Kluwer Law International, London.
OECD (1961) *Code on the Liberalisation of Current Invisible Operations*
   OECD/C(61)95; *Code on the Liberalisation of Capital Movements* OECD/C
   (61)96, periodically re-issued. OECD, Paris.
OECD (1962) *Draft Convention on the Protection of Foreign Property.* OECD,
   Paris. No.1563[6]7/Dec.1962; reproduced in *International Legal Materials*
   vol. 1–2, 241 (1962–3). The last revision of the draft Convention can be found
   in OECD Publication no.232081/Nov.1967 reproduced in *International Legal
   Materials*, vol. 7, 117 (1968).
OECD (1993) *National Treatment for Foreign-Controlled Enterprises.* OECD,
   Paris.
OECD (1994a) *OECD Guidelines for Multinational Enterprises.* OECD, Paris.
OECD (1994b) *National Treatment for Foreign-Controlled Enterprises.* Working
   Paper no. 34. OECD, Paris.
Potter, P. B. (1930) 'International Legislation on the Treatment of Foreigners',
   American Journal of International Law, vol. 24, 748.
Snyder, E. (1961) 'Protection of Private Foreign Investment: Examination and
   Appraisal', *International and Comparative Law Quarterly*, vol. 10, 469.
Snyder, E. (1963) 'Foreign Investment Protection: a Reasoned Approach',
   Michigan Law Review, vol. 61, 1087.
United Nations (1974) 'Charter of Economic Rights and Duties of States'.
   International Legal Materials, vol. 14 (1975), 251.
UNCTC (United Nations Centre for Transnational Corporations) (1988) *Bilateral
   Investment Treaties*. UN Sales No. E.88.II.A.I. United Nations, New York.

Waelde, T. (ed.) (1996) *The Energy Charter Treaty.* Kluwer Law International, London.

Wiesner, E. (1992) 'ANCOM: a New Attitude Toward Foreign Investment?', *University of Miami Inter-American Law Review*, vol. 24, 436.

Woolsey, L. H. (1948) 'The Problem of Foreign Investment', *American Journal of International Law,* vol. 42, 121.

World Bank (1965) 'Washington Convention on the Settlement of Investment Disputes Between States and Nationals of Other States'. *International Legal Materials*, vol. 4, 524; also in *United Nations Treaty Series*, vol. 575 (1965), 159.

World Bank (1985) 'Multilateral Investment Guarantee Agency Convention'. *International Legal Materials*, vol. 24, 1598.

World Bank (1992) 'Guidelines on the Treatment of Foreign Direct Investment'. *International Legal Materials*, vol. 31, 1363.

4 Defending the Legacy of Rio: the Civil Society Campaign against the MAI

Nick Mabey

The scale and strength of the world-wide campaign against the proposed MAI[1] demonstrated the fundamental impact of the 1992 Rio Earth Summit on international economic negotiations, and the importance of the core Rio principles of participation, consultation and sustainable development (UNEP, 1992). The MAI negotiation was initially followed by only a few NGOs, starting in mid-1996, but the network of interested groups grew at an amazing pace as its implications became widely known (WWF, 1996; CUTS, 1996; CI, 1996). The first formal NGO consultation with OECD negotiators in October 1997 was attended by over 70 people representing more than 30 organizations from all regions of the world. The joint statement arising from that meeting was endorsed by over 600 development, consumer, environment, citizens, human rights and indigenous peoples organizations (FoE-I, 1998a). The campaign also spread to encompass local authorities, state/provincial governments, parliamentarians, affected industries and developing country governments.[2] Unions, through their official representatives to the OECD, have generally not been against the MAI as a whole, concentrating their efforts on improving MAI clauses on labour standards. However, as opposition from other groups grew, more radical voices emerged, especially in France. A significant point of the campaign came in March 1998 when the European Parliament approved a resolution which was highly critical of the MAI by 437 votes to 8 (European Parliament, 1998).

This broad-based campaign emerged spontaneously, powered by mutually held concerns over how the MAI would institutionalize existing patterns of power and (under-)development; effectively preventing evolution towards sustainable development in a globalized economy. The common international NGO position was summarized in the Joint Statement (FoE-I, 1998a):

> There is an obvious need for multilateral regulation of investments in view of the scale of social and environmental disruption created by the

increasing mobility of capital. However, the intention of the MAI is not to regulate investments but to regulate governments. As such, the MAI is unacceptable.

The campaign was coordinated, and information shared, primarily through the Internet. This enabled groups who could actively follow and analyse the MAI negotiations to disseminate information to a global audience, and helped NGOs with fewer resources, especially in the South, to engage in a fast moving, highly technical international negotiation process and to collect up-to-the-minute material with which to lobby and inform their own governments, public and media. The importance of this new form of campaigning was underlined by the *Financial Times'* comment 'some think it could fundamentally alter the way international economic agreements are negotiated' (De Jonquieres, 1998).

This campaign was a significant factor in the decision to suspend negotiations in April and finally abandon them in December 1998; but the real NGO victory has been in moving the debate about the MAI away from narrow technical issues towards a wide-ranging discussion about the regulation of globalization. This shift was emphasized in the OECD ministerial statement (27 April 1998) which devoted only one paragraph to diplomatic and technical reasons for delay, and instead concentrated on the need for governments to engage in a discussion with 'interested groups in their societies' over the process of globalization and the implications of the MAI. It remains to be seen, however, whether this will be taken seriously. The speed with which the main MAI negotiators in the European Commission, Japan and the USA put forward proposals for the WTO to negotiate investment rules very much along the lines of the MAI suggests that they have not understood, or are reluctant to accept, the substantive criticisms of the MAI made by NGOs.

This chapter presents some of the principal components of the NGO critique of the MAI, although it does not aim to represent the views of any one organization, or be a consensus statement. As would be expected from such a diverse group of organizations, criticisms of the MAI cover many different issues, and range from analysis of textual ambiguities to fundamental questioning of the principles and assumptions underlying the treaty. However, whatever their focus all NGOs in the campaign agree that if implemented the MAI would have serious negative effects and irreversibly shape the world economically, environmentally, socially and culturally well into the twenty-first century. Undoubtedly, the future process and content of the MAI – or any other proposed international rules on investment – will form the litmus test of governments' real commitment to the Rio Principles of sustainable development and broader human rights.

My discussion of the main inadequacies of the MAI will focus on five main points: the secretive, exclusionary and undemocratic nature of the negotiating process; the MAI's granting of rights without responsibilities; its restriction on the ability of countries to choose their own appropriate development strategy; its failure to give citizens protections or rights to balance those of investors; and its conflicts with national and international environmental regulation. By drawing attention to these, it may be hoped that a new approach might begin to be charted, which would strengthen instead of weakening the regulatory framework for international investment. International flows of capital have the potential to improve people's lives, but only if preceded by adequate international and national regulation, designed to prevent restrictive business practices; protect and enhance environmental and labour standards; facilitate development at both national and local levels; and ensure investors respect human, cultural and community rights.

SUFFOCATED BY ITS OWN SECRECY: HOW A FLAWED PROCESS UNDERMINED THE MAI

The MAI emerged from a long tradition of non-binding investment agreements among OECD members. Its initial preparation period began in 1991 with the OECD secretariat and others working closely with business organizations such as the ICC on the initial research. Negotiations were formally launched in mid-1995, with completion initially planned for May 1997.

The MAI was seen by multinational companies as the way of achieving their ambitions on market access which were only partially realized in the GATS and TRIMS agreements. The position of international business was clearly stated in the 1996 ICC position paper on international investment rules: 'The preponderance of restrictions on foreign investment lie *outside the OECD area* ... Business needs the benefits of an international investment regime to include the fast-growing countries of Asia, central and eastern Europe, and Latin America' (emphasis added). Yet paradoxically, the use of the OECD as a negotiating forum for a free-standing international agreement which would be open to all was aimed to bypass the 'low standard' forum of the WTO where developing countries have equal representation – if not equal negotiating power. Although primarily a trade body, the remit of the WTO has been greatly widened, to open up all markets for goods and services, and there has been pressure for it to extend to investment liberalization. This has generally been resisted by developing countries, and the WTO has been limited to studying linkages between trade and investment. By starting the MAI negotiations, the OECD countries opened a twin-track process, hoping that the MAI would be both an alternative to and a blueprint for a WTO agreement. Despite the setback in 1998, this remains their strategy.

The OECD countries are the source of 90 per cent of outward investment flows, so they are obviously interested in gaining access for their investors to markets which are currently subject to various controls on inward investment, and to enhancing the security of these investments. This applies especially to financial services and manufacturing in Asia and Latin America, although ironically some of these aims have been achieved in South East Asia, even if only temporarily, through conditions laid down by the IMF on the bail-out loans after the 1997/8 financial crisis (Public Citizen, 1998). Developing countries are also being pressured to open up their economies through negotiations around the Free Trade Area of the Americas and the renegotiation of the Lomé Agreement. NGOs find this multi-faceted and concerted drive for unconditional investment liberalization deeply worrying, especially as those countries which liberalized in the late 1980s under Structural Adjustment Programmes saw little increase in foreign investment as a result (ODI, 1997). Liberalization aims at removing the power of governments in developing countries to gain added value from foreign investment through development conditions on market access.

The OECD strategy is fundamentally contradictory. On the one hand, OECD countries have argued that few non-OECD or developing countries will join the MAI, so their exclusion does not matter. However, these statements are undermined by both the business position quoted above and the public views of governments such as the UK and Ireland which are encouraging broad accession by developing countries.[3] Brazil, Argentina, Chile, Hong Kong, Slovakia and the Baltic States were accepted as observers to the negotiations and potential founder members of the agreement, and the MAI negotiators visited all corners of the world to hold 'informative sessions' with governments of key developing countries. Clearly, the ultimate aim of advocates of the MAI is a global agreement covering all investment flows.

The most fundamental NGO criticism of the MAI is that the OECD negotiations are attempting to impose an unfair and biased agreement on the rest of the world in order to benefit their own TNCs and speculators. The WTO is also seen as an inappropriate forum, biased towards liberalization, in which developing countries have little real power (Third World Network, 1998). NGOs instead urge that negotiations for rules governing international investment – not necessarily including liberalization provisions – should take place under the auspices of the United Nations inside a truly democratic and representative forum.

As well as excluding developing countries, the MAI was also hidden from governmental, public and parliamentary scrutiny in OECD countries throughout much of its negotiation. Indeed, by establishing the negotiation as a 'free-standing' one, it was even removed from the involvement of other OECD committees and their secretariats, notably those concerned with the environment and development. By the time they were drawn into the discussions, the basic structure of the agreement was established, so their contributions would either remain cosmetic or result in large 'carve-outs' (see Chapter 5 in this volume).

The first details of the MAI emerged in June 1996, a year after negotiations were started. All negotiating papers and texts were confidential until February 1998, but leaked copies of some documents were obtained by NGOs from around October 1996 – only six months before the treaty was originally meant to be signed. In most OECD countries responsibility for negotiating the MAI rested with the trade or finance departments. In very few countries were any other departments involved until NGOs began concerted lobbying in 1997. Even at the height of negotiations on environment and labour issues only two countries sent members of their environment departments to Paris, and only the UK had representatives of its development department present. This lack of coordination has been one of the main causes of problems with the MAI, because negotiators have not understood the implications of the agreement for other policy areas. The negotiators have resisted rather than welcoming broader expertise into the process, despite OECD ministerial declarations from 1991 affirming that:

> a key to sustainable development, and thus to ensuring sound environmental management, lies in the *full integration of economic and environmental policies*. ... There is a fundamental link between economic growth and the environment. Economic and environmental policies cannot be made and implemented in isolation (OECD, 1991; emphasis in the original).

Restatements of this principle in 1996 and 1997 explicitly included social issues as the third 'leg' of sustainable development that must be integrated inside policy development. Such integration has been absent from the MAI process, apart from a cursory and incomplete attempt at an environmental review and some late proposals for amendments on labour and environmental issues which, if agreed, would make a minor impact.[4]

National parliaments were not consulted about the MAI, and only after the NGO campaign and the increased publicity surrounding the negotiations did parliamentary questions result in governmental statements and some debates, although little serious analysis was carried out. The most impressive attempts at democratic oversight occurred in Canada, where the campaign was initially strongest (Canada, 1997), and then in the European Parliament which assembled a joint report from five of its committees (European Parliament, 1998). As well as calling for a halt to MAI negotiations pending a public review of its implications, this report highlighted its regret that the MAI negotiations had been conducted 'in the utmost secrecy', with national parliaments completely excluded.

The secrecy surrounding the MAI negotiations was a major factor contributing to its flawed and damaging approach. By failing to include experts and opinions from other government departments, parliaments and civil society, the MAI negotiators produced a treaty driven by narrow business interests and neo-liberal ideology. However, the acknowledgement of this deficiency by the negotiators in the 28 April statement, and the last-ditch attempt to undertake an environmental review, set a precedent for future negotiations. As was acknowledged by Sir Leon Brittan and President Clinton at the 1998 WTO Ministerial Meeting, international economic agreements cannot expect to obtain democratic support if they continue to be negotiated in secrecy. The campaign to expose the MAI negotiations has contributed to the sea change in the norms of international economic diplomacy by irrevocably opening the door to participation, policy integration and greater democracy.

'LICENCE TO LOOT'? HOW THE MAI WOULD ENHANCE CORPORATE RIGHTS WITHOUT RESPONSIBILITIES

The MAI would have given sweeping new rights and protections to foreign investors without any balancing responsibilities. The net effect of these new rights was characterized by one NGO as giving corporations a 'licence to loot' the human, social and environmental resources of the globe for their own profit (FoE-I/FoE-US, 1998b). Investors would gain the ability to sue governments directly if they felt their rights under the agreement had been breached, thus giving them the same legal standing as nation states. MAI negotiators have argued that this is not new, since investors can already sue states under many BITs. However, BITs are more limited treaties which generally define 'investor' more narrowly, and give no rights of market access, so they do not entail the same sweeping restrictions on government action as did the MAI.

Investor-state dispute settlement exacerbates the imbalance in legal rights written into the MAI. It means that large multinationals could directly intimidate countries by threatening costly disputes, without having to go through their own governments, as they do under the WTO. Given that even with government screening the WTO received some 130 cases during its first three years of operation, one can only expect the MAI would have generated even greater numbers. Abuse of such powers is already occurring under similar NAFTA investment rules. For example, in Canada the US Ethyl Corporation sued the Canadian Government for US$250 million for banning the import and sale of a petrol additive that was considered to be toxic. Other cases have been begun in Mexico by US companies objecting to restrictions placed on their operation of toxic waste sites (Nolan and Lippoldt, 1998).

The rights granted under the MAI cover four main areas: market access, performance requirements, expropriation and privatization. These go far beyond the non-discrimination principles of 'national treatment' and 'most-favoured nation' status which proponents of the MAI usually emphasize.

Market Access

The MAI would have granted foreign investors automatic access to any sector of a country's economy unless a specific exception had been negotiated, or there was a national security reason for denying access. Companies could use the dispute system to recover any costs they incurred during the 'pre-establishment' phase if they were denied access, as well as any 'lost' profit, whether or not any investment was actually made. Most existing investment treaties give equal treatment to investors only once they are established, and allow them to specify those sectors which are open. The MAI, in contrast, would have established a presumption of openness: failure to lodge an exception could not be rectified after the treaty was signed, and there would have been pressure on states to end national exceptions. NGOs have particular concerns over how this right of access might affect specific sectors, such as health or social security, as well as land and natural resources (see Chapter 6 of this volume).

Performance Requirements

The MAI would have removed the ability of governments to attach mandatory performance obligations on foreign investors, even if these were also applied to domestic firms. Banned requirements include: hiring a certain number of national employees; using a minimum amount of locally produced goods; transfer of technology; and obligations to enter into joint ventures. Some of these requirements could nevertheless be imposed in exchange for an 'advantage' – for example, tax breaks, or subsidies – so a company could refuse to accept such conditions by refusing the advantage. Essentially these restrictions would greatly increase the negotiating power of TNCs and their ability to gain preferential concessions and subsidies especially from small or weak economies. At present, countries can bargain with a foreign company to give access to lucrative sectors or resources in return for national and local benefits. By giving an unconditional right of access, the MAI would have increased the bargaining power and hence the profits of foreign investors, and decreased the power of governments to ensure national benefits from inward investment.

Expropriation

The MAI would have provided sweeping and absolute protection for the assets of foreign investors, including intangible and intellectual assets. Companies could sue for any reduction in the value of their investment, whether directly removed or through 'creeping' expropriation due to new taxation or regulation. Compensation would be payable whether or not expropriation were discriminatory or in the public interest, and must be made at market prices, in hard currency and with interest. Unlike existing customary international law, local remedies need not be attempted first. After heavy NGO pressure the OECD ministers realized that the original MAI text could have meant governments having to pay foreign investors when environmental and social standards were legitimately raised – as is happening under NAFTA. In response, MAI negotiators promised to include a 'right to regulate' clause which would limit the extent of the expropriation provision. However, the legal effectiveness of such a provision was doubtful, and uncertain.

Even with a 'right to regulate' clause the MAI would have undermined democratic rights to control sovereign policy. Since all contracts and investments – whether legitimate or illegitimate – would have gained full protection under the MAI, a democratic government would find itself bound to honour even 'sweetheart' deals or corrupt concessions made by previous regimes. This would have made recent efforts by the Indonesian government to renegotiate contracts with foreign investors which were signed under the corrupt Suharto regime contestable under the MAI. In this respect, the MAI gave foreign investors far more legal protection than domestic investors and placed all the risks for bad economic decisions due to corrupt practices and non-democratic governments onto the country's population, not the foreign investor. This could only increase perverse incentives for foreign investors to conclude 'sweetheart' deals with undemocratic and corrupt regimes.

Privatization

One of the most contentious areas of the MAI were proposals – championed by the USA – to open up all first-wave privatizations to foreign investors. The most radical proposals (which even OECD states may not have agreed to) would have banned policy instruments which aimed to produce an equitable redistribution of assets (voucher schemes and the like), or to retain some form of democratic control (such as a government retaining controlling or 'golden' shares). Experience all over the world has shown the difficulties of valuing nationalized assets, and of post-privatization regulation. Most countries which are privatizing are desperate to attract foreign capital and know-how, but are reluctant to give away valuable assets unnecessarily. The MAI did nothing to establish international standards or rules, while undermining the powers of governments to handle privatization so as to ensure maximum national benefit.

Such restrictions on the powers of governments are fundamentally undemocratic, especially since a state would have been locked in to the MAI for a minimum of five years, and even if it left, existing investments would have been covered by MAI rules and protections for another 15 years. The effect of rules on expropriation, performance requirements and privatization would be to ensure that a greater proportion of the net economic benefits from an investment flow to the incoming investor, not the host country. Inward investment is in great demand around the world, so such rules would be unlikely to expand investment to the poorest countries, but instead would affect those offering attractive investment opportunities which would have received flows anyway. The rules on market access and pressure to roll back sectoral exceptions would have exacerbated this, especially for resource-rich countries which are targeted by extractive industries from the OECD, for example, oil, coal, mining, forestry and agriculture.

In response to NGO concerns over the balance of rights and responsibilities in the MAI, negotiators pointed to the proposal to annex the MNE

Guidelines to the agreement. However, the Guidelines are non-binding and this status as reaffirmed in the draft MAI Preamble. A review of the Guidelines has begun at the OECD but there is no sign of an intention to make them evolve into a binding legal instrument such as the MAI. This is ironic because the Guidelines were initially agreed in 1976 as part of an overall package of voluntary OECD investment agreements, the other parts of which have been incorporated as binding into the draft MAI!

TNCs already have enormous economic power with which to support their interests, and the ability to play countries and regions off against each other in return for incentives and advantages. The MAI would have strengthened this economic power with legal sanctions, while doing nothing to limit abusive and anti-competitive or restrictive business practices: for example, cartels allocating markets or fixing prices, trade-restrictive technology contracts, abusive transfer pricing, or the use of tax havens and offshore centres to avoid taxes or other regulatory requirements. Although claimed to promote economic efficiency, the MAI failed to ensure an appropriate legal and competitive framework for this to happen, simply assuming that pure liberalization would by itself lead to more efficient outcomes. Thus, it would have exacerbated global inequality and distorted the conditions for capital investment, by giving special benefits to 'international' investors. It would also have created incentives for capital flight from developing countries, or for local investors to gain these benefits for themselves by 'round-tripping' through MAI members, and thus further have undermined the state's powers of regulation.

A prerequisite for any multilateral rules to increase corporate rights and enforce liberalization must be a binding international treaty on corporate responsibility. What is needed is an alternative framework for international investment which supports local and national sustainable development, empowers communities, and protects the environment, workers and consumers. Initial attempts to design such a legal framework are currently being undertaken by several groups (Clarke, 1998).

'PULLING UP THE DRAWBRIDGE': HOW THE MAI WOULD UNDERMINE THE ABILITY OF COUNTRIES TO DEVELOP

The unbalanced framework of the MAI would remove many of the powers needed by policy makers in developing countries to ensure they can successfully develop. No country has ever developed under the type of liberal open-access economic regime promoted by the MAI, because it would restrict the ability of countries to integrate strategically into the global economy in a way that serves their national interest. Because of this one NGO characterized the MAI as 'pulling up the drawbridge' between developed and developing countries by outlawing polices used in the past to stimulate national development (WDM, 1997).

The successful south-east Asian economies show that limiting access and adding conditionality to foreign investments can play an important part in stimulating the development of globally competitive national businesses, and ensuring that the benefits of growth are equitably distributed (Watkins, 1988). This is not to say that all discrimination is good for development, as shown by the use of import-substitution approaches in South America. However, the corollary is not to pursue unselective and overly rapid liberalization, which failed to help African countries attract investment when applied under structural adjustment programmes (Oxfam, 1998). Unregulated liberalization of financial flows can also create banking, currency and economic crises, as seen in Mexico and south-east Asia (see Griffith-Jones, Chapter 9 of this volume).

Contrary to the views of some radical free-market economists, governments can strategically manage their industrialization process in a way that is more beneficial than leaving everything to market forces. The lessons of 30 years of official aid flows also show that consultation, involvement and participation of local communities are vital if investment is to generate economic growth which benefits poorer groups. However, the simple market-orientated philosophy of the MAI did not acknowledge these complexities, except by providing a blanket exception from MAI provisions for official aid programmes.

In response to these arguments, the MAI's advocates did not deny the inappropriate nature of the MAI rules for developing countries, but either pointed to the possibility of national exceptions, or conceded that it would only be suitable for a few, more 'advanced', developing countries. However, the vigorous 'outreach' sessions held by the OECD did not attempt to take the views of developing countries on the MAI on board, but were essentially a selling exercise designed to encourage countries to join. This intellectual schizophrenia was also shown in the surprising conclusion of a report on the development implications of the MAI produced for the British government (Fitzgerald, 1998), which argued that countries without the MAI stamp of approval would fail to attract new foreign investment, and hence advocated its extension to all developing countries.

Even more disingenuous was the attitude of the business community, which argued against including environmental and labour issues in the MAI on the grounds that this would discourage developing countries from joining. Thus, a joint letter from BIAC and the ICC to the *Financial Times* (15 January 1998) argued: 'The agreement risks being encumbered by excess baggage that would dilute business enthusiasm and discourage non-OECD members from acceding ... OECD governments should be careful not to discourage developing countries from joining the agreement.'

However, the main argument of NGOs is that foreign investors should operate to minimum international standards, thereby benefiting local populations, and not gain profit from lower environmental and labour standards. Compliance with minimum international standards would not damage the interests of developing countries, but instead create a true level playing field where economic competitive advantage would determine investment flows, not a country's willingness to deregulate or accept low standards from desperation to attract investment.

The choice of the OECD as the negotiating forum was fuelled by the worst type of economic power politics. By avoiding a negotiation with developing countries *en bloc* in the WTO, it aimed to persuade them one by one on a take-it-or-leave-it basis, thus minimizing developing countries' negotiating power. Negotiators claimed that all countries would have the choice whether to join the MAI or not, but in reality this choice would have been highly limited. The 11 or so developing countries already receiving substantial OECD investment would be pressured by investors to join such a 'gold standard' agreement or risk disinvestment. Countries which are not in this group would have joined the MAI hoping that it would provide the magic catalyst to attract investment. Developing countries would face a Catch-22 situation where they would have to balance the costs of entering into premature liberalization and restrictions on economic policy, against the costs of potentially being shut off from global investment flows.

Only after four years of preliminary discussions and three years of negotiation did the OECD countries finally begin to analyse the impact of the MAI on developing countries, rather than the opportunities their investors could exploit from opening up new investment opportunities. The OECD finance and development directorates were to produce new research by October 1998, building on a report commissioned by the UK Government which was heavily criticized by NGOs and others (Fitzgerald, 1998; WDM, 1998b; WWF, 1998c). However, it was not clear how the OECD could reform the MAI – or its relationship to developing countries – in a way that would remove negative impacts and empower countries to ensure that they received high quality inward investment.

PRIVILEGING THE POWERFUL: HOW THE MAI REJECTED CITIZENS' SOCIAL AND CULTURAL RIGHTS

In contrast to the rights given to corporate actors the draft MAI gave no protection or rights to citizens or sub-national groups. One of the main advances of the Rio conference was the explicit recognition that governments should not be the sole arbiters of their citizens' interests on the international stage. Rio defined a series of 'major groups' including NGOs, youth, women, indigenous peoples, industry and unions, which should be consulted and included in decision making.

Under the MAI only investors would have had the standing to use the MAI dispute mechanism. Citizens would have no right to initiate complaints about corporate behaviour or even to participate in the investor-state arbitrations. MAI negotiators dismissed calls for such rights, perhaps for fear that they could lead to pressure that investors' rights be conditional on their compliance with international standards or guidelines. For example, the UK Trade Minister in response to a parliamentary question on 25 February 1998 replied: 'Investors, like others, are subject to the national laws of the countries in which they operate. Therefore, there is no need for workers, consumers or others to use the Multilateral Agreement on Investment dispute settlement mechanism for disputes against investors.'

This response clearly showed the double standards at work in the MAI. The argument for a strong investor-state MAI dispute procedure – especially for expropriation claims – was that investors lack confidence in the strength and fairness of national courts. However, these are the very same flawed systems that citizens are being urged to use in order to secure environmental and social protection. Ironically, negotiators argue in favour of investor-state disputes on other issues because these take the politics out of economic issues and increase the power of smaller countries, but reject the same reasoning for citizens!

The double standards surrounding dispute resolution reflect the disregard of MAI negotiators both for citizen representation, and the impact of investment on local populations. The MAI was intended to be a 'high standard' agreement, but this only holds for levels of investor protection and liberalization. In contrast, countries would not have been required to obey core international labour standards, or even to enforce their own domestic environmental laws effectively, in order to accede to the treaty. This explicitly decoupled investors' rights from social and environmental standards. Not only was this against OECD statements on policy integration, but it reduced the pressure which could be put on repressive regimes to reform their domestic practices.

The MAI would also have removed the right of governments and local authorities to refuse to allow companies with bad human rights or environmental records to invest in their communities. Any discrimination – such as used in campaigns against investment in South Africa under apartheid, or against Burma – would have been banned. The draft MAI even appeared to restrict countries from requesting information about a company's record of operation overseas, to those for 'informational purposes'.[5] This could lead to investors with a long track record of destructive behaviour, for example in forestry or toxic-waste management, being allowed into these sectors with no additional safeguards. Also, by prohibiting inquiries about companies' overseas operations, the MAI could undermine the enforcement of safeguards against tax evasion and restrictive business practices.

The neo-liberal thrust of the draft MAI also means that it would have promoted cultural homogeneity. For example, it would ban regulation which attempts to counteract the overwhelming commercial power of foreign investors through controls on advertising and other marketing methods. There is a distinct difference between a local firm and a foreign firm advertising a product such as cigarettes, medicines or baby food. The foreign firm can imbue the product with 'Western glamour', thus encouraging far more purchasing, as has been seen by the explosion of sales by US cigarette companies in developing markets. Laws governing such activity would inevitably be challenged as overtly, or in practice, discriminatory under the MAI, limiting countries' ability to protect the health of their citizens and their local cultures. For example, under MAI the Bahamas could have been prevented from taking a recent decision not to allow McDonalds to open a branch there.

The French and Canadian governments argued against complete open access by proposing a 'cultural' exception. However, this only covered investment in cultural industries, and seemed likely to be limited to the audio-visual sector. Even so, this amendment was firmly resisted by US film and TV distributors. The only other cultural rights referred to in the MAI were those of indigenous peoples. This is because many governments recognize that their laws covering indigenous peoples would have been in conflict with the MAI, mainly because they confer exclusive rights over natural resources or traditional economic activities. The USA, Canada, Australia, New Zealand, Norway, Sweden and Finland registered some type of exception for indigenous peoples. These individual exceptions could be subsumed under a general 'aboriginal exception' protecting all nominated groups.

On the other hand, the MAI curiously defined a new set of privileged actors: 'managers' (defined as those who can hire and fire people, and control budgets) and 'technical specialists' (who have advanced and specialized knowledge). These two groups of company employees, though nominally bound by existing immigration procedures, would have been given priority access under the MAI into a country. The MAI therefore implied a rather Brave New World: a free-moving global elite servicing capital; indigenous groups protected at the bottom; and the remainder of the global population in between with no cultural rights.

The MAI set up huge tensions by neglecting citizens' and cultural rights. These were expressed by demonstrations against the treaty on the streets of Paris, and stimulated probably the fiercest resistance to the agreement. NGOs consider that cultural diversity is a vital component of sustainable development, and so must be protected along with other citizens' rights. The MAI would not cause cultural homogenization, but rather attempted to remove the power of communities to make their own decisions to prevent or slow it. NGOs prefer to see international investment rules which could protect citizens' and community rights by levelling the playing field between powerful corporations, weak or corrupt governments and local people. The MAI failed to achieve this and indeed would have entrenched and expanded the rights of powerful groups.

GROWTH BEFORE ENVIRONMENT: CONFLICTS BETWEEN THE MAI AND ENVIRONMENTAL LAWS

Despite official assurances to the contrary, NGOs considered that the MAI could undermine much national and international environmental legislation, and would do nothing to promote rising global standards of environmental protection. The draft MAI could undermine the environment in four ways: by overturning national environmental laws; conflicting with multilateral environmental agreements (MEAs); allowing companies to sue for expropriation when faced by rising environmental standards; and undermining attempts to transfer environmentally sound technology and raise global environmental standards.

The draft MAI would only allow environmental and natural resource legislation if it is neither explicitly (*de jure*) nor in effect (*de facto*) discriminatory against foreign investors. However, many legitimate environmental laws exist which are discriminatory and must remain so for sound regulatory reasons. The MAI therefore arbitrarily elevated economic goals above environmental regulation. Examples of existing *de jure* discriminatory environmental laws include requirements for foreign investors to provide greater amounts of information on environmental performance than resident companies, and the levying of higher environmental bonds against potential future environmental liabilities on non-resident companies, for example, for cleaning up toxic waste and restoring forests. Requirements on companies to use best technologies, or restrictions on novel processes (such as biotechnology) not currently used domestically, could also be challenged as *de facto* discrimination under the MAI.

Countries may wish to exclude foreign investors from some sensitive sectors altogether. Such policies are used to protect unique environmental assets from 'cut-and-run' exploitation, and to preserve traditional livelihoods and cultures dependent on their sustainable use; for example, artisan fishing rights, traditional herding and farming practices, or toxic waste disposal operations. The UK and six other EU countries asked for an exemption from the MAI for their fishing regulations. Yet it would not be certain that any developing country signing the MAI would have been allowed to exempt special rights of access by nationals to land or other natural resources. Yet international agreements such as the UN Convention on the Law of the Sea accept and even mandate the priority of nationals to exploit resources such as fisheries.

The draft MAI would over-ride many existing MEAs because they include provisions which aim to ensure that the benefits of environmental protection are spread evenly between parties, and not allocated purely by market forces. The Rio principle of 'common but differentiated responsibility' allocates obligations and benefits between countries on the basis of their level of economic development. This extremely important principle should be regarded as basic to any international economic agreement. These differentiated responsibilities, which include financial resource and technology transfer obligations, can translate into discrimination between investors from developing and from industrialized countries. Examples of MAI conflicts with MEAs include:

- The Convention on Biological Diversity (CBD) mandates the use of 'benefit-sharing agreements' under which the profits from exploiting genetic resources will be split between national governments and the (usually foreign) companies which directly exploit them. Experience of such agreements is that they can only be constructed in a way that could be considered discriminatory under the MAI.
- Under the Kyoto Protocol, industrialized countries can transfer 'climate friendly' technology to developing countries in return for 'carbon credits'. Yet under the MAI, developing countries – such as Argentina – taking part in such an exchange could be sued by multinationals from countries which were not eligible under the Protocol – such as Korea. This is because the restriction that credits can only go to some parties to the Kyoto Protocol constitutes a discriminatory

subsidy which could be regarded as violating the most-favoured-nation clause of the MAI.

- The Montreal Protocol provides different levels of funding and tech-nology-transfer to foreign-owned and domestic firms in specific coun-tries, in order to encourage the elimination of ozone-depleting substances. Such discrimination could be outlawed by the MAI's national-treatment and most-favoured-nation provisions.

As explained above, since companies could sue governments directly under the MAI for expropriation of their investments, whether or not it is discriminatory, profit reductions due to environmental (and social?) legis-lation could become a form of expropriation which must be compensated. This concept is already a controversial issue in the USA where companies and landowners have attempted to gain similar recompense under the US constitutional right to compensation (see Tshuma, Chapter 6 of this volume).

The result would have been many costly disputes. For example, foreign-owned water companies in the UK might sue for full market-value compensation if they lose water abstraction licences under the current gov-ernment review. In contrast, compensation for UK-owned companies is governed by the polluter-pays principle, and so may not give full market recompense. Similar issues arise if landowners were required to protect biodiversity, which they might argue effectively expropriates some of their productive assets. Arbitration under the MAI would have been able to over-rule national decisions on these matters, which might slow the evolu-tion of much environmental legislation. The response of the OECD nego-tiators to these points was to propose a 'right to regulate', restricting the protection against expropriation. This was welcome, but it still left the MAI and its dispute mechanisms – not national parliaments – to decide what is a proper regulation.

The MAI negotiators made much of the 'non-lowering of standards' clause which they said would prohibit 'any lowering of environmental or labour standards in order to attract investment'.[6] However, even if the pro-posed binding clause had been agreed it would have had little practical impact. This is because the clause would not apply to general changes in environmental laws, but only to failures to enforce them in relation to *par-ticular* investments. The clause would therefore not prevent lowering of standards in particular sectors (such as mining or offshore oil) or in sub-jurisdictional geographic areas (such as free trade zones). The clause could also be evaded by drafting laws with local discretionary powers. Addition-ally, as mentioned above, disputes could only be initiated by governments, excluding NGOs and citizens from protesting against lowering of standards.

Experience of similar clauses in NAFTA shows this would be likely to reduce its effectiveness greatly. Meanwhile other parts of the MAI would continue to work against higher environmental standards: for example, restrictions on the ability of governments to specify transfer of technology, joint ventures, use of local suppliers and training of local personnel. The OECD itself cited these factors as essential if increased foreign investment is to raise global environmental standards (DAFFE/MAI(97)3), but then the MAI negotiators proceeded to outlaw them!

The draft MAI would do virtually nothing to prevent competitive deregulation, and in fact would restrict policies at both the national and international level to transfer environmentally sound technology to developing countries. Its emphasis on protecting the investments – both material and intellectual – of foreigners is at odds with the collaboration needed to address environmental problems.

TOO LITTLE, TOO LATE: THE MAI NEGOTIATORS' RESPONSE TO ENVIRONMENTAL CONCERNS

After 18 months of rejecting the NGO analysis outlined here, MAI negotiators finally responded by instructing each country to carry out an environmental review by the end of January 1998 (DAFFE/MAI/RD(97)51). However, these studies were not comprehensive and by April 1998 only the UK, Finland, South Korea and France had submitted any material. The secretariat also performed short studies on the relationship with MEAs (DAFFE/MAI(98)1) and the broader relationship of foreign investment with the environment (DAFFE/MAI(97)3).[7]

However, enough concerns had been substantiated for the MAI high-level meeting in February 1998 to issue a statement pledging that a 'right to regulate' would have been preserved and for several amendments to the treaty to be tabled. This political realization led to a Chair's text on Environment and Labour (DAFFE/MAI(98)10) which attempted to deal with these problems. This text represented the most progressive amendments proposed, but was still subject to negotiation. However, it failed to address NGOs' main concerns adequately.

In short, the proposed amendments would still open up environmental laws to challenge under the MAI for discrimination, and the burden of proof they would have to surmount remained unclear. Experience with similar clauses under the GATT system shows that an environmental regulation has never survived a challenge from an international economic agreement (WWF *et al.*, 1998). As yet, the negotiators had not adequately dealt with the expropriation or MEA conflicts, and the issue of binding environmental standards on companies was yet to be addressed. Of all the issues raised by NGOs, environmental concerns received most attention from the negotiators. This is due partly to their high public profile, but also to the relatively powerful constituency of environmental ministries and international organizations which have been mobilized in support of these positions. Despite this effort the negotiators' record was still very poor, with measures to review and patch up the treaty only being attempted four months before it was meant to be signed!

CONCLUSIONS AND REFLECTIONS

The MAI was a highly complex and multifaceted agreement which would have touched every part of society. In fact the over-ambitious and sweeping range of the treaty caused most of its problems. By neglecting and excluding other government departments and civil society, the negotiators constructed a legally unworkable treaty which relied on a multitude of 'exceptions' and 'interpretative footnotes' to avoid conflicting with other laws and policy goals. Nevertheless, it failed to achieve this, and the rights of investors and concern for economic growth would still have over-ridden the needs of workers, communities, consumers and the environment.

The MAI was clearly a false start in the search for a framework to regulate global investment flows. NGOs formed an impressive coalition of interests, engaged many different groups in society and delivered a devastating critique of the MAI. A new start should begin from the interests of people, not those of corporations, and should aim to balance rights and responsibilities in a genuine manner. This task will require the involvement of all interested groups, and is not the privileged task of investment experts alone. The NGOs involved in the MAI campaign are working to begin this process. We believe that if such regulation were in place the world would have been better placed to evolve in a sustainable manner, and this would have benefit the environment, societies, the economy and even multinational corporations in the long run.

NOTES

1.	Throughout this chapter reference is made to the MAI draft as of 13 February 1998 (DAFFE/MAI/NM(98)2) and subsequent proposed amendments which are individually referenced.

2. For example: several UK Local Authorities voted anti-MAI resolutions (WDM, 1998); the provincial government of British Columbia publicly rejected the agreement (CoC, 1998); UK parliamentarians initiated critical debates on the MAI (House of Commons, 1997); French cultural industries were highly active in protesting against MAI liberalisation proposals (Ecoropa, 1998).

3. The official Irish position stated: 'We would like to see as many countries as possible acceding to the MAI' (Ireland, 1998). The UK government also explained: 'The MAI has its roots in the OECD. A great deal of effort has also been put into outreach events, looking towards countries which are not part of the process. We are playing a prominent role in that' (Roche, in House of Commons, 1997: 885). At the international level the OECD Ministerial Declaration of May 1997 concluded: 'The Ministers express their determination ... iii/ to pursue intensified dialogue with non-member countries, particularly those interested in joining the MAI'.

4. The terms of reference for the environmental review are given in the OECD document DAFFE/MAI/RD(97)51. No country met the timetable of completion by January 1998, and by April 1998 only four countries had tabled their reviews. See WWF papers (1998a&b) for a critique of the review and existing country responses. The draft Chair's proposals on Environment and Labour are contained in DAFFE/MAI(98)10, and analysed in WWF (1998b).

5. The Transparency provision states that the Agreement should not prevent states from 'requiring an investor of another Contracting Party, or its investment, to provide routine information concerning that investment solely for information or statistical purposes'. This suggests that other provisions, presumably the National Treatment article, would restrict information requests, and if such requests are for regulatory rather than informational or statistical purposes they are not saved by the Transparency article. This provision has aroused the concern of some, for example the US Environmental Protection Agency.

6. Reply by the British Trade Minister, Lord Clinton Davis, to a parliamentary question, 4 November 1997.

7. Detailed critiques of these review papers are available from WWF.

REFERENCES

Canada (1997) *Canada and the MAI.* Report of the Committee on Foreign Affairs and International Trade of the Canadian Parliament, December (available from www.parl.gc.ca).

Clarke, Tony (1998) *Towards a Citizens' MAI.* Polaris Institute, Canada.

CoC (Council of Canadians) (1998) 'BC Tells Ottawa No to MAI', 23 January 1998; Internet communication on MAI *ad hoc* list server. Up-to-date information available from enquiries@canadians.org.

CI (Consumer International) (1996) *Briefing on the OECD Multilateral Agreement on Investment.* London.

CUTS (Consumer Union for Trust and Solidarity) (1996) *Globalising Liberalization without Regulations!* July Briefing on the OECD Multilateral Agreement on Investment, Delhi.

De Jonquieres, G. (1998) 'Network Guerrillas', *Financial Times*, 30 March. London.

Ecoropa (1998). Internet communication on MAI *ad hoc* list server. Up-to-date information available from ecoropa@magic.fr.

European Parliament (1998) 'European Parliament's Committee on External Economic Relations' DOC_EN\RR\347\34768. Brussels.

Fitzgerald, E. K. (1998) *The Development Implications of the Multilateral Agreement on Investment (MAI)*. DFID, London, March.

FoE-I (Friends of the Earth – International) (1998a) *Updated Joint NGO Statement on the Multilateral Agreement on Investment (MAI) to the Organization for Economic Cooperation and Development*. Internet communication on MAI *ad hoc* list server 10 February 1998; up-to-date information available from MValli@aol.com.

FoE-I/FoE-US (Friends of the Earth – International/United States) (1998b) *Licence to Loot*. Washington DC.

House of Commons (1997) *Investment (OECD Multilateral Agreement)*. Parliamentary Debates (Hansard), 23 July, 865.

Ireland (1998) Department of Enterprise, Trade and Employment, *Multilateral Agreement on Investment: State of Play and Irish Orientation*, January.

Nolan, Matthew and Lippoldt, Darin (1998) 'Obscure NAFTA Clause Empowers Private Parties', *National Law Journal*, 6 April, B8.

ODI (Overseas Development Institute) (1997) *Foreign Direct Investment Flows to Low Income Countries: a Review of the Evidence*. ODI Briefing paper 1997(3), London, September.

OECD (1991) 'An Environmental Strategy in the 1990s'. Environment Committee meeting at ministerial level, 31 January 1991. Press Release SG/PRESS(91)9.

Oxfam (1998) *Briefing on the OECD Multilateral Agreement on Investment*. Oxford.

Public Citizen (1998) *The Multilateral Agreement on Investment (MAI) Will Impose the Same Rules on the US that the IMF is now Imposing on Asia*. Washington DC, January.

Third World Network (1998), *Oppose MAI Move to WTO*. Petition circulated 5 May 1998; details and list of organizations signed on available from twn@igc.apc.org.

UNEP (1992) *The Rio Declaration on Environment and Development*. Geneva.

Watkins, Kevin (1998) *Economic Growth with Equity. Lessons from East Asia*. Oxfam-UK, Oxford.

WDM (World Development Movement) (1997) *Pulling up the Drawbridge – the OECD Multilateral Agreement on Investment*. WDM, London.

WDM (1998a), Internet communication on MAI *ad hoc* list server. Up-to-date information available from wdm@gn.apc.org.

WDM (1998b) *WDM Critique of 'The Development Implications of the Multilateral Agreement on Investment (MAI): E. K. Fitzgerald, University of Oxford, UK'*. WDM, London.

WWF (1996) *OECD Briefing on the Multilateral Agreement on Investment*, October. WWF, Geneva.

WWF (1998a) *Enhancing the Environmental Review of the Multilateral Agreement on Investment*. WWF-International, Geneva.

WWF (1998b) *The OECD Multilateral Agreement on Investment: Ripe for Reform or Ready for Rejection?* WWF-International, Geneva.

WWF (1998c) *WWF-UK Response to the Environmental Component of the United Kingdom Department for International Development (UK-DFID) Commissioned Paper: 'The Development Implications of the Multilateral Agreement on Investment (MAI): E. K. Fitzgerald, University of Oxford, UK'*, WWF, Godalming.

WWF, Oxfam-GB, CIEL (Center for International Environmental Law) and CNI (Community Nutrition Institute) (1998) *Dispute Settlement in the WTO: a Crisis for Sustainable Development.* Discussion Paper, May, Geneva.

5 A Critical Assessment of the MAI

Sol Picciotto

This chapter offers a critical analysis of the MAI, to show why a new approach is needed towards the establishment of a multilateral framework for international investment. It argues that the negotiations for a MAI at the OECD were misconceived, as became clear with the failure to reach agreement on a text for approval by the OECD Ministerial Council in May 1998, and the suspension of the negotiations in October, with the withdrawal of the French government. The draft text of the MAI was the product of the mandate given to the 'high-level negotiating group' in May 1995, following four years of preparatory work. The group was asked to draw up an agreement which would 'provide a broad multilateral framework for international investment with high standards for the liberalization of investment regimes and investment protection and with effective dispute-settlement procedures'. The fundamental flaws in the resulting draft can be traced to that initial and little-noticed decision.

That decision was mistaken on three grounds.

1. The choice of the OECD as a forum, while aiming for a 'free-standing' agreement open to accession by all states, whether developed or developing, repeated the tactic of using a negotiation among like-minded developed countries to set the terms for wider global agendas. In this instance, however, it succeeded only in highlighting the problems even within the OECD area of the one-sided pursuit of liberalization, while discrediting the OECD as an illegitimate forum to negotiate an agreement aiming to encompass countries outside its own membership.

2. The aim of a 'high standards' agreement was either intended or interpreted to mean one which would constrain government powers of intervention in market mechanisms. As a result, the negotiations failed to address the central problem of globalization, which is how to balance liberalization with a positive framework of regulation.

3. By entrusting the negotiations to a special group operating outside the OECD's normal committee structure, the implications of liberalization commitments for many areas of regulation, such as taxation or intellectual property protection, appear to have been brought home to the negotiators only late in the day. Consultations with sectoral specialists

attempted to accommodate some regulatory issues through large carve-outs or special provisions, or took place at national level, so that their objections were rolled into national negotiating positions for specific exceptions. The result was a gruyère cheese of an agreement, which many said had more holes than cheese.

Thus, the MAI was a false start. A new approach should aim at beginning to construct a more balanced framework, which makes liberalization conditional on strengthened international regulatory standards and arrangements for their enforcement. This is the only way to build a sufficiently strong foundation of political support and public confidence, on which safe and secure markets must rely. The failure of the MAI in this respect is evident not only from the growing political opposition it faced, but also in the very texture of the draft agreement itself. This chapter aims to demonstrate this through an analysis of the structure and main provisions of the draft agreement,[1] and an evaluation of its implications and effects against the claims made for it by its advocates. Despite suspension of the OECD negotiations, similar proposals will undoubtedly be put forward elsewhere, and a detailed understanding of their implications is important.

THE MAI'S BROAD OBLIGATIONS

The MAI was based on two central obligations: (a) the protection of investments, and (b) the liberalization of investment rules. These would impose broad restrictions on how states could treat investors from MAI members and their investments, very broadly defined to include contractual as well as property rights. It would establish a general non-discrimination standard based on National Treatment (NT) and Most Favoured Nation (MFN) treatment for such investments. It required a guarantee against expropriation of investments (direct and indirect), and the right for foreign investors to repatriate all profits and other returns without restriction. To ensure that these rights would over-ride local laws, both foreign investors and their home states would be given the right to binding international arbitration of their claims.

The negotiators aimed to establish these obligations at as high a level as possible, taking the strongest precedents from existing investment treaties. The implications of establishing strong versions of these principles as a global legal standard, especially if backed by binding dispute-settlement, would indeed be far-reaching. They would impose obligations, or 'disciplines', on states, and give rights to investors, without any balancing obligations or regulatory standards. Their effects would be negative, in undermining many existing national regulatory arrangements, without putting anything in their place. Furthermore, they would be unpredictable and would create uncertainty rather than the reliable and predictable basis of rules that business firms say they require. This is because the very breadth of the principles would create potential conflicts with a whole swathe of existing national regulations, and lay specific rules and decisions open to attack, either through pressures on government bodies, or legal actions in local courts, or through the dispute-settlement procedures. The MAI resulted from the neo-liberal ideas of the 1980s, and embodied an approach which is inappropriate for the contemporary face of globalization.

In reply to the often vehement criticisms of the MAI, its defenders stressed equally strongly that a wider framework is needed to provide 'predictable and transparent laws and regulations'.[2] However, when critics pointed to its potentially far-reaching effects, the MAI's advocates gave the low-key response that it was largely based on existing agreements. The agreement did indeed build on prior practice, especially the network of bilateral investment treaties (BITs) negotiated initially by OECD members, and more recently by other states.[3] However, although there are now many hundreds of BITs, very few include all the key elements which made the MAI distinctive.[4] It also adopted an approach very different from that of the main recent multilateral treaty affecting these matters, the General Agreement on Trade in Services (GATS).[5] Nevertheless, it was stressed from the beginning that, despite being negotiated at the OECD, it was intended to be a free-standing multilateral agreement, which would establish a global 'gold standard' for investment protection. Developing countries were to be encouraged to join and, given the competition to attract investment, few could afford to be excluded. Yet the inappropriate character of the agreement was underlined by the difficulties experienced in reaching agreement even between the OECD countries.

In their pick-and-mix from available precedents, the MAI negotiators essentially aimed at a highest-common-factor approach, rather than a lowest-common-denominator. Hence, in attempting to establish a new global standard based on provisions so far agreed by rather few countries, the MAI negotiators were very ambitious. In essence, they attempted to push the logic of investor protection and investment liberalization as far as it would go. In doing so they exposed its severe limitations.

Definition of Investment

The breadth of the obligations begins with the wide definitions of investor and investment proposed in the MAI. These included all types of assets or contractual rights acquired in a country by a person or firm resident in any MAI state, however financed, and even if routed through third states. The common image of international investment pictures it as a cross-border inflow of new resources, usually thought of in money terms. Most of the attention is directed at foreign direct investment (FDI) by transnational corporations (TNCs), which essentially involves managing business assets or operations under a system of common corporate control. In fact, between 30 per cent and 70 per cent of the estimated value of FDI flows are accounted for by cross-border mergers and acquisitions: in 1996 they were 47 per cent of the estimated $350bn of FDI (UNCTAD, 1997: 9). Such acquisitions do not entail the establishment of any new operations, but create repayment obligations to be met by asset sales or through the higher profits which might be generated by a reorganization. In their favour it is said that such acquisitions bring in new managerial expertise or a more efficient organization of the business concerned, yet research shows that mergers often fail, and do not generally generate a higher rate of profit. Far from creating employment, they are likely to result in job losses.

Thus, the MAI is concerned with protecting proprietory, contractual and other rights acquired by foreigners, regardless of whether the acquisition entailed any actual inflow of money or other new resources. The definition of investment includes, for example, an authorization or licence granted to a foreigner; patents, copyright or other intellectual property claimed by a foreigner; as well as claims to money, and contractual rights of all kinds. A footnote suggests that an interpretative note would indicate that to qualify, an asset must have 'the characteristics of an investment, such as the commitment of capital or other resources, the expectation of gain or profit, or the assumption of risk'. This would still mean that no commitment of capital or resources would be necessary under such a definition, only 'the expectation of gain or profit'. Purely speculative transactions would also be included, as they involve 'the assumption of risk'.

A further important aspect of the broad definitions in the MAI is the inclusion of assets 'owned or controlled directly or indirectly' by a foreigner; the only requirement was that the ultimate rights of control must be held by either an individual who is a national or permanent resident of a MAI party, or a company or other legal entity formed under its laws. This also was taken from the US model BIT; in most BITs, the investment must be actually owned by a legal entity or a national of the state concerned.[6] This apparently small point makes a great difference to the legal enforceability of the treaty rights. In practice, TNCs and other investors almost always use affiliates or shell companies as intermediaries in organizing foreign investments and owning foreign assets, mainly to avoid tax and other regulations. These intermediary holding companies would not normally benefit from the protection of a BIT. This may be one reason for the very small number of actual claims brought, at least until recently, under the dispute-settlement provisions of the BITs. The legal drafting in the MAI therefore would help to legitimate the use of intermediary companies for tax avoidance purposes, and make it more likely that legal claims would be brought under the MAI than has been the case under most BITs.

The obligations in the MAI would establish constraints on state action, since they would provide a basis for investors to claim that policies adopted by states, ranging from administrative decisions to legislation, are illegal because of the MAI. This could occur as part of the usual process of lobbying, by investors or by their home states, backed up by threats of legal action. In many countries, where treaties are incorporated into national law, legal claims based on the MAI could be brought in the ordinary national courts. However, the MAI would go much further than this, by giving foreign investors privileged access to international arbitration. Although an international arbitration procedure for investors is already provided in some treaties, notably the BITs, it has been relatively little used, at least until recent years. However, the MAI would contribute to the strong recent trend of legalization of international economic affairs, as has been seen for example in the rapid growth of conflicts referred to the WTO dispute-settlement procedures. However, in the MAI as in the WTO, these procedures generally aim not at ensuring that firms or states comply with positive international standards, but at striking down existing national laws if they are thought to involve 'obstacles' to market forces.

THE OPEN DOOR

The main innovation in the MAI was the 'Open Door' obligation on states to allow free entry of foreign business. Although most BITs include general NT and MFN obligations and a political commitment to 'promote investments as far as possible', they generally create no obligations towards foreigners prior to admission, and indeed many BITs state explicitly that their obligations apply only to approved investments. The MAI contained an apparently innocuous but far-reaching provision, based on the US model BIT, which was transplanted into the NAFTA. It would create a right of entry, by extending the requirement of 'national treatment' to the establishment and acquisition of investments, as well as their subsequent operation. This entails a substantial departure from existing international law, which accepts that state sovereignty gives the right to control entry.

The right of establishment has until now been confined to regional economic integration agreements, for very good reasons. Firstly, most if not all states have some laws which explicitly restrict entry by foreign firms, or acquisition of economic assets by foreigners. These include

- powers to block takeovers in key economic sectors or those essential to national security (e.g. shipbuilding or aerospace), or cultural and media industries
- restrictions related to particular assets or sectors such as land or natural resources
- limitations on the percentage of foreign shareholding in companies or restricting foreign investors to participation in joint ventures with local state or private parties (e.g. in China, most east European countries, and many in Asia and Africa)
- 'screening' requirements necessitating specific approval for foreign investments (in many developing countries) (See generally Muchlinski, 1995: ch. 6.)

Such explicit restrictions would be invalid in principle under the MAI, but the draft included exceptions which the OECD countries considered important. The General Exceptions article excluded actions necessary to protect 'essential security interests', measures in compliance with UN obligations for the maintenance of international peace and security, and a limited exception for action 'necessary for the maintenance of public order'. The privatization article, the scope of which was controversial, seemed likely to allow special share arrangements or other procedures which favour particular groups such as small purchasers or employees, provided they are not discriminatory against foreigners. The articles on State Monopolies and on Concessions were also the focus of bargaining as OECD states sought to control the potential impact of the Open Door requirement.

However, the pre-entry national treatment obligation would go beyond explicit controls on entry. It would enable a foreign firm to object to any internal laws which could be said to be indirectly discriminatory (see further below, pages 92–5). This point has been made perhaps most clearly in relation to the media and cultural industries. This is the reason for the proposal, on which the French government insisted, to exclude 'policies designed to preserve and promote cultural and linguistic diversity'. This would exempt not only explicit restrictions on foreign ownership of the media, but also rules which might be argued to be indirectly discriminatory against foreign-owned firms, such as those requiring TV stations to carry a proportion of material made locally or in the national language.

Regulation of entry by national and local state bodies is also central to the conservation of natural resources and access to land. This was argued within the MAI negotiations by Norway, which pointed out the conflicts between the MAI and the sovereign rights of states to control natural resources under international law, and in particular the regime for conservation and management of sea and seabed resources established by the UN Convention of the Law of the Sea (UNCLOS). This gives the coastal state a primary role in the exploitation and conservation of the maritime resources of the Exclusive Economic Zone, as well as requiring it to give special consideration to developing and landlocked states and those whose nationals have habitually fished the zone. Norway's suggested safeguards clauses, to allow UNCLOS to prevail over MAI, to exclude fishing and natural resources ownership, and to reaffirm the overriding responsibilities of states for the conservation and management of natural resources, were not accepted. Instead some countries, such as the UK, tabled national exceptions for fishing, while Norway proposed that MAI be limited to a country's land, internal waters and territorial sea.

These arguments are part of a larger issue about how to ensure an optimal balance between conservation and exploitation of natural resources. At least two points can be made in support of retaining the right of states to maintain some discrimination in regulating access to natural resources. The first is straightforwardly that local communities should have priority of access to these resources, since land and other natural resources are the key elements of life for a large proportion of the world's people. The second is that conservation is more likely to be effective if priority is given to exploitation by locals. The increased economic efficiency which is the aim of a liberalized regime of non-discriminatory access inevitably creates great risks of over-exploitation. In many ways, effective enforcement of conservation rules becomes much more difficult if exploitation is in the hands of globally footloose operators, who have no strong commitment to maintain the renewability or optimal levels of exploitation of specific local resources. Here the aims of the MAI in promoting global liberalization to improve economic efficiency came into conflict with sound ecological principles aiming at sustainable development (see Chapters 4 and 6 of this volume).

INVESTMENT PROTECTION AND LIMITS ON
GOVERNMENT ACTION

A further potential restriction on the powers of democratically elected governments stemmed from the MAI's obligations on states to allow free withdrawal of profits and other returns, as well as its broad prohibition of expropriation, which covered 'direct and indirect' expropriation and 'measures having an equivalent effect'.

This revived in a new form the dispute which has long raged about the powers of governments and their obligation to compensate the losses of foreign investors and speculators. Since the early nineteenth century, foreign investors and speculators, complaining about defaults on government bonds, cancellation of concessions or nationalization of their businesses, have turned to their home governments for political and often military support. However, these appeals were viewed with some caution, and the British government's policy was expressed in Lord Palmerston's famous statement in 1848 that 'the losses of imprudent men who have placed mistaken faith in the good faith of foreign governments would prove a salutory warning to others' (Lipson, 1985: 44). In any case, the experience has been that economic and commercial pressures generally provide a more effective remedy than political intervention, since states which are considered to have dealt unfairly with investors find it hard to access international markets. There were often very good reasons for governments to cancel concessions obtained under dubious circumstances, or to nationalize businesses in key economic sectors. Latin American governments, in particular, put forward the Calvo doctrine, under which foreign investors were required to accept that their rights would be governed by local law. This entailed a view that foreigners were entitled to the same treatment as nationals, no more. On the other hand, capital-exporting countries argued for a minimum standard of treatment under international law for foreign-owned property, which was essentially an attempt to establish the limits of legitimate action by host governments (Lipson, 1985: 55). The high standard proposed in the MAI, which would become entrenched in the domestic laws of many states and would be backed by the right of access to the dispute-settlement procedure, would enable investors to challenge the actions of democratically elected governments, and thus to try to restrict their legitimate powers.

Thus, the MAI could be used to entrench a minimalist, neo-liberal view of the role of state intervention. It was certainly intended to establish a new global standard very different from that laid down in the most authoritative statement in international law until now, the Charter of Economic Rights and Duties of States, adopted by the UN General Assembly in 1974. The well-known article 2 of this Charter affirms the right of every state to 'full permanent sovereignty ... over all its wealth and natural resources', and

> to regulate and exercise authority over foreign investment within its national jurisdiction in accordance with its laws and regulations and ... to nationalize, expropriate or transfer ownership of foreign property, in

which case appropriate compensation shall be paid...taking into account...all circumstances that the State considers pertinent.

The Charter was approved at the height of the assertion of economic nationalism by developing countries, and especially the wave of nationalizations of oil, mining and other natural resources. While these entailed a forced divestment of ownership rights, foreign companies generally received substantial compensation, and often maintained or regained an extensive role in managing the same operations (Lipson, 1985: 121–2). The MAI aimed to articulate standards regarded as more appropriate to a climate which was considered to be more welcoming to foreign investment. However, this both overestimates the extent to which the economic nationalism of the 1970s was hostile to foreign investment, and underestimates the importance of a continuing role for the state in regulating economic activity.

The investment-protection provisions proposed in the draft MAI go well beyond what is needed to safeguard investors against unfair or arbitrary confiscation. By creating a basis for legal challenges to the validity of a wide range of national and laws government regulation, they would undermine the security and predictability of the regulatory framework on which markets rely. The MAI included in its definition of expropriation any actions which 'directly or indirectly' have that effect, as well as 'measures having equivalent effect'. Combined with the broad definition of 'investment', which as I have already mentioned includes contractual rights, licences or authorizations granted to an investor, this would make it possible to challenge any administrative or legislative act which could be said to reduce the scope of an investor's expectations. Under the equivalent provisions of the NAFTA, for example, the US company Metalclad initiated a $90m action challenging the decision of the Governor of a Mexican province to close a waste disposal facility which was considered potentially contaminating (Nolan and Lippold, 1998). Regardless of the merits of the issue, the point is that a foreign investor is given the right to make a legal challenge to an otherwise valid state action, if it can be argued to interfere with an asset – in this case, a licence to operate a waste disposal facility. The wide definitions of 'expropriation' and of 'investment' would therefore give foreign investors the basis of a legal claim whenever they consider themselves to have been deprived of an expectation of profit. This could fire an unpredictable guided missile into national legal systems of states.

It is noteworthy that there have been two major expropriation disputes between OECD member countries taken to the International Court of

Justice (*Barcelona Traction* ICJ 1970, and *Elettronica Sicula* ICJ 1989). Both were claims of 'indirect' or 'creeping' expropriation, and concerned the terms of liquidation or refinancing of companies which had run into financial difficulties (Picciotto, 1998: fn 63). Although the claims of the investors were rejected under international law at the time of those cases, they would probably succeed under the more stringent provisions of the MAI. This treaty would, therefore, greatly strengthen the power of international investors, who are often large TNCs, to object to decisions validly taken in democratic countries by courts, administrative authorities, and local or national governments and legislatures. An immediate case in point is a special tax, such as the windfall profits tax enacted by the new Labour government in the UK in 1997. Among the arguments made by those objecting to this proposal was that it constituted a retrospective taking of property, and such arguments would have been strengthened if the MAI had been in existence. The draft MAI text attempted to safeguard against this through an interpretative note, which stated *inter alia* that a tax measure will not be considered to be expropriatory 'where it is generally within the bounds of internationally recognized tax policies and practices'. This would mean that a government's right to introduce a new tax must be judged according to a vague standard of what is 'internationally recognized', and could be subject to the decision of an arbitration tribunal.

Rather late in the day, it seems, the negotiators also discovered a number of potential conflicts between the MAI and intellectual property laws. Intellectual property rights (IPRs) are legal monopolies granted by the state, which must carefully balance special protection for scientific or artistic innovation against the general economic and social interests of free competition and circulation of new ideas. Countries take different views on how this balance should be struck, so there are many large and small differences in the operation of national IPR systems, and a number of international agreements have developed over the past century or more, attempting to co-ordinate them (Cornish, 1993). National laws provide for action to be taken to restrict IPRs in cases of abuse or inadequate exploitation by the rights-holder, for example by granting compulsory licences, or regulating royalty rates. Such action may well be argued to fall within the definition of expropriation in the MAI. Once this issue was addressed, there was difficulty in reaching agreement,[7] which is not surprising given the contentious nature of the issues, and the complexities of the existing international agreements on the matter. The compulsory licensing issue has been especially contentious, and a hard-fought compromise was only reluctantly accepted by developing countries in the TRIPS agreement because it was part of the bigger package in the Uruguay Round.[8] The broad provisions of the MAI could disrupt the delicate compromises in both national and international IPR systems, if they are used to further entrench technology monopolies (see Chapter 8 of this book).

These potential conflicts with other areas of law such as taxation or intellectual property are not an incidental or technical matter, but result from the basic principles of the MAI. IPRs are by their nature exclusive property rights granted by the state, and are necessarily limited and subject to constraints, which may extend to limitation or cancellation of vested rights. Viewed in the MAI's optic of protection of property rights, any such interference with vested rights or assets could amount to an expropriation. In relation to both taxation and IP, the negotiators attempted to repair the potential damage by resorting to exclusions for 'normal governmental activity'. This still leaves the danger that foreigners would be able to challenge decisions taken by democratic political processes, on the basis of the MAI's property-protection standards, and a state would have to justify its policies as complying with the standard of 'normal governmental activity'.

DISCRIMINATION AND REGULATION

The most apparently plausible argument for the MAI was that it would not intrude on national sovereignty, but merely sought a 'level playing field', or equal treatment for investors. This was done through clauses requiring Most Favoured Nation (MFN) treatment, and National Treatment (NT), principles perhaps best known from the General Agreement on Tariffs and Trade (GATT). Thus, MAI would require a member state to give investors from any other MAI country *at least as good* treatment as it gives *either to its own* investors, or those from *any other* country.

The first problem with this provision is that it would not establish equal treatment between national and foreign investors at all, but a minimum standard of treatment for foreign investors. In fact, the drafting of the NT and MFN rules in the MAI meant that foreign investors from MAI countries would be guaranteed the highest level of treatment available under the laws of a host country. Thus, the MAI's 'high standard' is high from the point of view of foreign investors. It entails rejection of the strict NT standard of the Calvo doctrine, discussed above.

This is more than a minor legal point, since it relates also to the failure of the MAI to tackle one of the most distortive factors for international investment, the competition among states to offer investment incentives. Under the MAI states would be free to continue to offer foreign investors generous incentives even if these are not available to national businesses. The competition to attract mobile investments by offering special financial or tax inducements is one of the main distortions of investment flows, and is especially disadvantageous to poorer countries. It was apparently considered too prickly a nettle to grasp, even though the OECD had previously handled National Treatment and Investment Incentives as related issues,[9] and even though the desirability of some action on this point in the context of the MAI had been pointed out (UNCTAD, 1996b: 59). The provision on investment incentives misleadingly stated that they would be subject to both the MFN and NT requirements, but since the MAI only required *at least* National Treatment, it would not prevent preferential treatment of foreign investors. This is hardly establishing a 'level playing field'.

More generally, the NT provision would pose a threat to a wide range of existing national regulatory arrangements, which could be challenged as involving *de facto* discrimination. The experience with general non-discrimination requirements repeatedly shows the difficulties of establishing with clarity whether a distinction may validly be made between persons or situations with some aspects in common. Thus, a rule that does not explicitly discriminate against a foreigner may be argued to do so in practice or *de facto*. For example, a local sourcing requirement, requiring a certain proportion of inputs to be locally produced, may be expressed to apply to all firms without distinction as to their ownership, but may be considered to discriminate *de facto* against foreign-owned firms.[10] Conversely, exemptions or positive discrimination are sometimes needed to *ensure* competitive equality. For example, if a foreign bank wishes to set up a local operation, it may be unfair to subject it to the same prudential rules, such as reserve capital requirements, as local banks, without regard to the consolidated capital or prudential provisions applied to the group as a whole. A different approach to defining discrimination has been adopted in the GATS. Its NT provision (article XVII) accepts that national treatment can take the form of 'either formally identical treatment or formally different treatment', the test being whether it 'modifies the conditions of competition in favour of services or service suppliers of the Member compared to like services or service suppliers of any other Member'. Surprisingly, this provision was not included in the MAI.

Foreign investors *are* in many respects different from local firms, and it is because of those differences that many countries establish special rules aimed at them. Under the MAI, regulations which distinguish on the basis of such differences could be challenged as discriminatory, so *creating* uncertainty. That is why the MAI also had a number of special provisions, carve-outs and exceptions (see next section). Just as the expropriation provision could be used to challenge government actions which might be considered to interfere with the freedom of a foreigner to make profits from an asset, so the MFN and NT non-discrimination rules create broad principles which could threaten many regulatory arrangements. The same problem has arisen with the application of the MFN and NT principles of the GATT to many areas of state regulation, referred to as 'non-tariff barriers'. Perhaps the best-known example is the Tuna-Dolphin case, in which a GATT panel decided that US rules forbidding sales of tinned tuna which did not meet dolphin-friendly fishing standards were unfairly discriminatory. More recently, the EU's prohibition of hormone-treated beef was thrown into doubt by decisions under WTO dispute-settlement procedures.

The GATT agreement itself includes a list of exceptions under article XX for certain categories of government measures, provided that they do not constitute an 'arbitrary or unjustifiable discrimination ... or a disguised restriction on international trade'. In contrast, the general exceptions in the MAI were restricted to national security and public order, although as a result of NGO pressures one delegation proposed an additional clause on Labour and the Environment, using wording very similar to that in the GATT. It would at least have been a step forward for the MAI to include a more substantial set of General Exceptions, which could include not only Labour and the Environment, but also the Culture clause, and other types of regulation which are important to maintain local and national specificity and diversity in an age of globalization.

Such a clause would establish a counterweight to the presumptions of liberalization which were given such a strong impetus in the MAI. However, the GATT experience shows that this is far from adequate, since it leaves the validity of national regulations to be decided on a case-by-case basis. The experience with GATT/WTO dispute-settlement procedures shows that national government rules are almost always regarded as discriminatory and restrictive when viewed from the perspective of an institution committed to liberalization. MAI arbitrators would most likely be as pro-investor as GATT/WTO panels are pro-trader. However, the WTO has moved to a new model, with the elaboration of more detailed agreements as part of the WTO package. In particular, the agreements on Technical Barriers to Trade (TBT), and on Sanitary and Phytosanitary Measures (SPS), establish more detailed criteria against which the validity of national measures should be evaluated. Indeed, they go further, and create linkages to internationally agreed standards, creating a presumption that national measures complying with such standards are deemed to be valid from a free-trade viewpoint.[11] While there is much about these arrangements that needs improvement, they do at least begin to create linkages between compliance with internationally agreed standards and rights of access to global market-places.

EXCEPTIONS, CARVE-OUTS AND DISCIPLINES

In order to deal with the potential incompatibility of its broad obligations with many areas of national regulation, the MAI was riddled with exceptions, exclusions and special provisions. These fell into three broad categories: (a) carve-outs, (b) specific provisions or 'disciplines' and (c) country-specific exceptions. All of these entail trying to identify potential conflicts in advance.

Broad exclusions were few. General Exceptions, which would exclude any type of government measure with certain objects, were limited to national security and perhaps public order, as already mentioned. However, in addition, a few types of government action were 'carved out' in their entirety. One concerned transactions in pursuit of monetary and exchange rate policies by central banks or other monetary authorities, but this covered *transactions* (that is, 'open market' sales or purchases of currencies or government debt) not regulations such as exchange controls. In contrast, foreign exchange or capital movement controls, which would be likely to be considered discriminatory against foreign investors as well as contrary to the requirement to allow free transfers of funds, would be permitted only as temporary safeguards and only if compatible with IMF obligations. The inadequacy of this approach has been revealed since the start of the financial crises in Asia in 1997, following which many leading economists advocated controls on short-term international capital flows (see Chapter 9 of this volume). Even the IMF's annual international capital markets report (IMF, 1998) accepted that such controls can be helpful, although their effects might be temporary as investors find ways of circumventing them. This indicates that countries may need to modify or change their controls, but this would be prohibited if they were validated only by a national exception under MAI, which would be subject to 'standstill'. A carve-out was also proposed for public debt rescheduling, although there were differing views on what form it should take. Another general carve-out was taxation, although the carve-out expressly excluded the expropriation provisions, so that (as discussed above) a tax could be regarded as expropriatory. A further carve-out was requested by the EU, to allow its members to extend each other a more favourable level of treatment by means of regulatory harmonization, without having to extend these benefits to others under the MFN requirement. The US requested a converse exclusion for measures by sub-national levels of government (state and local government), perhaps intended as a bargaining counter.

Following strong pressures from trade unions and NGOs and widespread criticism of the draft agreement, a proposed clause was put forward on Non-Lowering of Standards, covering both environmental and labour standards. However, this was not drafted as an exception, but merely to preclude any relaxation of such standards in order to attract a *specific* investment. Since other investors could in any case object to such privileged treatment of an investor under the NT or MFN clauses, this provision would be little more than cosmetic. In particular, it would not prevent states from establishing or maintaining special economic zones, within which all firms could be given exemptions from labour or environmental laws. Thus, the MAI would do little to protect states from pressures to accept lower standards in a short-sighted bid to attract investments.

More extensive were the special provisions listed in the agreement under Special Topics, sometimes referred to as 'disciplines', since they elaborated further restrictions on government powers. The very uneven character of these shows that the MAI was at most an international investment framework in the early stages of gestation. Perhaps the most elaborate provisions were those developed for Financial Services, which grew from a short clause exempting national prudential measures for financial services in the January 1997 draft, to an entire and substantial section which nevertheless remained problematic. To begin with, these provisions raised rather sharply the question of the relationship of the MAI to the GATS, under which an annex on financial services was agreed in December 1997. Although the MAI would apply only to services provided through some form of establishment in a host state, there would be a clear overlap with the GATS. This at least raised the question of whether MAI members would be obliged to extend its advantages to WTO members under the MFN clause of the GATS (discussed above). More seriously, it reinforced the point that a MAI negotiated by OECD countries is an inappropriate way to tackle the question of financial-services liberalization. The continuing financial crisis demonstrated that liberalization of financial flows must be carefully handled, and that a strengthening of regulatory arrangements is an essential pre-requisite. The deregulatory thrust of the MAI could further destabilize a global financial system that many consider to be dangerously under-regulated and volatile (Bhagwati, 1998). For example, a World Bank study has indicated that some restrictions on the entry of foreign banks may be important to prevent cream-skimming and ensure more equal competition

(Barfield, 1996: 246), but such ownership restrictions would not be likely to qualify as 'prudential measures' under the MAI's exemption.

The discipline on Performance Requirements also involved an overlap and potential conflict with another WTO agreement, that on Trade-Related Investment Measures (TRIMS). The TRIMS agreement affirms the GATT principles of national treatment and prohibition of quantitative restrictions and provides an 'illustrative list' of trade-related investment requirements deemed inconsistent with them. In contrast, the approach in the MAI was to abandon any connection with equal treatment between foreign and domestic investors, by establishing a flat prohibition of export, domestic-content, domestic-purchase, trade-balancing or foreign-exchange-balancing requirements. Yet such provisions could be seen as a means of ensuring fair competition in the domestic market between TNCs and local firms. The MAI would also go beyond trade-related requirements and prohibit in addition obligations such as technology transfer, the location of headquarters or of research and development facilities, or the hiring of nationals. However, such requirements would be permissible if made as conditions for the 'receipt of an advantage'. Combined with its failure to discipline the use of investment incentives, these provisions seem calculated to exacerbate the international competition for investments, and hence worsen the position of poorer countries less able to afford the offer of 'advantages'.

Employment and immigration laws were also subject to a limited discipline in the provisions on rights of 'temporary entry, stay and work' of investors committing a 'substantial amount of capital', and of their executive, managerial or specialist employees, if they are 'essential to the enterprise'. This does not exclude the application of immigration and work permit laws, but states would be restricted from applying these laws on the basis of labour market or other economic needs tests, or quota systems, for such key personnel. Investors would also be given the freedom to appoint employees of their choice regardless of nationality. Although a footnote indicated that this is not to be taken to exclude national anti-discrimination laws, unless spelled out in the article itself, it would create uncertainties. In the USA in particular, there has been litigation over the conflict between the rights of foreign investors under treaties and equality-of-opportunity laws, especially over the preference of some foreign-owned companies to appoint home-country nationals to senior positions.

In addition to exceptions, exclusions and special provisions which would apply to all parties (including any which join subsequently), a procedure would be established for each individual country to specify its own exceptions. These country-specific exceptions[12] are subject to Standstill (prohibition of any new measures inconsistent with MAI) and Rollback (negotiated reduction of national exceptions). Thus, every member would have its own Schedule, which would list any measures which it wished to maintain although they might be contrary to the basic obligations of the MAI. Thus, the MAI was designed as a 'top-down' agreement, unlike in particular the GATS, which applies only as and when states make specific commitments, and is therefore considered 'bottom-up'. A bottom-up agreement would establish a framework within which the economic and regulatory implications of liberalization could be considered sector-by-sector, as is occurring through the GATS. The MAI's obligations could be binding for up to 20 years, since parties would not be allowed to withdraw for five years from its entry into force, and it would continue to apply for 15 years from the date of notification of withdrawal to investments made by that date. Much therefore depends on the initial national schedules of exceptions, which the MAI parties spent a considerable time negotiating, with the aim of reaching an acceptable 'balance of commitments'. The later accession of states that were not initial parties to the agreement would be subject to negotiation by such candidate state with the Parties Group.[13] Such applicants would obviously be in a very weak bargaining position.

The MAI therefore would require states to make a leap into the unknown. The inevitable consequence was that the negotiations over national schedules among the OECD negotiators became protracted and helped to seal the fate of the treaty. One way to reduce the pressure, as suggested by some states (notably, the USA) would be to relax the Standstill requirement, by allowing states to separate their exceptions into List A and List B, and allowing later additions or amendments to List B measures. In this approach, List A measures would be subject to the full rigours of the downward ratchet of standstill and rollback, while measures under List B could still be expanded later. The disagreement on this point was evidence of the difficulties created by the MAI's top-down approach, and the reluctance of some governments to make the irrevocable commitments that it would entail. The Rollback process also could take various forms: it could be unilateral, by agreement, or automatic. Unilateral changes by states involving liberalization would need to be published under the agreement's transparency obligation, but the negotiators differed on whether there should be an obligation on states also to notify such changes by amending their Exclusions Schedule. There would also probably be a review process, allowing states mutually to renegotiate their exceptions lists. The draft did not envisage a time-limited automatic elimination of national exceptions, which would be hard to agree, since states would be tightly locked in to commitments under MAI.

MISSING FROM MAI: POSITIVE STANDARDS

The flaws in the MAI were structural, and flowed from the assumptions which guided the initiative, the neo-liberal dogmas of the 1980s. These are that economic development can best be assured by removing barriers to the free flow of market forces, coupled with stringent and extensive protection of property rights. The MAI sought to entrench these principles into the constitution of the global economy. However, markets require regulation for their very existence, as well as to provide stability and certainty through public confidence that they are accountable and responsive to social needs. The strong investment-protection and liberalization provisions of the MAI would have a destabilizing effect on existing state and international regulatory arrangements. Consequently, as this chapter has tried to show, the agreement was largely made up of exceptions, carveouts and special provisions which attempted to reconcile its basic assumptions with the realities of existing forms of regulation. As the negotiations progressed, these various derogations became more numerous and complex. They were also very skilfully drafted, to concede as much as seemed necessary, but no more, to this or that pressure group. The result was a spatchcock of a document, which many found entirely undigestible.

What is the alternative? It has long been known (ever since the failure of the Havana Charter) that the missing element in global economic governance is a basic framework of rules for international investment. Indeed, as international economic integration has deepened, and trade and investment have become intertwined, some of the tentacles of the trade regime have begun to cover investment issues also. Many assume therefore that the next step is to widen the ambit of the WTO into investment regulation, and that issue was placed on its agenda, by the creation of a Trade and Investment Working Group, due to report in late 1998 or early 1999. The decision by the French government in October 1998 to withdraw from the MAI negotiations, based on the analysis of the Lalumière report (France, 1998), switched attention to the WTO as a possible alternative forum.

The lessons of the MAI, however, should be that we need a more positive agenda for international regulation of global business, and not an approach focusing only on liberalization, which is essentially negative. A positive framework should aim at establishing internationally and democratically agreed standards of social responsibility and accountability in the conduct of business, and strengthening state capacity and international arrangements for the enforcement of such standards. Many of the elements of a positive regulatory framework have been slowly developed over the past quarter century, in response to the growth of international investment. However, in the neo-liberal climate of the 1980s, they often received half-hearted or even derisory support. The result has often been watered-down principles, and international soft-law codes of conduct. Nevertheless, where such standards have been the focus of active campaigns by elements in international civil society, they have been relatively effective despite their lack of formally binding obligations or state-enforced sanctions. This can be exemplified not only by campaigns such as that around the Babymilk Code, but also by the anti-Money Laundering principles, which have been quite effectively established and policed by the Financial Action Task Force. However, rules for the prudential regulation of the banking and financial system have evolved very slowly, and mostly in reaction to publicized scandals, from Banco Ambrosiano to BCCI and Barings (Picciotto, 1997; BCBS, 1996, 1997).

What is now needed is a more coherent and comprehensive approach. By prioritizing liberalization and investment protection, the MAI tries to put the cart before the horse, since it would undermine existing local and national state controls without putting anything in their place. If the aim is to ensure a more efficient international allocation of capital, what is primarily needed is to reduce the distortions created by the presently very weak disciplines over investment incentives, abuses of international tax and financial regulation, and restrictive practices and abuse of dominant position by large firms. The so-called 'offshore' finance system continues to thrive, and attempts to prevent its use by organized crime will fail as long as its facilities for avoidance and evasion of tax and financial supervisory requirements are allowed to continue. If an investment fund in the UK or USA makes a speculative investment in emerging markets which would not be permitted under its own country's prudential rules, through a shell company in an unregulated jurisdiction, should that investment be entitled to protection? The enforcement both of prudential financial regulation and tax-avoidance provisions are greatly hampered by the reluctance of governments to sign up to international agreements establishing comprehensive standards and cooperation to enforce them. The OECD itself helped draft a Convention for Cooperation in Tax Matters a decade ago, and yet it has been ratified by only a handful of states. The UK could set an example by doing so now, and applying its provisions to the UK dependent territories. The argument in the past has been that there will always be some small territory willing to provide such avoidance facilities. However, if we begin by setting global standards of transparency and probity, and then find the means to ensure that those who do not live up to those standards forfeit the right to protection, we would be establishing a sounder foundation for the global economy.

So, a new approach to the MAI should be in a more comprehensive international forum, and an agreement for investment protection should be part of a package of agreements setting regulatory standards for investment. There has been a variety of international efforts to establish and enforce such standards, but they are hampered by inadequate arrangements for ensuring compliance. Some countries may also face substantial difficulties in meeting regulatory standards, whether financial, social or environmental. For this reason, standards may establish both minimum requirements and higher levels to be reached after transitional periods, and their attainment could be facilitated by technical assistance and debt relief.

A new start to the MAI should be based on a bottom-up approach to establish fair international standards which are industry-specific and function-specific. They should not just aim at the chimera of equal treatment, but at fair treatment, based on internationally agreed minimum standards, covering responsibilities and requirements as well as rights for business. Over the past quarter-century some progress has been made in agreeing a variety of agreements and codes establishing such standards, though it has been a tortuous path. But the MAI experience shows that we should not be tempted by what seems like a shortcut – it might lead into the deepest forest, inhabited mainly by litigious lawyers.

NOTES

1. References are to the Consolidated Text of 28 April 1998, DAFFE/MAI/ NM(98)2/REV1, which was made available on the OECD website (www.oecd.org); the Commentary was also later published on this site.
2. See for example 'The Case for MAI', by the OECD Secretary-General Douglas Johnston in the *Financial Times*, 24 February 1998, written in response to that paper's leading article 'Bye Bye MAI?' of 19 February.
3. Since most BITs have been concluded with developing countries, and not among OECD members themselves, it may have seemed plausible to consider an intra-OECD multilateral treaty, although some had reservations (Brewer and Young, 1995: 74–7). However, a majority of OECD states are members of the EU bloc (the 15 members of the EU itself plus Norway and Iceland, which form the European Economic Area), which already has a stronger set of rules and institutions than those envisaged by the MAI. Rules very similar to those proposed in the MAI already apply between the three NAFTA states (Canada, Mexico and the USA). If the MAI were seen as a super-NAFTA extended to the EU block, it should be considered in relation to the parallel negotiations for a Transatlantic Economic Partnership. Rather different issues arise in relation to the various other OECD members: Australia, Japan, New Zealand, Switzerland and Turkey, plus the Czech

Republic, which was admitted in 1995, and Hungary, Korea and Poland, which joined in 1996, making 29 OECD members in all.

4. The UNCTAD database included 1330 such treaties among 162 countries at 1 January 1997 (UNCTAD, 1997: 19; UNCTAD, 1998). This appears to include agreements which have not been ratified and thus are not in force, such as that between the USA and Russia. The negotiation of BITs was initiated in 1959 by Germany, and then taken up by other European countries. These agreements have been mainly political documents, attempting to strike a compromise with developing country governments anxious to attract foreign investments (Guzman, 1998). In the 1990s, Central and Eastern European countries and some developing countries began concluding such agreements amongst themselves (UNCTAD, 1997: 19). There was a significant shift with the publication of the US model BIT in 1980, which broke new legal ground, especially in requiring the Open Door (discussed below). However, comparatively few countries signed up to the US model. The USA had previously relied on treaties of Friendship, Commerce and Navigation (FCN), which date back to the nineteenth century. Some treaties of this type were negotiated after 1945, but developing countries proved reluctant to accept them; the last such treaties were concluded by the US with Togo and Thailand in 1966, and an unsuccessful negotiation was attempted with the Philippines in the early 1970s (Salacuse, 1990; Dolzer and Stevens, 1995: 4). Few states signed up to the 1980 US model BIT until the early 1990s (the latest version of 1994 is reprinted in UNCTAD 1996–III). By January 1998 the US had negotiated 41 such treaties, but only 31 had been ratified. Russia had not yet ratified the treaty signed in 1992, and of the rapid-growth economies in east Asia and Latin America, only Argentina had ratified a BIT with the US (in 1991, coming into force in 1994). The Argentine treaty was a significant break-through, entailing the virtual abandonment of the doctrine enunciated by the Argentine jurist Carlos Calvo a century earlier, that property rights are a matter of the internal affairs of a country, and foreigners are not entitled either to diplomatic or military protection by their home country. As a remaining obeisance to the Calvo doctrine, the treaty includes a provision exceptional in US BITs, in its article III, reserving the right to regulate the admission of investments 'provided, however, that such laws and regulations shall not impair the substance of any of the rights set forth in this Treaty'. Although Argentina has experienced a growth in FDI, it has been surpassed by Brazil, which has far fewer BITs, and none with the USA (UNCTAD, 1997: xxii, 366). There seems no evidence that acceptance of a high-standards BIT is important in increasing economic growth; if anything, the contrary (UNCTAD, 1998).

5. Despite its name, the GATS deals with market access for service providers which is not restricted to 'trade' (that is, cross-border provision), but by any of four 'modes of supply', one of which is 'through commercial presence', which covers investment. The GATS is based on a 'positive list', or bottom-up system, in that its National Treatment obligation only applies to those sectors and modes of supply for which states make specific commitments (and subject to exceptions they may make either generally or for a sector) (article XVI). However, its most-favoured-nation obligation (article II) is immediate and unconditional, although exemptions may be listed, which are subject to

review after five years and regarded as limited 'in principle' to ten years. Thus, OECD members would be obliged to extend to WTO members the benefit of any changes they make to their internal investment regimes as a result of a MAI which improved the rights of establishment for providers of services, unless services were excluded from the MAI, or unless a new exemption from GATS article II were agreed in respect of the MAI, which would require a 75 per cent majority of WTO members (Wimmer, 1996: 117–19). It might also be possible for each MAI member to ensure that its GATS commitments were in line with its MAI obligations by listing appropriate country exceptions under the MAI.

6.   Most model BITs protect investments made by investors 'of' the other contracting party, usually defined as individuals who are its nationals, or legal entities formed under its laws or having their seat there (see for example the model agreements of Austria, Chile, China, Denmark, Germany, Hong Kong and the UK, in Dolzer and Stevens, 1995, and UNCTAD, 1996-III). The Dutch, French, Swiss and US models, however, do include legal entities formed in third countries but owned or controlled even indirectly by investors of a contracting party (see discussion in Dolzer and Stevens, 1995: 36–42, and UNCTAD, 1998: 37–41).

7.   The alternatives under consideration by May 1998 were either a general text 'clarifying that expropriation does not include normal government regulatory activity', or a specific IP text. The former begs the question of what is 'normal', while the latter raises major issues of compatibility with and linkages to existing international IP agreements.

8.   Historically, technology-importing countries have considered that failure to work a patent through local production could be treated as an abuse, which could result in forfeiture of the patent or compulsory licensing. Under article 5 of the Paris Convention, as amended, compulsory licences can only be non-exclusive and cannot be granted until four years after the patent application; and forfeiture is only possible if licensing would be an inadequate remedy, and not before two years after the first compulsory licence. The TRIPS agreement requires patents to be enjoyable without discrimination as to whether products are imported or locally produced (article 27), while article 31 lays down detailed conditions for the granting of compulsory licences, emphasizing that they should be non-exclusive and adequately remunerated.

9.   In 1976 the OECD Council adopted the Declaration and Decisions on International Investment and Multinational Enterprise, which included as an Annex the Guidelines for Multinational Enterprises. The two main Decisions were on National Treatment, and Investment Incentives and Disincentives. The NT decision is a forerunner of the MAI's NT provisions, but no comparable effort has been made to develop 'disciplines' on investment incentives, although some delegations have argued that the problem of positive discrimination should be tackled in the MAI's anodyne draft provision on incentives.

10. However, due to the uncertainty of how far this argument might be pushed, 'performance requirements' such as local content rules were not dealt with as an aspect of national treatment in the MAI, but by a specific article, discussed below.

11. Generally, the WTO agreements refer to international standards as criteria for the validity of national rules, and thus tend to create a presumption against

the validity of national standards which diverge from them. However, they are also an encouragement to national states to adopt such standards, and have had the effect of focusing more attention on the relevant standard-setting bodies, such as the Codex Alimentarius Commission, which is responsible for food safety standards. The TBT is more stringent, in requiring states to use international standards where they exist as a basis for their technical regulations 'except where such international standards ... would be ... ineffective or inappropriate' (article 2.4). The SPS allows national measures 'which result in a higher level of sanitary or phytosanitary protection than would be achieved by measures based on the relevant international standards, guidelines or recommendations, if there is a scientific justification', which must be shown by a formal risk assessment process – see also GATS article VI(5)(b). These agreements use international standards as limits on national regulation. In contrast, the TRIPS agreement establishes a minimum level of IP protection which WTO states must provide, based on existing international agreements, with some extensive new requirements, especially on enforcement. This type of 'positive linkage' to international standards should, I argue, be used to strengthen a wider range of national state regulation, to provide a more secure foundation for international trade and investment (see further Picciotto, 1998).

12. These were previously termed reservations. The terminology has been changed to make it clear that, unlike normal reservations to treaties, they do not operate reciprocally, although a country may list an exception which is subject to reciprocity. For example, if country A lists as an exception that foreign banks must have local partners with at least 50 per cent of equity, this would not mean that banks from country A would also be subject to this requirement in other MAI countries. However, country A could limit its entry requirement to those countries which also maintained such restrictions.

13. Accession decisions would apparently be made normally by consensus, but where this proves impossible, either by a three-quarter or two-thirds majority. The EU would have a number of votes equivalent to the number of EU states which ratify the treaty, which would give it potential dominance.

REFERENCES

Barfield, C. E., ed. (1996) *International Financial Markets. Harmonization versus Competition.* American Enterprise Institute, Washington DC.

Barcelona Traction, Power and Light Company (New Application: 1962) (1970) Belgium v. Spain. *ICJ Reports*, 3.

BCBS (Basle Committee on Banking Supervision) (1996) *The Supervision of Cross-Border Banking.* Bank for International Settlements (BIS), Basle.

BCBS (1997) *Core Principles for Effective Banking Supervision.* BIS, Basle.

Bhagwati, J. (1998) 'The Capital Myth: the Difference between Trade in Widgets and Dollars', *Foreign Affairs*, vol. 77, 7–12.

Brewer, T. L. and Young, S. (1995) 'Towards a Multilateral Framework for Foreign Direct Investment: Issues and Scenarios', *Transnational Corporations*, vol. 4, 69–83.

Cornish, W. R. (1993) 'The International Relations of Intellectual Property', *Cambridge Law Journal*, vol. 52, 46–63.

Dolzer, R. and Stevens, M. (1995) *Bilateral Investment Treaties.* Nijhoff, The Hague.

Elettronica Sicula S. P. A. (1989) United States v. Italy. *ICJ Reports*, 15.

France (1998) *Rapport sur l'Accord Multilatéral sur l'Investissement (AMI).* Rapport Intérimaire – Septembre 1998; Catherine Lalumière, Jean-Pierre Landau, Emmanuel Glimet, made available on website of French Ministry of Finance, October 1998: http://www.finances.gouv.fr/.

Guzman, A. T. (1998). 'Why LDCs Sign Treaties that Hurt Them: Explaining the Popularity of Bilateral Investment Treaties', *Virginia Journal of International Law*, vol. 38, 639–88.

IMF (1998) *International Capital Markets. Developments, Prospects, and Key Policy Issues.* IMF, Washington DC.

Lipson, C. (1985) *Standing Guard: Protecting Foreign Capital in the 19th and 20th Centuries.* California University Press, Berkeley.

Muchlinski, P. (1995) *Multinational Enterprises and the Law.* Blackwell, Oxford.

Nolan, Matthew and Lippoldt, Darin (1998) 'Obscure NAFTA Clause Empowers Private Parties', *National Law Journal*, 6 April, B8.

Picciotto, Sol (1997) 'Networks in International Economic Integration: Fragmented States and the Dilemmas of Neo-Liberalism', *Northwestern University Journal of International Law and Business*, vol. 17, 1014–56.

Picciotto, Sol (1998) 'Linkages in International Investment Regulation: the Antinomies of the Draft Multilateral Agreement on Investment', *University of Pennsylvania Journal of International Economic Law*, vol. 19.

UNCTAD (1996) *International Investment Instruments: a Compendium*, 3 volumes. United Nations, Geneva.

UNCTAD (1996b) *Incentives and Foreign Direct Investment.* United Nations, Geneva.

UNCTAD (1997) *World Investment Report. Transnational Corporations, Market Structure, and Competition Policy.* United Nations Conference on Trade and Development, Geneva.

UNCTAD (1998) *Bilateral Investment Treaties in the Mid-1990s.* United Nations, Geneva.

Wimmer, A. M. (1996) 'The Impact of the General Agreement on Trade in Services on the OECD Multilateral Agreement on Investment', *World Competition*, 109–20.

Part II
Broadening the Agenda

6 Implications of the MAI for Use of Natural Resources and Land

Lawrence Tshuma

A recent 'Money Report' in the *International Herald Tribune* analysed how international investments in land could produce double-digit returns, at a time when yields in Western stock and bond markets are low, and the Asian crisis is making many investors nervous about traditional securities in any of the emerging markets. The lead article argued that:

> The risks are formidable and the barriers to entry extensive, but with land values across Central and Eastern Europe a mere fraction of those in the West, private investors are actively investigating long-term investment opportunities in former Communist countries (Wall, 1998: 15).

The barriers alluded to in the report are common to regimes governing the use of natural resources and land in many countries. They are inconsistent with the standards of investor protection and rights of access which the negotiators of the MAI sought to entrench, as discussed elsewhere in this volume.[1] This chapter argues that the neo-liberal principles which informed the MAI treat land and natural resources purely as commodities, and that such treatment is inappropriate and also inimical to sustainable development. It further argues that these basic principles of investor protection and rights of access which the negotiators sought to entrench in the MAI run counter to the integrated principles and practices governing the use of natural resources and land established in the main international environment and development instruments (which I refer to as 'the Instruments'):

- Rio Declaration on Environment and Development
- Agenda 21
- Biodiversity Convention
- Convention on Combating Desertification
- Forestry Principles[2]

NATURAL RESOURCES AND SUSTAINABLE DEVELOPMENT

Sustainable development is one of the greatest challenges facing humanity at the end of the twentieth century. The World Commission on Environment and Development defined sustainable development as the satisfaction of the needs of current generations without compromising the needs of future generations (WCED, 1988). This definition has gained common currency in the last decade and has been adopted in the Instruments. It is predicated on the principles of inter-generational responsibility and justice in the use and conservation of natural resources. The concept of development includes raising living standards and improving the quality of life, eliminating poverty, increasing food production, preserving biodiversity and improving human settlements.

Natural resources are a key element of sustainable development. This chapter will focus on renewable resources – land, soil, water, flora, fauna as well as other biological resources with actual or potential use or value for humanity (Schrijver, 1997: 12–16). Their key role in sustainable development is underscored by the Forestry Principles which state that forest resources and forest lands are essential for meeting the social, economic, ecological and spiritual needs of present and future generations. These needs are wood and wood products, water, food, fodder, medicine, fuel, shelter, employment, recreation, habitats for wildlife, landscape diversity and carbon sinks and reservoirs.

Natural resources generally are finite and are increasingly being exploited to meet growing human requirements. Large proportions of the population in many countries are dependent on land and natural resources for their food needs and livelihoods. Yet, although in some regions (notably Africa), land-labour ratios are low, and in others new technologies have helped to improve yields, land ownership is generally very unequal, and demand for land and pressures on natural resources are growing. Estimates suggest that the world's population will increase by 75 per cent to more than 9800 million between 1997 and 2050. Arable land per capita in developing countries is projected to fall from 0.65 hectares to about 0.4 hectares between the late 1990s and 2010. In the meantime, overgrazing, erosion, soil salinity and waterlogging are damaging or destroying millions of hectares of productive land and natural resources (FAO, 1997: 1). In addition, more land is required for human settlements. The finiteness of land and natural resources, and the increasing human demands placed on them, lead to competition which, in turn, leads to social conflict.

SOVEREIGNTY, LOCAL EMPOWERMENT AND SUSTAINABLE DEVELOPMENT

For these reasons, natural resource and land use occupy a prominent place in the development policies and strategies of many countries. Since the

1950s, this has been articulated in international law in the principle of national sovereignty over natural resources. As Schrijver (1997: 369) observes, the principle was developed partly to secure the benefits arising from exploiting natural resources for peoples living under colonial rule and partly to provide newly independent states with a defence against infringements upon their sovereignty by foreign states and companies.

The two-fold origins of the principle were expressed in a number of General Assembly Resolutions, notably the Resolution on Permanent Sovereignty over Natural Resources (1803/XVII). The link between self-determination and natural-resources management has also been articulated in the two International Human Rights Covenants of 1966, which provide that all peoples have a right to self-determination and may for their own ends freely dispose of their natural wealth and resources, and there is a similar provision in Article 21 of the African Charter on Human and Peoples' Rights.

The emphasis subsequently shifted to national sovereignty, rather than the rights of peoples. As Schrijver (1997: 370) observes:

> It is symptomatic of this shift that during the period from the adoption of the 1962 Declaration to 1985, with the exception of the resolutions on the rights of specific peoples under 'foreign occupation, colonial domination or apartheid', the permanent sovereignty-related General Assembly resolutions are addressed exclusively to States as subjects of the right to permanent sovereignty over natural resources.

Thus, in the 1960s and 1970s the self-determination of peoples in the planning and management of natural resource and land use disappeared from the formulation of the principle.

It is therefore not surprising that until recently most developing countries considered natural-resource and land use as under the control of central government. The dominant top-down paradigm of development of that period viewed the state as the locus and engine of development. The centralized, and at times authoritarian, policies and plans of the 1960s and 1970s concerning use of land and natural resources were made at the level of central government and then transmitted to regional and local levels for implementation.[3] Too much power was concentrated in central government with very little delegation to local authorities. Within central government, the management of natural-resource and land use was scattered among different ministries, leading to institutional confusion and fragmentation.

Over the last decade, there has been renewed interest in the principle of self-determination of peoples in the management of natural resources. Notably, the 1986 UN Declaration on the Right to Development recalls the right of people to exercise sovereignty over all their natural wealth and resources; and the Draft Declaration on the Rights of Indigenous Peoples proclaims the right of indigenous peoples to self-determination and confers on them a number of resource rights (Schrijver, 1997: 370–1). In addition, the Instruments, while they reiterate the sovereignty of states over natural resources, also impose obligations on states to promote and provide opportunities for the participation of local communities, indigenous people, industries, labour, non-governmental organizations, and individual men and women in the planning and implementation of natural resource and land use policies.[4]

In this emerging trend, states are increasingly under an obligation to exercise their right to permanent sovereignty over natural resources in the interest of national development and to ensure that the benefits of natural-resource use spread across the whole population (Schrijver, 1997: 391). In the context of sustainable development, local communities, women, indigenous peoples and non-governmental organizations – linked in multi-level frameworks with international institutions and states – are coming to be seen as deserving recognition as the objects of the traditional state-centred international law.

In parallel, a new development paradigm which emphasizes popular participation and empowerment has replaced the centralized and statist model at the national level, as many governments have begun decentralizing power to local authorities. Such countries include Nepal, India, the Philippines, Venezuela, Chile, Colombia, Zimbabwe, Côte D'Ivoire and Tanzania (UNDP, 1996: 5). Indeed, '[t]he present level of interest in decentralization is pervasive in that out of 75 developing and transition countries with populations greater than 5 million, all but 12 claim to have embarked on some form of transfer of political power to local units of government' (UNDP, 1996: 3). Decentralization of power and popular participation in decision-making and implementation are important elements of good governance which, in the 1990s, has come to be recognized as a precondition for sustainable development, although vigilance is necessary to ensure that effective power is actually devolved. Not surprisingly, there is a discernible trend towards decentralization and popular participation in natural-resource-and-land-use policies.

INTEGRATED AND SUSTAINABLE DEVELOPMENT VERSUS THE COMMODITIZATION OF RESOURCES

In contrast to the neo-liberal principles that underpin the MAI, which would treat land and natural resources as commodities like any other, the

Instruments advocate an integrated approach to the planning and management of natural-resource and land use. This is because land and natural resources serve a variety of purposes which interact and may conflict with each other.[5] Integrated natural-resource and land use seeks to balance social, economic, ecological, cultural and spiritual needs and purposes. It allows informed choices and trade-offs to be made by all parties concerned with particular natural-resource and land uses. In addition, the Instruments advocate popular participation in natural-resource and land use through a range of measures such as delegating policy-making to the lowest level of public authority consistent with effective action and other locally driven approaches. They also provide for the establishment of innovative procedures, programmes, projects and services that facilitate and encourage the active participation of those affected in the decision-making and implementation process, especially of groups that have, hitherto, often been excluded, such as women, youth, indigenous people and their communities and other communities.[6]

Hence, the Instruments seek to promote a spirit of partnership, solidarity, cooperation and coordination in natural-resource-and-land-use planning and management at subregional, regional and international levels as well as among all levels of government, communities, non-governmental organizations and individuals.[7] They propose cooperation in the provision or facilitation of access to, or transfer of, environmentally sound, economically viable and socially acceptable technologies that are relevant to the conservation and sustainable use of natural resources.[8] Access to and transfer of technology to developing countries should be provided or facilitated under fair and most favourable terms including concessional and preferential arrangements where mutually agreed and subject to adequate and effective protection of intellectual property rights. Furthermore, the Instruments provide for the exchange of information, from all publicly available sources, relevant to the conservation and sustainable use of natural resources.[9] The information contemplated includes the results of technical, scientific and socio-economic research, as well as data on training and surveying programmes, specialized expertise, and indigenous and traditional knowledge. In addition, they provide for the promotion of appropriate capacity-building, which is defined as institution-building, training and the development of relevant local and national capacities.[10] Another form of cooperation that is proposed is the provision of financial support by developed countries to enable developing countries to meet the costs of implementing measures advocated in the Instruments.[11] The proposals also envisage mechanisms to facilitate the provision of financial resources to developing countries on a grant or concessional basis.[12]

Among the innovations of the Desertification Convention is the prominent role accorded to non-governmental organizations (NGOs) in the conservation and sustainable use of natural resources and land. The principles that provide guidance to the parties to the Convention require them to develop – in a spirit of partnership – cooperation with, amongst others, NGOs (Article 3c). Governments, with the support of NGOs, are obliged to promote awareness and facilitate the participation of local communities, particularly women and youth, in efforts to combat desertification (Article 5d). In their national action plans, governments are enjoined to provide for effective participation, at the national and regional levels, of NGOs in policy-planning, decision-making, implementation and review (Article 10f). With regard to information collection, analysis and exchange, governments are required to make full use of the expertise of competent intergovernmental and non-governmental organizations to disseminate relevant information and experiences among target groups. In promoting capacity-building for local people, governments are enjoined to cooperate with NGOs (Article 19a). The Convention exemplifies the growing acceptance that civil society in general, and NGOs in particular, have an important role to play in promoting sustainable use of natural resources.

The Instruments emphasize the critical importance of popular participation for the success of conservation and sustainable natural-resource use. They are premised on the view that the greater the degree of the control by people over the natural resources on which they rely, the greater will be the incentives for social and economic development as well as environmental protection. In broad terms, the Instruments seek to promote

- the achievement of wider access to land, water and forest resources in order to ensure equal rights for women and other disadvantaged groups;
- the assignment of clear titles, rights and responsibilities over natural resources in order to encourage investment by individuals or communities;
- the initiation and maintenance of community groups for natural-resource planning, management and conservation to assist in identification of problems, development of technical and management solutions, and project implementation;
- the development and implementation of programmes to remove and resolve the physical, social and economic causes of natural-resource depletion.

The negotiators of the MAI were not oblivious to the concerns expressed in the Instruments with regard to sustainable development. Various preambular formulations (not agreed at the time of writing this chapter) acknowledged that investment can play an important role in ensuring that economic growth is sustainable when accompanied by appropriate and sound environmental policies; and expressed a desire to implement the MAI in accordance with international environmental law and in a manner consistent with sustainable development, as reflected in the Rio Declaration and Agenda 21. The footnotes indicate disagreements among the negotiators regarding the emphasis that should be given to sustainable development and environmental protection. Certainly, formulations were proposed that would express the desirability of implementing the MAI in a manner consistent with environmental protection and conservation; and reaffirming the parties' commitment to the Rio Declaration and Agenda 21, and such principles, of relevance to investment, as the polluter pays; the precautionary approach; public participation and the right of communities to have access to information; and the avoidance and relocation and transfer of activities which cause severe environmental degradation or are found to be harmful to human health. Crucially, however, there was strong opposition to any suggestion that obligations in the Instruments or other environmental treaties should have precedence over obligations in the MAI. Nor did the negotiators apparently even consider the possibility that any rights given to investors under the MAI should be made subject to compliance with national or international environmental standards.

Despite the proposed preambular statements, the substantive provisions of the MAI would have implications inimical to integrated and sustainable development. As defined in the MAI, investment is quite broad and includes every kind of asset owned or controlled, directly or indirectly, by an investor, including any other tangible and intangible, movable and immovable property, and any related property rights, such as leases, mortgages, liens and pledges. Undoubtedly, natural resources and land are some of the assets contemplated by the above definition. The definition also includes rights conferred pursuant to law or contract such as concessions, licences, authorizations and permits. Rights such as timber licences and concessions and fishing permits are covered by the definition. This definition would impinge on natural-resource management and conservation. The question of concessions was a controversial one during the negotiations, and one of the delegations took the view that the granting of authorizations, licences and concessions in both the petroleum and fisheries sectors involves measures relating to the conservation and management of natural resources, and should fall outside the mandate for the negotiation of the MAI.

RIGHTS, PRIVILEGES AND PARTICIPATION

This proposal illustrates the problems inherent in the asset-based definition of investment. It lumps together property rights and contractual rights
with privileges granted by the state to do what would normally be forbidden. As the Supreme Court of the Philippines pointed out in the *Minors
Oposa* case (1994), timber licences are merely a privilege to do what
would otherwise be unlawful. They are not contracts; neither are they
property or property rights. The same applies to concessions and permits.
As privileges granted by the state, they may be revoked, amended, modified or replaced in the ordinary exercise of regulatory powers of the state –
the so-called 'police powers' in American jurisprudence. To include them
in the definition of investments, and give them the strong protection envisaged in the MAI, would greatly impair the exercise of the day-to-day powers of the state in the regulation of natural-resource use. As the *Minors
Oposa* case illustrates, unregulated timber licences granted for commercial
logging purposes have largely contributed to the depletion of rainforests in
South East Asia and other parts of the world. The MAI would make it very
difficult to withdraw or modify such concessions.

Furthermore, the principle of the Open Door to foreign investment
which is basic to the MAI would require states to give foreigners equal
rights of access to resources with local people. Yet natural resources are
often fundamental to the livelihoods of communities. Furthermore, balanced and sustainable exploitation of resources is more likely to be
secured if priority of access is given to local people. This is recognized in
relation to fish and other ocean resources, in the UN Convention on the
Law of the Sea, which gives the coastal state special rights and responsibilities in the management of these resources. Even the British government, which was one of the strongest advocates of the MAI, reserved
priority of access to its fisheries.

In contrast, the Instruments emphasize that sustainable natural-resource
and land use should be carried out in a participatory way, at the international, national and local levels. The planning and management of natural-
resource and land use are inherently political processes involving decisions
about conflicting interests. Decisions relating to conflicts over natural-
resource and land use are better made through processes which allow the
participation of affected and interested parties at every level. This is best
achieved through the decentralization of power and decision-making to
local government. Agenda 21 appreciates this, by making provision in its
Chapter 28 for local Agenda 21 initiatives. Local communities are better
able to determine the sustainability or otherwise of natural-resource and

land uses. International and national institutions, however, can play an important role in providing technical expertise, financial resources and information that may not be available at the local community level.

Australia's National Landcare Programme is a good example of a natural-resource-use approach that has successfully harnessed federal, state and local communities in collaboration. This is a community-based, self-help approach to natural-resource use. Public policy provides a framework for the identification of shared problems via a group approach, allocation of responsibilities and coordination of activities. The programme emphasizes integrated and cooperative natural-resource-use measures, involving partnerships between governments, landowners and managers, and community groups. Zimbabwe's Communal Areas Management Programme for Indigenous Resources (CAMPFIRE) is yet another example of a successful multi-tiered approach to natural-resource management. CAMPFIRE seeks to devolve the management of natural resources, such as wildlife and forests, to local communities in order to promote sustainable rural development.

Where the regulation of natural-resource and land use is decentralized, this is usually achieved through national legislation which delegates subsidiary law-making and regulatory functions to local authorities. Regulations for natural-resource and land use may therefore differ among local authorities as a result of different developmental, resource or environmental factors. The uniform national-treatment standard that MAI seeks to impose would militate against the delegation of subsidiary law-making and regulatory functions to local authorities in the area of natural-resource and land use. Chapter 11, the investment chapter, of the NAFTA, treats all local government measures as general exceptions. The MAI had no similar general exception.

The MAI would also over-ride the restrictions on access to land by non-local people which are found in land-tenure systems in many countries. Unlike Western countries which generally enjoy uniform land-tenure systems, in many developing countries received Western land-tenure systems coexist with customary tenure systems which, in many cases, vary from region to region. Under customary land-tenure systems, land usually vests in the community and individual rights and entitlements to use land are embedded in, and defined within, the community. Community membership is therefore a *sine qua non* for access to land.

By its very nature, customary tenure excludes non-community members from enjoying rights of use to communal land. In many developing countries, non-citizens are not permitted to acquire customary land, for example under the Tanzanian National Land Policy (Tanzania, 1995). Similarly, the basis for the regime of land law in Vanuatu is custom. The constitution of Vanuatu prohibits foreigners from acquiring perpetual ownership of land (Ghai, 1985). National land policies and laws which prohibit foreign acquisition of customary land are inconsistent with the national-treatment standard of the MAI as it presently stands. Opening up customary land to foreign ownership is likely to cause conflict which would be inimical to sustainable development. Applied to regimes governing natural-resource and land use, the national-treatment standard is a blunt principle that does not take into account national and local factors which impinge on sustainable development.

The issue of customary tenure is linked with the definition of natural resources and land. While the Instruments adopt an integrated approach which acknowledges the different functions and meanings attached to natural resources and land by different societies and communities, the MAI definition concerns itself exclusively with the view of natural resources and land purely as commodities and factors of production that should be subject to the laws of the market. The Instruments accept that natural resources and land, in addition to their economic functions, have social as well as cultural functions and meanings. For example, land plays an important role in the self-understanding and identity formation of many societies and communities. Hence in many countries land and natural resources are either not commoditized or are semi-commoditized. The OECD negotiators put forward proposals for clauses to deal with the special rights of 'indigenous peoples' (discussed by Nick Mabey, in Chapter 4 of this volume), but took no real account of the very different view of the world's resources taken by many other peoples.

The Instruments enjoin governments to review and refocus existing measures to achieve wider access to natural resources and land. Sustainable development is predicated on the enjoyment of access to primary resources by all members of society, and is often crucial to sustainable livelihoods for the majority of people. Many countries use citizenship or residence as a factor in the management of the competition for access to scarce or valuable land or other resources. Restrictions on foreign acquisition and ownership of land range from outright prohibitions to requirements for government approvals for land acquisitions beyond a specified ceiling. For example, Pakistan does not permit foreign investors to own land for agriculture or irrigation, while New Zealand requires the approval of the Overseas Investment Commission for foreign investment that results in the control of land over five acres or worth more than NZ$ 10 million. In some countries non-citizens can only acquire land through joint ventures or leasehold agreements (Tanzania, 1995). Regardless of whether they are intended to ensure access to land by citizens in order to promote sustainable development, restrictions on foreign acquisition and ownership of land would be inconsistent with the investor protection and rights of access of the MAI as it stands today.

The Instruments are consistent with the emerging human-rights jurisprudence on economic, social and cultural rights which views the issue of human-rights implementation from the perspective of state obligations. The state is considered to have three obligations (Van Hoof, 1984).

1. *The obligation to respect* requires the state to refrain from any action which prevents people from satisfying their needs themselves when they are able to. It could well be argued that statist regimes governing natural-resource and land use denied people the right to make decisions about how to utilize their resources and thus prevented them from satisfying their needs in circumstances where they were able to do so. Decentralized natural-resource and land use on the other hand gives people the scope to decide how best to use their resources. The granting of timber licences or fishing permits on an open-market basis would amount to a violation of this obligation if it caused the depletion of these resources to a point where communities which were once self-sufficient in meeting their food requirements ended up being unable to do so.

2. *The obligation to protect* requires the state to prevent others from depriving people of their main resource. Thus, the state has an obligation to prevent the socially powerful from depriving local communities of their main natural resource, such as land, rainforests or fish stocks.

3. *The obligation to promote* requires the state to take appropriate legislative, administrative, budgetary and other long-term measures towards the full realization of economic, social and cultural rights. It could be argued that the measures recommended in the Instruments regarding natural-resource and land use amount to an obligation to promote the economic, social and cultural rights of local communities, women and indigenous people.

THE REGULATION OF LAND USE AND THE TAKINGS QUESTION

The other provisions of the MAI which impinge on land-use regulation are those which deal with expropriation and measures having an equivalent effect, giving investors rights which could allow them to claim damages in national courts, as well as being enforceable through international arbitration.

It is generally accepted that states enjoy sovereign powers for the compulsory acquisition of land for public purposes subject to paying the owner the fair market value of the land. This is the so-called 'power of eminent domain' in American jurisprudence. The circumstances under which land can be acquired compulsorily and the procedures for acquisition are often set out in the constitution. One clause in the MAI which is of interest to land use for sustainable development is the seemingly innocuous one which prohibits 'measures having equivalent effect' to expropriation. This could have extensive effects on the power of governments to regulate land development. Not surprisingly, this issue has been extensively explored in US case law. Should the MAI come into force, US lawyers will not be slow to exploit its provisions and bring cases challenging the validity of land-use regulations which interfere with the 'free' use of land and natural resources by an owner.

At issue are the limits of legitimate land regulation. Land-use planning law and development controls frequently impose conditions, either on the title to the land or through a development permit. These conditions require the performance of specified activities on or in connection with the land. In addition, they may set out standards for measuring the quality of performance of the specified activities. Examples of activities which may be imposed by land-use planning-and-development instruments include the erection of buildings, the design and structure of the buildings to be erected, the type of materials to be used, and the use to which the buildings should be put. Usually, the specified activities have to be performed within given time periods. Another popular planning-and-development control instrument is the development agreement. This is an example of what has come to be known as public-private partnerships in the provision of public infrastructure. Under development agreements, planning authorities may make the grant of a development permit conditional upon the developer's consent to make a contribution to public infrastructure or some other benefit.

Landowners and developers often claim that restrictions and regulations on development are tantamount to the taking of private property without compensation. Claims that public authorities have taken property without paying compensation include cases where

- the government occupies the land in order to build something such as a road;
- regulatory action creates hazards or noise which can be said to amount to an invasion of the property;
- regulations seek to confer a benefit on the public;
- regulation reduces the value of the property (Beatley, 1994: 190–208).

US court decisions illustrate the type of claims for compensation arising out of land-use regulations which investors might make. US lawyers have employed a number of theories to determine whether restrictions amount to takings (Beatley, 1994: 190–208; Munzer, 1990: 442–69). These may revolve around rather indeterminate concepts, such as whether the regulation is intended to prevent a harm, in which case compensation is not required, or to secure public benefits, when payment must be made (Beatley, 1994: 200). For example, in the *Nollan* case, the US Supreme Court upheld a challenge to the California Coastal Commission's policy of ensuring beach access to the general public, by conditioning seafront building permits on the provision of public rights of passage. The Supreme Court did not regard the Commission's decision as substantially related to legitimate state interests and decided that if the Commission wanted the right of passage across the property, it had to pay for it (Munzer, 1990: 464–5).

The dominant test is the so-called 'diminution of value' test, an economic criterion which is likely to be relied upon by investors claiming compensation under the MAI. This focuses on the extent to which the government regulation reduces or diminishes the value of land. The test has been modified by the concept of reasonable 'investment-backed expectations' which was introduced in 1978 by the Supreme Court in the *Penn Central* case. The Penn Central Company argued that the city's historic district regulations, which prevented the company from building a 55-storey building on top of Grand Central Station, amounted to a taking of its property. Under the modified test, in addition to the diminution of value occasioned by the land-use restriction, it is also important to determine the extent to which the expectations of such use are reasonable. As the restrictions did not interrupt the existing uses of the property, the court found that no taking had occurred (Beatley, 1994: 202). However, in the *Lucas* case, a developer who owned two small pieces of beachfront found that he would not be allowed to construct a beachfront home on either property as a result of a new law. He sued the Council for compulsorily acquiring his properties without compensation. The Supreme Court issued a majority opinion which reinforced the idea that when a regulation serves to preclude all reasonable use, a taking will have occurred (Beatley, 1994: 202–3).

Relying on the MAI protections against expropriation and measures with equivalent effect, foreign investors are likely to impede government land-use regulations, or claim compensation for government land-use measures which they deem to amount to takings. Indeed, this has already happened under the similar provisions of the NAFTA (Nolan and Lippoldt,

1998). Most relevant is the claim against the government of Mexico by Metalclad, a US corporation with Mexican subsidiaries, which is involved in waste treatment and disposal. In 1993 Metalclad purchased a Mexican hazardous-waste-disposal facility in the state of San Luis Potosi. The Mexican company that Metalclad purchased had a history of pollution and conflict with local communities. Given continuing concerns about the safety of the site, the Mexican federal government delayed giving Metalclad approval to operate the site until December 1995. The state government of San Luis Potosi continued to block the project.

In January 1997, Metalclad filed an investor-state claim before an ICSID arbitral panel under the NAFTA investment chapter, seeking monetary damages on the grounds that Mexico had expropriated its hazardous-waste landfill located in the community of Guadalcazar by not allowing it to operate the facility. Metalclad is claiming damages equal to the landfill's fair-market value, estimated to be in excess of US$ 50 million. This claim illustrates the point that investors will use the MAI dispute-resolution provisions to challenge land-use measures which they deem to be expropriatory in effect. Delays in granting land-use permits and approvals for investment projects would be considered as expropriatory in effect. This is likely to be the case where investors can argue that the land-use regulations in question interfere with their investment-backed expectations.

CONCLUSION

Over the last decade, the international community has made great strides in establishing principles of sustainable development. The time has come for sustainable-development norms to be integrated into the globalization agenda. It should be emphasized that sustainable development should not be subsumed under globalization. The two processes are at times supportive and at times contradictory. Thus a cursory reference to the Rio Declaration and Agenda 21 in the preamble of the MAI does not mean that sustainable-development concerns have been taken into account in the globalization agenda of the latter.

As regards natural-resources and land use, their special character and integral role in sustainable development indicate the limitations of a definition which sees them purely as an ordinary investment that should be subject to extensive investor-protection standards and open-market acquisition rights. While there is no denying that private property rights in natural resources and land serve important social and economic functions, there is also no denying that such rights should be subject to collective constraints decided at the national level in accordance with a country's specific circumstances and exercised at the local level. Thus, an integrated approach which is sensitive to the social and cultural embeddedness of natural-resource and land use is to be preferred to the narrow neo-liberal approach of the MAI. This is not to argue that global standards are unimportant. On the contrary, global standards in the regulation of investment are called for more than ever before. Such standards need to be informed by an integrated approach similar to the one that underpins the Environment and Development Instruments.

What is required is a multi-tiered framework which integrates global standards, national sovereignty and local empowerment concerns. While global standards will necessarily make inroads into the principle of national sovereignty, they should at least recognize and enhance the capacity of the state to regulate economic activity in a developmentally sustainable manner. Global standards similar to those articulated in the Environment and Development Instruments are also critical to local empowerment. For example, international standards on environmentally and socially sustainable technologies, as well as the methods and terms of their transfer, are critical to local empowerment. What is called for is not a neo-liberal multilateral framework exemplified by the MAI, whose sole concern is with the commoditization of all natural resources. Rather, what is called for is a framework that seeks to create multi-level synergies and to knit together global standards, national sovereignty and local empowerment. The solution is neither a top-down nor down-up approach. Rather, it is a combination of both.

NOTES

1. Although individual country exceptions can be negotiated to the MAI, and countries may be allowed to preserve their land-use and natural-resources management systems, the very fact that these have to be treated as exceptions that would be subject to standstill and rollback shows that they run counter to its principles.
2. Principles for a Global Consensus on the Management, Conservation and Sustainable Development of All Types of Forests (not legally binding). These Instruments, as well as a range of other documents and resources, are available through the Greenpeace Globelaw website, http://www.globelaw.com/sources.htm.
3. For an excellent critique of authoritarian land-use policies, see Tanzania, 1994.

4. See Principle 10 of the Rio Declaration, Articles 8(j) and 10(c) and 10(d) of the Biodiversity Convention, Principle 1(d) of the Forestry Principles, and Articles 3, 5, 10, 13, 17 and 19 of the Desertification Convention.
5. See for example Chapter 10(3) of Agenda 21; Principle 1(b) and 6 of the Forestry Principles; Articles 2(2), 4(2)(a) of the Desertification Convention.
6. See for example Principle 10 of the Rio Declaration, Chapter 10 of Agenda 21; Article 3(a) of the Desertification Convention; Principles 1(d) and 5(a) of the Forestry Principles; Articles 8(j) and 10(c) and (d) of the Biodiversity Convention.
7. For example Principle 7 of the Rio Declaration; Article 3 of the Desertification Convention; Chapters 10 and 14 of Agenda 21; Principles 3(b) and 9(a) of the Forestry Principles; Articles 5, 16, 17, 18 and 20 of the Biodiversity Convention.
8. See Article 16 of the Biodiversity Convention and Article 18 of the Desertification Convention.
9. Article 17 of the Biodiversity Convention and Articles 20(2)(c) and (6) of the Convention on Combating Desertification.
10. See Article 19 of the Desertification Convention. Capacity-building is defined as institution-building, training and the development of relevant local and national capacities.
11. Article 20 of the Biodiversity Convention; Articles 6(c) and (d) and 20(2), (3), (4) and (5) of the Desertification Convention.
12. Article 21 of the Biodiversity Convention and Article 21 of the Desertification Convention.

REFERENCES

Beatley, T. (1994) *Ethical Land Use: Principles of Policy and Planning.* The Johns Hopkins University Press, Baltimore and London.

FAO (Food And Agriculture Organization) (1997) *Chapter 10: Integrated Approach to the Planning and Management of Land Resources.* Progress Report, Rome.

Ghai, Y. (1983) 'Land Regimes and Paradigms of Development: Reflections on Melanesian Constitutions', *International Journal of the Sociology of Law*, vol. 13, 393–405.

Lucas v. South Carolina Coastal Council (1992) US vol. 505, 1003.

Minors Oposa v. Secretary of the Department of Environment and Natural Resources (DENT) International Legal Materials vol. 33, 177 (1994).

Nolan, M. and Lippoldt, D. (1998) 'Obscure NAFTA Clause Empowers Private Parties', *The National Law Journal*, 6 April.

Nollan v. California Coastal Commission (1987) *Supreme Court* vol. 107, 3141.

Munzer, S. (1990) *A Theory of Property.* Cambridge University Press, Cambridge.

Penn Central Company v. City of New York (1978) *US* vol. 438, 104.

Schrijver, N. (1997) *Sovereignty Over Natural Resources: Balancing Rights and Duties.* Cambridge University Press, Cambridge.

Tanzania, United Republic of (1994) *Report of the Presidential Commission of Inquiry into Land Matters,* vol. 1. Ministry of Lands, Housing and Urban

Development in cooperation with the Scandinavian Institute of African Studies, Uppsala.

Tanzania, United Republic of (1995) *National Land Policy*. Ministry of Lands, Housing and Urban Development, Dar es Salaam.

United Nations Development Programme (1996) *Decentralized Governance Programme, Strengthening Capacity for People-Centred Development*. Management and Governance Division, New York.

Van Hoof, G. J. H. (1984) 'The Legal Nature of Economic, Social and Cultural Rights: a Rebuttal of Some Traditional Views' in Alston, P. and Tomasevski, K. (eds) *The Right to Food*. Martinus Nijhoff, Utrecht.

Wall, B. (1998) 'Reaping the Fruits of the Land in Eastern Europe, England and Asia', *The International Herald Tribune,* Saturday-Sunday, February 21–22.

World Commission on Environment and Development (1988) *Our Common Future*. Oxford University Press, Oxford.

7 Improving Investor Accountability

Dominic Ayine and Jacob Werksman

INTRODUCTION

This chapter explores how international standards, especially those for protecting the environment, may be more effectively enforced, in relation to international economic activity and corporate behaviour. It argues that measures to create more open and competitive world markets, such as the proposed MAI, must be accompanied by arrangements to strengthen the enforcement of environmental standards. Although the international community has made great strides, in the past two decades, in recognizing the importance of the principle of sustainable development, and embodying it in more specific standards, effective enforcement is too often lacking. To a great extent this is because the costs of environmental damage may be external to the firm or state causing it, creating the temptation to free-ride. The consensual nature of international law, and the competitive character of capitalist economic relations, create difficulties for effective enforcement of standards which protect public interests. However, these are certainly not insurmountable. The increased integration of the world economy can and should be accompanied by more effective means for coordinating the enforcement of those standards for environmental protection which are now recognized as essential to ensuring the sustainability of economic development.

The dangers of pursuing economic liberalization without an adequate reinforcement of regulatory standards have been made apparent in the debate over the MAI. As shown by other chapters in this book, the MAI aimed to introduce strict 'disciplines' on the powers of states to regulate international investors and investments, very broadly defined. As a corollary, it would have given those investors legally enforceable rights. In response to widespread criticisms of the one-sidedness of the draft agreement, the negotiators put forward some proposals recognizing social and environmental issues, but these were largely window-dressing (see Mabey, Chapter 4). Statements in the Preamble 'reaffirming their commitment' to international instruments such as the Rio Declaration, Agenda 21, and the Copenhagen Statement of the World Summit on Social Development would have no binding force. Even the proposed 'non-lowering of standards' article would only prevent derogation from a state's own regulations in respect of a specific investment, and not a general reduction of standards. It seems that no consideration has even been given to including measures which would hold either firms or governments responsible for ensuring compliance with environmental standards, or liable for damage caused by their breach.

This chapter examines the general issue of the accountability of transnational corporations (TNCs) for environmental damage. It begins with a consideration of the way in which the broad liberalization obligations envisaged in the MAI, combined with its 'top-down' approach to investment liberalization, would undermine the ability of national governments to regulate access to and use of their natural resources, and their ability to hold foreign corporate investors accountable for negative environmental and development impacts. The second section deals with problems and prospects of enhancing TNC accountability for environmental damage at different levels – host country, home country and at the international level. The third section examines the need for a multilateral framework for investment (MFI) that broadly incorporates environmental concerns, norms and principles and thus widens the possibilities of holding TNCs accountable for environmental damage.

THE MAI'S TOP-DOWN APPROACH

The MAI's 'top-down' approach to liberalization of investment rules undermines the ability of national governments to regulate access to and use of their natural resources, and their ability to hold foreign corporate investors accountable for negative environmental and development impacts. The MAI would require contracting parties to accept sweeping non-discriminatory obligations with regard to National Treatment (NT) and Most Favoured Nation (MFN), backed by a compulsory state-to-state and investor-state dispute-settlement regime.

The NT and MFN obligations are intended to prohibit both measures which are explicitly discriminatory, and those that are formally neutral but may disadvantage foreign investors in their effect. The MAI would empower foreign investors, either through their home governments, or directly through an international arbitration procedure, to challenge as discriminatory any of the host country's regulations that had not been expressly exempted.

Contracting parties that wish to preserve their sovereign discretion to make distinctions between foreign and domestic investors must therefore identify specific environmental and other measures that deviate from the MAI's NT and MFN obligations. These must be negotiated and agreed with the other contracting parties prior to signature or accession. The bargaining over these national exceptions among the countries participating in the OECD negotiations began in mid-1997, and the difficulty in reaching agreement on a 'balance of commitments' seems to have been one of the reasons for the failure to conclude the agreement by April 1998. Although the MAI would be open for accession by other states, including developing countries, they would have to negotiate the terms of their accession with the existing members, through a so-called Parties Group.

Theoretically, this system of country-specific exceptions, if generously applied, could exempt any existing measures that discriminate between domestic and foreign investors, in order to achieve a variety of policy goals, including environmental protection. For example, the parties to the North American Free Trade Agreement (NAFTA), under a similar legal arrangement, have exempted their fisheries and other environmentally related sectors from that Agreement's NT provisions.

However, experience under other liberalization agreements points to the difficulty of drafting exceptions or waivers precisely enough to avoid challenges based on the broad non-discrimination principles of NT and MFN. For instance, the European Union applied for and was granted a waiver from GATT non-discrimination rules (on which those of the MAI are based), in order to allow the EU to extend favourable treatment to, among others, certain banana-exporting developing countries. The favourable treatment was justified, in part, on the basis of the more sustainable agricultural practices of these countries. However, a group of American-owned TNCs operating large-scale banana plantations prompted a number of governments to challenge these measures as discriminatory. The WTO Panel hearing the dispute construed the European waiver narrowly, and has required the EU to adjust its banana regime to remove the offending provisions.[1]

Moreover, the MAI's top-down approach is aimed at narrowing the number and level of national measures which might be discriminatory, by encouraging countries to negotiate them away through 'stand-still' and 'roll-back' requirements. Thus, any country wishing to accede to the MAI after the OECD adopts the Agreement is likely to be under pressure to catalogue legitimate but potentially discriminatory measures, and commit to phasing them out.[2] Such an approach might be more appropriate in a small group of countries, such as NAFTA, which has a history of cross-border investments, and which can liberalize trade and investment in the context of an active programme of regulatory cooperation on matters such as the environment. In such a context, the need to distinguish between domestic and foreign investors declines as social and legal integration advances and mutual confidence improves in each party's environmental standards, and their capacity to enforce them.

A more appropriate model for liberalizing investment laws in a multilateral context, which involves countries with different national traditions and at very different stages of economic development, is the approach taken by the Uruguay Round negotiators when designing the General Agreement on Trade in Services (GATS). This covers the provision of services not only across borders but also through a foreign establishment, which involves investment: hence the GATS would have significant overlaps with the MAI. However, the GATS is designed from the 'bottom up', allowing countries to opt in to its rules specific sectors of their economies one by one, through rolling negotiations. It also includes procedures for coordination and harmonization of regulatory arrangements (such as professional qualification requirements), which helps to establish a sounder regulatory basis for liberalization.

In contrast, the OECD negotiators have continued to view the top-down approach as a key element of the MAI. This makes the agreement inappropriate for developing and transitional states, that are still in the process of building their domestic regulatory capacity. Moreover, as concerns TNC accountability for environmental damage, the top-down approach undermines the ability of national governments to regulate access to and the use of their natural resources.

The NT and MFN obligations of the MAI would create rights which could be used by TNCs to 'chill' the development and implementation of existing environmental standards and/or to prevent the strengthening of these standards. They could do so by lobbying against proposed new standards on the grounds that they might contravene the MAI, and in the last resort by using the investor-state dispute-settlement mechanism. This has already been the experience under NAFTA, which has a similar procedure, under which several cases have already been brought (Nolan and Lippoldt, 1998). The problems which can be created are vividly illustrated by the case brought by the US multinational, Ethyl Corp., against Canada.

Ethyl challenged the Canadian ban on both the import and interprovincial transport of MMT, a fuel additive that increases the octane level in gasoline while decreasing nitrogen-oxide levels. MMT is produced in the USA and processed in Canada by Ethyl's Canadian subsidiary. Ethyl's claim was that the ban constituted a violation of its investment rights since the ban treated American companies worse than Canadian ones. Also, since it would have completely eradicated Ethyl's Canadian business,

Ethyl argued that the law was an 'expropriation' of its assets or an action 'tantamount to expropriation' because it would have eliminated Ethyl's expected profit earnings through Canadian sales of the fuel additive (Nolan and Lippoldt, 1998: 6). Ethyl sought at least $250 million in damages. The government of Canada settled the suit for $13 million, dropped the ban and apologized to Ethyl for its action (Public Citizen, 1998). Ethyl thus effectively deployed the NAFTA dispute settlement mechanism to 'chill' the Canadian government's environmental measure of banning MMT in the public interest.

In view of the close similarity of NAFTA's Chapter 11 dispute-settlement mechanism to the proposed investor-state dispute-settlement provisions of the MAI, this case is a foretaste of what might occur under the MAI. By October 1998, four suits had been filed under NAFTA Chapter 11. Beside Ethyl, two other corporations, Metalclad Corp., of Newport Beach, California, and Desechos Solidos (DESONA), also based in California, had brought proceedings against Mexico for damages for 'expropriation' of their businesses (Nolan and Lippolt, 1998). The details of these cases are still secret, but they are apparently based on the withdrawal of waste-disposal licences by local government authorities. Another American chemical corporation, Ohio-based S. D. Myers Inc., also invoked the procedures against Canada for the ban placed by Canada on the export of PCB.[3]

Ironically, as will be explored in the rest of this chapter, the legal difficulties inherent in holding TNCs accountable for environmental harm at home-country, host-country and the international level significantly undermine efforts to make TNCs pay for environmental damage. The MAI would thus create a simple win-win situation for foreign investors.

ENHANCING TNC ACCOUNTABILITY IN THE HOST AND HOME COUNTRIES

A defining characteristic of TNCs is that they consist of a network of many, often hundreds, of affiliates or subsidiaries, based in a wide variety of countries around the globe. Legally, a TNC is not a single entity, but many, each of which may be subject to different jurisdictions, either due to its place of incorporation (sometimes thought of as its nationality), or its residence (location of its central management or headquarters), or where it does business. Thus, TNCs sometimes complain they are subject to multiple and often conflicting rules. Indeed, proposals have been put forward for inclusion in the MAI to deal with the problem of 'conflicting requirements'.

However, no one state is responsible for overall jurisdiction. Because jurisdiction is often unclear, it is often difficult, if not impossible, to exert effective legal control over the group as a whole. Moreover, TNCs have become adept at manipulating jurisdictional rules and regulatory differences between states, and using intermediary companies incorporated in convenient 'havens', to evade or avoid many regulatory requirements. The absence of a world-wide jurisdiction over TNCs, coupled with the availability of certain procedural and substantive legal impediments, has greatly hampered the use of law and the legal system to ensure TNC accountability for environmental damage. This problem is starkly revealed when environmental damage occurs in a developing country, which may be anxious to encourage investment and economic growth, may lack adequate administrative systems to ensure environmental protection, and whose legal system may be incapable of providing effective remedy for the damage caused.

In this part, it is proposed to examine the problems and prospects of holding TNCs accountable for environmental damage at the host-country, home-country and international levels.

Limits of TNC Accountability in the Host Country

Most TNC foreign investments are made either directly (through a branch) or through the use of separately incorporated subsidiaries. These are usually wholly owned, but are sometimes joint ventures with local firms, private investors or government entities. The TNC is often able to dominate the activities of the local firm, even if it has only minority shareholding, since it usually provides the technology and often the top management personnel. Legally, however, the local firm is a separate entity, and the TNC is only a shareholder, not directly liable for its actions. In some cases, indeed, the links are merely through contracts, as in the case of franchising operations such as McDonald's or Benetton.

The question of TNC accountability at the host-country level is both a political and a legal question. Politically, host-country governments, especially developing-country governments desirous to attract foreign investment, may be cautious about imposing environmental standards and requirements that might drive away much-needed potential foreign investment. Even where existing standards have been violated by a foreign TNC and/or its local subsidiary, the political will to pursue vigorous enforcement might be lacking for the same reason. Further, local communities and individuals affected by any environmentally harmful investment activity of a multinational are often reluctant to take action, since local jobs and livelihoods are often at stake. Even if a local group wishes to act, it may be politically powerless to effect necessary policy changes that could halt the investment activity or minimize its deleterious effects, or to use the law to obtain compensation for personal injury or environmental damage.

Legally, the question of TNC accountability often reduces itself to whether and to what extent the parent corporation can be held liable for damage which results from activities which are directly the responsibility of the subsidiary. Establishing the accountability of the parent faces both substantive and procedural legal obstacles, not only in the host state, but under both public and private international law. The main substantive legal obstacle is the principle of separate legal personality already mentioned, which will be discussed further below.

The procedural legal obstacles are rooted in the principle of public international law, under which state sovereignty limits the extra-territorial application of domestic law, so that a state cannot itself enforce its laws against persons or property located in another state. Thus, it is only possible to use the national law of a host state directly against a foreign parent corporation to the extent allowed by treaties between the home and host states. Thus, even if the parent can be added as a defendant in a legal action in a host state against the subsidiary of the TNC, damages recovered may be limited to the assets available in the host state, unless the home-state courts are willing to cooperate to enforce the judgement and orders of the host-state courts.

The Bhopal case clearly demonstrates both the political and legal limits of TNC accountability for environmental damage, due to the division of jurisdiction. In this case, toxic fumes known as methyl isocyanate leaked from a chemical plant owned and operated by Union Carbide, India Limited (UCIL), killing over 2000 people and causing injuries to a further 200 000. UCIL was jointly owned by the Union Carbide, a US multinational (50.9 per cent) and the Government of India (49.1 per cent) and was incorporated under Indian law as a subsidiary of Union Carbide since 1934 (Yakpo, 1989: 139; Cassels, 1993). With the help of US lawyers, the victims brought about 100 different suits in 13 states in various courts of the United States against Union Carbide for tort damages for injury and death caused by the gas leak (Yakpo, 1989). The suits were subsequently consolidated for trial before the Southern District Court of New York. Union Carbide challenged the institution of proceedings in the United States instead of India as inappropriate, and the New York courts dismissed the case on the ground that India, rather than the United States, was a more suitable place to try the case against Union Carbide and its

Indian subsidiary, UCIL, relying on the doctrine of *forum non conveniens* (inconvenient forum).

Back in India, victims brought actions against Union Carbide and UCIL, but while these were pending, the Indian government, which had arrogated to itself the power to enter into any compromise with Union Carbide under Section 3(2)(b) of the Bhopal Act of 1985, eventually settled the case for $470 million. This covered all past, present and future claims arising in relation to the Bhopal case (Anderson, 1995: 157). This was a fraction of the damages that a US court would have awarded, and caused only a small dent in Union Carbide's profits.

As pointed out by Michael Anderson (1995), right from the outset, people in Bhopal were largely excluded from the litigation process. To him, the distance of the people of Bhopal 'from the putative mechanisms of accountability may be traced in three aspects of the litigation':

- Many of the worst-affected areas were effectively slums whose inhabitants possessed neither the institutional skill nor the financial resources required to proceed against the corporation; the court hearings on appropriate forum took place in the United States, well beyond the reach not only of the victims but also of civil society groups in Bhopal.
- By its passage of the Bhopal Act, the Indian government effectively excluded these civil society groups from any participation in the process of accountability.
- During the settlement negotiations, Bhopal groups were neither represented nor consulted as to their content (Anderson, 1995: 156–7).

A critical analysis of the Bhopal case shows not only the limits of legal mechanisms of accountability, but also that the political mechanisms deployed by both the Central Government of India and the political activism of Bhopalian civil society proved highly insufficient in relation to the enormous and irreparable damage caused. The central government's conduct was based on short-term political considerations (Anderson, 1995: 158) which could not be altered by the political activism of local groups. Indeed, the settlement took the possibility of corporate accountability completely out of their reach both in legal and political terms.

Events in Bhopal following the dismissal of the case by the US courts demonstrate that host states, especially developing countries with weak political, economic and legal systems, may be incapable of providing effective regimes for holding TNCs accountable for environmental damage caused by their subsidiaries in foreign countries. The marginalization of civil society, the absence of judicial determination of liability and the settlement 'extracted' from the Indian government by Union Carbide all point not only to the weak nature of host (developing)-country systems of accountability but also to the enormous power wielded by TNCs over governments in particular and society as a whole.

The MAI would exacerbate this already precarious situation by giving more power to TNC investors without at the same time imposing commensurate responsibilities on them towards societies in host states. The investor-state arbitration envisaged in the MAI, and already in effect under NAFTA, allows a parent company to over-ride any inconvenient limitations of local law and bring its complaints directly against the government. However, no complementary procedures are envisaged to hold parent companies accountable for the operations of their local subsidiaries. For example, in the Ethyl case, discussed above, if the Canadian government or some other person or group of persons in Canada sought monetary damages against Ethyl of USA for pollution caused by its subsidiary in Canada, nothing in the NAFTA Chapter 11 procedures would allow this.

To improve TNC accountability at the host-country level, there is need for home-country intervention to control the foreign investment activities of their multinationals. Such control is already being exercised over some aspects of TNCs' foreign activities. For example, OECD countries in 1997 drafted a Convention on Combating Bribery of Foreign Public Officials in International Business Transactions. The Convention criminalizes bribery of foreign public officials by individuals and companies and obliges participating states to impose criminal penalties on companies under their jurisdiction for complicity in or authorization of such bribery. In appropriate cases, therefore, this could penalize parent companies for involvement in bribery, even if it is done by their foreign agents or subsidiaries and takes place abroad, although only if the complicity of the parent or its offices can be shown.

The OECD Bribery Convention follows the pattern of the Foreign Corrupt Practices Act (FCPA) of the USA which penalizes US-based corporations for bribery of foreign public officials. The FCPA in a sense legislated extra-territorially by holding American corporations to home-country standards for activity carried out abroad. Thus, the FCPA complements possible weaknesses of host-state governments and legal systems in combating corruption of their officials by American TNCs. Similarly, nothing prevents states from, either unilaterally or collectively, taking steps to hold TNCs to home standards of environmental regulation so as to complement the efforts of host states such as India or Ghana (see generally Neff, 1990).

Host states, especially those in the developing world, could enhance the possibilities of holding TNCs and/or their subsidiaries accountable for environmental damage by imposing home-state standards of environmental regulation and by enabling civil society groups to proceed against corporations responsible for such damage. However, since unilateral actions along such lines may trigger diversion of investments to other states not applying similar high standards, the solution lies in taking collective action to impose comparable standards.

Enhancing TNC Accountability in the Home Country

In the absence of strong host-state regulatory and political regimes that ensure TNC accountability for environmental damage, the home state of the TNC becomes the next resort. But though home-country legal and political systems are, as a general rule, stronger and thus hold greater promise of accountability, victims of environmental damage should not be surprised to find certain legal obstacles that would frustrate their attempts to sue in home-country courts. Our analysis of the Bhopal case has shown that the actions against Union Carbide and UCIL in the US were rejected on the basis of the doctrine of *inconvenient forum*. Although traditionally courts were reluctant to refuse to accept a civil action validly brought against a person within their jurisdiction, in the past few years courts in developed countries (especially the US) have increasingly accepted arguments on behalf of TNCs that a claim should be rejected if a more convenient forum exists to hear it (Muchlinski, 1987: 141–4; Prince, 1998).

A second major procedural difficulty is caused by the requirement of *standing*. This refers to the right of a person to bring an action before a court of law. To demonstrate standing, a litigant must establish at least that:

- s/he has personally suffered some actual or threatened injury as a consequence of the illegal conduct of the defendant;
- the injury fairly can be traced to the challenged action; and
- the injury is likely to be redressed by a favourable decision (Robbins, 1995: 13).

In environmental litigation, the first of these minimum requirements means that individuals and groups must show that they have suffered, or are imminently threatened with, some harm to their particular personal interests, as opposed to the interests of the general public. The second requirement places a burden on the plaintiff to establish the causal connection between the act complained of and the claimed injury. The damage must not be too remote or too speculative. Finally, the plaintiff must demonstrate that the remedy sought is substantially likely to redress the said damage. This may be because an irremediable damage renders the court's decision ineffectual.

The problem of standing is also linked to the question of whether the parent is liable for acts which were directly the responsibility of the subsidiary. In the Bhopal case, for example, Union Carbide argued that the Indian plaintiffs only had standing to sue UCIL and other persons immediately involved with operation of the plant which it argued had caused the disaster; evidence that the cause was the plant's initial design would have established a stronger case against Union Carbide.

Choice of Law

A foreign plaintiff who has successfully cleared the obstacles regarding standing and inconvenient forum discussed above may still be faced with the problem of choice of substantive law. The question here is which law to apply in resolving the dispute: the law of the place where the injury occurred or the law of the court trying the dispute?

This depends on the rules of private international law as interpreted by domestic courts. Generally, courts apply the law of the forum where the litigation takes place (probably because they are in a much better position to do so) but public policy concerns and the principle of non-discrimination may affect the choice (Kiss and Shelton, 1991: 367). According to the latter principle, in no circumstance may the plaintiff's case be judged in accordance with rules less favourable than those which would be used to judge the case in the place of origin of the allegedly illegal conduct of the defendant. The principle does not preclude the application of rules more favourable to the plaintiff than those that obtain in the place where the illegal conduct took place. However, since this principle is not applied by some jurisdictions, it is possible that unfavourable substantive rules of law pertaining to the jurisdiction where the environmental harm occurred might haunt the plaintiffs wherever they go.

In the absence of uniform rules, the problem of choice of law remains an inherent one due to the divergent policies of sovereign states (Kiss and Shelton, 1991: 367) and adds to the woes of a foreign plaintiff seeking to hold a TNC accountable for its injury to the environment.

Parent-Subsidiary Liability Rules

As already mentioned, the main obstacle to TNC accountability is the principle of separate legal personality of each separately incorporated affiliate within the TNC corporate group. Courts are generally reluctant to 'lift the corporate veil' and make a parent company directly liable for acts attributable to its subsidiaries, either for their contractual liabilities (such as debts), or for their negligent or other tortious acts.

Nevertheless, the parent can be sued if it can be shown to have participated or been involved in the activity concerned. For example, in the Bhopal case, the claim against Union Carbide was partly based on its responsibility for the original design of the plant, and for supervising its operations. Recently, the British Court of Appeal accepted legal actions brought against Cape Industries, on behalf of workers and local residents in South Africa alleging that they had contracted mesothelioma as a result of Cape's asbestos mines and mills operated through its South African subsidiaries (*Lubbe et al.* v. *Cape Plc*, 1998). However, this depends on being able to prove that the parent company knew, through its directors or officers, of the health risks created by the operations conducted by its subsidiary.

Some courts, however, have gone further, and accepted that where a TNC can be shown to be run as an integrated group under central control, then the parent can be sued directly. Thus, following the massive oil spill caused off the coast of France by the tanker *Amoco Cadiz* in 1978, US courts accepted an action brought by the French local authorities and businesses who had been affected, not only against the tanker's direct owner Amoco Transport Co. (a company registered in Liberia), but against Standard Oil of Indiana, the ultimate parent. The court concluded:

> As an integrated multinational corporation which is engaged through a system of subsidiaries in the exploration, production, refining, transportation and sale of petroleum products throughout the world, Standard is responsible for the tortious acts of its wholly owned subsidiaries and instrumentalities.
>
> ('The *Amoco Cadiz*', 1984: para. 43)

A similar approach was adopted by the Indian courts in the Bhopal case, before the Indian government accepted the settlement, in taking the view that Union Carbide's majority shareholding and managerial control over its subsidiary justified lifting the corporate veil between them (Muchlinski, 1995: 328). Another argument which produces similar results is based on the concept that the control exercised by the parent is such that the subsidiary amounts to its agent (Fawcett, 1985). However, proving control may be difficult given the often highly complex structural characteristics of TNCs. In the United States, courts are in conflict over this issue. While some courts regard the mere capacity of a parent to control the subsidiary as sufficient, others require proof that the parent did exercise actual control over the subsidiary for the purposes of piercing the veil (Brown, 1996).

The foregoing makes clear that workers and communities who suffer damage from the operations of a TNC already face enormous problems in their quest for justice, mainly because TNCs are able to hide behind the fiction of separate legal personality of their subsidiaries, and often insist that they should be responsible only under the local law of the host state. The MAI's dispute-settlement mechanism does nothing to help resolve these problems. On the contrary, the MAI would give the foreign parent strong new legal weapons to restrict local laws. The MAI would recognize the transnational nature of a TNC, by proposing a procedure for international arbitration of disputes over the rights it would create. However, it creates rights only for investors against governments. The MAI would give no rights of action against investors, and would not even give citizens or concerned groups any access to the dispute-settlement procedure.

ENHANCING TNC ACCOUNTABILITY AT THE INTERNATIONAL LEVEL

International dispute-settlement regimes fall far short of providing effective mechanisms of TNC accountability for environmental damage. The proposed MAI dispute-settlement mechanisms only propose investor-state and state-state dispute resolution in relation to investors and their investments. Similarly, the World Trade Organization (WTO) Dispute Settlement Understanding (DSU) can only be invoked by states, although they often do so on behalf of business interests. Therefore, private individuals and civil society organizations such as international non-governmental organizations (NGOs) do not have legal standing to invoke the dispute-settlement mechanisms of either the MAI or the WTO, nor even to be involved in the proceedings.

This limitation has recently been demonstrated in the Shrimp-Turtle case brought by four developing countries against the United States under the WTO. Since this case raised important global commons issues, NGOs such as the Worldwide Fund for Nature (WWF) attempted to present a brief for consideration by the Disputes Panel, intervening as *amicus curiae* (friends of the court). This was rejected by the Panel, despite its authority under Article 13 of the Dispute Settlement Understanding to access outside expertise. Although the MAI's state-state dispute-settlement procedures would allow an arbitration panel to call upon scientific and technical expertise, either at the request of the disputants or on its own initiative, it fails to take into account that disputes between governments can often affect interests and perspectives that reside not with governments but with individuals and non-governmental organizations.

Thus neither the investor-state nor the state-state dispute-settlement procedures envisioned for the MAI reflect the widely accepted decision-making principles, designed to ensure accountability and respect for overarching interests such as environmental protection and sustainable development. The experience of GATT and the WTO has shown that international arrangements dedicated to liberalization tend to prioritize immediate economic interests, rather than the longer-term concerns of sustainable development and environmental protection. This is reinforced by the lack of access provided to civil society groups, which could more effectively represent such concerns.

The lack of legal standing for individuals and organizations whose vested interests may be adversely affected by international agreements such as the MAI or the WTO Agreement drains these agreements of any accountability to the global society. At best they ensure accountability only to the narrow interests for which they were established – trade in the case of the WTO and investment in the case of the MAI. The secrecy which would be likely to attend dispute settlement under the MAI further undermines its transparency and calls into question its democratic character.

The participation of international civil society groups in dispute-settlement regimes of international arrangements such as the MAI should be made possible through the granting of legal standing to individuals and organizations who can show an identifiable interest which is threatened or harmed by an investor or investment. For instance if a multinational engaged in mining pays inadequate compensation to persons displaced by its mining activities, such persons ought to be allowed to invoke the same procedures against the mining company as the latter would have done if its investment in those activities were expropriated. There appears to be no justification for the difference in treatment between investors, and individuals and organizations capable of demonstrating that their vested interests have been, or will be, affected by an investor or investment.

The link between trade and investment on the one hand and environmental protection on the other is widely recognized. As major transnational actors in both trade and investment, TNCs stand at the centre of any attempts to bridge the widening gap between trade and investment liberalization, entrenched in the WTO and envisaged in the MAI, and environmental protection. International trade and investment regimes must therefore come to firm grips with this unavoidable interconnection by incorporating environmental concerns and thus creating a basis for cooperation in the enforcement of environmental norms.

As other contributions to this book also demonstrate, it is necessary to look beyond the narrow liberalization concerns of the MAI, towards a broader multilateral framework for investment (MFI). Such a framework should incorporate environmental principles agreed upon by the world community, including the OECD countries who were the main architects of the MAI. For instance the basic principles of Rio, accepted by all OECD countries, of polluter pays and precautionary decision-making, should be an integral element of any such a MFI, so that they could be applied by its dispute-settlement procedures. Ways should be found to ensure that any rights granted to investors would be conditional on their acceptance of responsibility to comply with such internationally agreed standards. It is time that international agreements aiming to increase the degree of liberalization and the power of economically dominant firms should also reflect global concerns about the impact of foreign investment on other aspects of global cooperation, not least the environment.

CONCLUSION

The text of the MAI, as it emerged from the OECD negotiations, largely ignored concerns regarding the accountability of multinational enterprises for damage to the environment consequent upon their investment activities. The MAI would confer rights on corporate and other investors, including rights to natural and environmental resources, without concomitant responsibilities or obligations towards the environment. Its dispute-settlement regime would not offer any opportunity for action against investors for environmentally harmful investment.

Against the backdrop of environmental disasters such as Bhopal, and the lessons they teach about attempts to hold corporate giants accountable for such disasters, it would be a mistake to establish any MFI which fails to integrate global principles of environmental protection and sustainable development. More specifically, such a MFI must provide for access to justice by individuals and organizations seeking to protect the environment from harmful investments or to obtain compensation for damage resulting from such investments.

NOTES

1. *European Communities – Regime for the Importation, Sale and Distribution of Bananas,* WT/DS27/R/USA (92070) 22 May 1997, available from the WTO web-site at: www.wto.org.

2. The experience of China and Russia in their continuing and lengthy accession negotiations to the WTO shows the leverage that original signatories are likely to have on developing and transition economies wishing to accede to the MAI.
3. See *BNA, International Environment Reporter,* vol. 21, no. 18, p. 848.

REFERENCES

Anderson, Michael, R. (1995) 'Public Interest Perspectives on the Bhopal Case: Tort, Crime or Violation of Human Rights?' in D. Robinson and J. Dunkley, *Public Interest Perspectives in Environmental Law.* Wiley and Chancery, London.

Brown, John, M. (1996) 'Parent Corporations' Liability under CERCLA Section 107 for the Environmental Violations of their Subsidiaries', *Tulsa Law Journal,* vol. 31, 819.

Cassels, J. (1993) *The Uncertain Promise of Law. Lessons from Bhopal.* Toronto University Press, Toronto.

Fawcett, J. J. (1985) 'Jurisdiction and Subsidiaries', *Journal of Business Law,* 16–25.

Government of Canada Statement on MMT, 20 July 1998, http://www.intrasec.mb.ca.

Kiss, A. and Shelton, D. (1991) *International Environmental Law.* Graham and Trotman, London.

Lubbe et al. v. Cape Plc (1998) Court of Appeal, 30 July.

Muchlinski, P. (1995) *Multinational Enterprises and the Law.* Blackwell, Oxford.

Muchlinski, P. (1987) 'The Bhopal Case: Controlling Ultrahazardous Industrial Activities Undertaken by Foreign Investors', *Modern Law Review,* vol. 50, 545.

Neff, Alan (1990) 'Not in Their Backyards, Either: a Proposal for a Foreign Environmental Practices Act', *Ecology Law Quarterly,* vol. 17, 477.

Nolan, Matthew and Lippoldt, Darin (1998) 'Obscure NAFTA Clause Empowers Private Parties', *National Law Journal,* 6 April, B8.

Prince, P. (1998) 'Bhopal, Bougainville and Ok Tedi: Why Australia's Approach to *Forum Non Conveniens* is Better', *International and Comparative Law Quarterly* vol. 47, 167–84.

Robbins, Deidre, H. (1995) 'Public Interest Environmental Litigation in the United States', in D. Robinson and J. Dunkley, *Public Interest Perspectives in Environmental Law.* London, Wiley and Chancery.

'The *Amoco Cadiz*' (1984) 2, *Lloyd's Law Reports* 304. US District Court, N. E. Ill.

Yakpo, E. K. M. (1989) 'Application of *Forum Non Conveniens* in the United States – Bhopal and its Lessons for Developing Countries', *Revue Africaine de Droit Internationale et Comparé* vol. 1, 153.

8 Transfer of Technology and Competition Policy in the Context of a Possible Multilateral Investment Agreement

Pedro Roffe[1]

The growth of foreign direct investment (FDI) is at the core of the globalization process. The total volume of FDI has kept increasing; by the end of 1996, FDI stock exceeded $3.2 trillion in book value. Developing countries have become important players in this process. FDI to developing countries has increased significantly: from an average of $20 billion annually during the period 1983–8 to $129 billion in 1996, although these flows continue to be heavily concentrated in a few countries of Asia and Latin America (see Balasubramanyam, in Chapter 2 of this volume). A further significant trend in FDI during the 1990s has been the increase in outward investment by firms based in developing countries. Whereas approximately 6 per cent of all FDI outflows originated in developing countries during the period 1983–8, this share rose to almost 14 per cent in 1995–6, mainly from South-East Asian firms (UNCTAD, 1998a).

The increased importance of FDI, and the role it can play in economic growth and in the development process, have led to a renewed interest in dealing at the international level with foreign investment and related issues – an interest which has manifested itself recurrently throughout the past 50 years, starting in 1948 with the Havana Charter. At UNCTAD IX (1996), governments recognized that

> The importance of FDI for development has dramatically increased in recent years. FDI is now considered to be an instrument through which economies are being integrated at the level of production into the globalising world economy by bringing a package of assets, including capital, technology, managerial capacities and skills, and access to foreign markets. It also stimulates technological capacity-building for production, innovation and entrepreneurship within the larger domestic

economy through catalyzing backward and forward linkages. Another trend of importance is that a number of countries in all regions have put into place, or are in the process of doing so, elements of a regional and, in some areas, interregional framework for FDI. There is no comprehensive, multilateral framework that covers a great majority of countries. The desirability, nature, issues and scope of such a multilateral framework, and especially its development dimensions, are increasingly being analysed and discussed (UNCTAD, 1997b).

Initiatives have been taken, particularly by leading industrial countries, aimed at the negotiation of an international treaty based on high standards for the liberalization of investment regimes and investment protection. Concerns have been voiced at the same time, however, as regards the advantages that developing countries may derive from such a prospective agreement, particularly in view of the fact that essential elements of the development dimension have, at least thus far, been either kept outside the negotiations or insufficiently addressed. This chapter attempts to explore the possibilities opened by, and challenges involved in, a possible new multilateral framework on investment (MFI), particularly as regards issues of direct relevance to developing countries such as competition policy and transfer of technology, which have been addressed within UNCTAD's programme of work on a possible MFI.

Transfer of technology and competition law are indeed two separate but interrelated issues that have been identified as being directly relevant to the operation of international firms. The purpose of this chapter is therefore limited: it aims at examining how the development dimension, as illustrated by competition policy and transfer of technology, could best be tackled and incorporated in an eventual MFI. To this end, it reviews the process of FDI and its international treatment so as to ascertain the relevance of restrictive business practices and transfer of technology and their implications for the regulation of international investment and business more generally. The chapter draws heavily on the research and analytical work that has been carried out in the United Nations, particularly in UNCTAD, over the past 10 years.

INTERNATIONAL RULE-MAKING IN THE AREA OF FDI

Despite the growing convergence of national policies in recent years, there are still significant differences in national characteristics and conditions. This partly explains the difficulties experienced in reaching an acceptable consensus at the international level on investment regulation, even among OECD countries. Although, as pointed out above, no comprehensive multilateral framework governing FDI exists yet, there is an array of bilateral, regional and multilateral agreements and general declarations or resolutions of international organizations dealing with diverse aspects of international business activities and covering different aspects of the treatment of FDI in host countries (UNCTAD, 1996).

At the bilateral level, more than 1400 treaties on the reciprocal promotion and protection of investment have been concluded (compared to 50 in the 1960s). Initiatives in this regard were first taken by major capital-exporting countries – aimed principally at receiving a minimum level of investment protection in host countries, but in recent years, a considerable number of bilateral treaties have also been concluded between developing countries. By 1996, more than 400 BITs had been signed among developing countries and countries of Eastern Europe, compared to less than 20 in the 1960s (UNCTAD, 1998a).

At the regional and subregional levels, investment issues now occupy a more prominent place in trade-related agreements than was the case in the past. Recent examples are the NAFTA Treaty (1992) in which an entire chapter is devoted to investment issues, the Energy Charter Treaty (1994), and initiatives to deal with the subject by the APEC countries, and MERCOSUR, as well as the recent launching of a proposal for a free trade area of the Americas.

As regards current attempts at designing a new MFI, three distinct approaches can be distinguished. The first is that adopted in the MAI-OECD process, which aims to consolidate the radical policy changes that have taken place since the mid-1980s at the national and regional levels geared to the liberalization of FDI regimes. As discussed in other chapters in this volume, this approach entails setting non-discrimination and property-protection standards for government policies; encouraging or requiring further liberalization; establishing procedures for monitoring and enforcing governments' compliance with such an agreement; and simplifying the complex nature of the existing network of bilateral and regional agreements.

A second approach is taken by those who harbour doubts over the advisability of a comprehensive approach to liberalization of investment flows, as envisaged in the OECD's negotiations. It is argued that the existing differences in national approaches call for differentiated approaches to regulatory frameworks for FDI so as to reflect each country's development strategy. From this perspective, international disciplines should not over-restrain national initiatives or reduce the degree of freedom that countries need to regulate investment so as to pursue their development objectives (Third World Network, 1996). More generally, countries may legitimately prefer an approach in which the starting assumption is not the foreign investor's right to invest but the host country government's capacity to allow them to do so. National policies developed without multilateral constraints leave more room for carefully calibrated approaches to policy issues in the area of FDI (UNCTAD, 1996: section VI). National regimes on FDI, supplemented by existing bilateral agreements, are thus adequate to deal with these matters.

A third approach seeks to examine the potential offered by international instruments if these address other issues that could become part of a new arrangement beyond the setting up of non-discrimination and property-protection standards for public policies. UNCTAD's *World Investment Report 1996* suggested that international cooperation, both among states and between states and international firms, is particularly important in areas where the efforts of a single state would not be sufficient and a degree of international cooperation would be indispensable (the subsidiarity principle). Prominent among these are restrictive business practices, transfer pricing and taxation, technology transfer, employment, protection of the environment, illicit payments, consumer protection and information disclosure. Under this third perspective, a multilateral approach appears thus to be warranted provided that it tackles, in particular, development-related issues that have thus far been neglected in current discussions. This chapter, in dealing with a possible MFI, focuses on this third approach.

A number of the subjects listed above have occupied the attention of the international community over the past few decades (see UNCTAD, 1996a). Some of them are discussed in other chapters of this book. As proposed above, the rest of this chapter will deal with only two aspects, namely competition policies and transfer of technology.

COMPETITION POLICIES[2]

Recent international discussions reflect a growing recognition of the links between FDI policy, trade policy and competition policy, as a means of maintaining contestable and competitive markets. This is underlined in particular by the decision taken at the December 1996 Ministerial Conference of the WTO in Singapore to establish a working group charged with examining the relationship between trade and investment, and another to study issues raised by member states with respect to the interaction between trade and competition policy, including anti-competitive practices, in order to identify areas that may merit further consideration within the WTO framework.

Competition Law and Foreign Direct Investment

The main objective of competition law is to preserve and promote competition as a means to ensure the efficient allocation of resources in an economy, resulting in the best possible choice of quality, the lowest prices and adequate supplies for consumers. In addition to promoting efficiency, many competition laws make reference to other related objectives, such as controlling the concentration of economic power, promoting the competitiveness of domestic industries, stimulating innovation, supporting small and medium-size enterprises and encouraging regional integration.

The main interface between competition law and FDI occurs when a foreign affiliate is established by means of a significant merger, acquisition or joint venture. Competition law is concerned with FDI not only at the entry stage but also once it has been established, since it may result in anti-competitive behaviour. In fact, even in a national framework in which trade and investment are fully liberalized, the possibility of anti-competitive practices provides a justification for competition laws. In other words, the removal of international barriers to trade and investment would not by itself ensure competitive behaviour in all instances. Therefore, while the initial entry of FDI may not raise concerns from a competitive point of view, or it may even be beneficial in itself, it could, nevertheless, raise competition problems in the longer term.

An important effect of FDI liberalization has been greatly to reduce the role of traditional mechanisms used by host countries, especially developing countries, such as screening at the time of entry, closing certain activities to FDI and foreign-ownership restrictions. The central presumption underlying these controls was that FDI entry should be allowed only if it is beneficial to the domestic economy and is specifically approved by host governments. The opening of countries world wide to FDI, and their increasing competition to attract it, has challenged the ability to apply such controls, although perhaps not their underlying rationale. In a world of liberalized investment regimes the priority becomes to ensure an increase in inward FDI flows, efficiency gains for the host economy and, ultimately, a positive impact on welfare. Competition policy can, in this respect, be an essential component of the process of liberalization, notably to ensure that markets are kept as open as possible to new entrants (both foreign and local), and that firms do not frustrate this by engaging in anti-competitive practices. In this manner, a strong competition law can provide reassurance that FDI liberalization will not leave a government powerless against anti-competitive transactions.

The question arises, however, whether the international community requires a strengthened framework of regulatory arrangements governing restrictive business practices, in an era of deep integration and globalization of markets and production structures. The liberalization of trade and investment flows and the globalization of economic activity raise potentially complex issues in relation to dominant positions and restrictive practices of firms in international markets, and the rules governing their operations and behaviour in host countries. This has, in turn, aroused a renewed interest in exploring options for strengthening international cooperation in competition policy. It is widely recognized that the liberalization of FDI policies could promote competition among firms. However, in order to benefit fully from such liberalization, countries need to ensure that, as legal obstacles to market entry are reduced, they are not replaced by anti-competitive practices of international firms. This was recognized most notably in the setting up of the European Community, which from the beginning established and progressively has developed a strong system of competition law, to ensure that the creation of a more open and competitive European market is not negated by restrictive practices or the abuse of dominant positions by firms. A possible multilateral framework on investment also needs to acknowledge this.

International Cooperation in the Field of Competition Policy

Proposals to control restrictive business practices by private enterprises date back to Chapter V of the Havana Charter and to the initial GATT negotiations on the subject in the 1960s, which however were inconclusive. Chapter V of the Havana Charter dealt with business practices affecting international trade which restrain competition, limit access to markets or foster monopolistic control. Practices deemed to be anti-competitive were to be subject to the decision of the prospective organization after consultation and investigation procedures. The Charter referred in particular to practices such as

- price-fixing, excluding enterprises from, or the allocation or dividing up of, any territorial market or field of business activity;
- discriminating against particular enterprises;
- limiting production or fixing production quotas;
- preventing by agreement the development or application of technology or inventions;

- extending the use of intellectual property rights;
- similar practices which the organization may declare to be restrictive business practices.

(See Article 50 (1) of the Charter.)

The OECD Guidelines for Multinational Enterprises, adopted in 1976 as part of the Declaration on International Investment and Multinational Enterprises, recommend that enterprises refrain from abuses of market power such as anti-competitive acquisitions, predatory behaviour and anti-competitive abuse of industrial property rights, and refrain also from participating in restrictive cartels that are not in accordance with relevant laws.[3]

Sectoral and regional liberalization agreements also include competition policy provisions, although few are as strong as the European Community measures mentioned above. In Chapter 15 of the NAFTA, members agreed to maintain national measures to prohibit anti-competitive behaviour by firms. Mutually agreed competition rules, however, are not included.[4] MERCOSUR, on the other hand, envisages cooperation on competition policy through the establishment of mechanisms of consultation, information exchange and joint investigation of anti-competitive practices. The Energy Charter Treaty calls for the adoption of competition laws and policies, and for cooperation on exchange of information and consultation among the signatory countries. In the context of the Asia Pacific Economic Cooperation (APEC), a dialogue has started with a view to developing cooperative approaches in the area of competition policy.

The UNCTAD Set of Multilaterally Agreed Equitable Principles and Rules for the Control of Restrictive Business Practices (1980) is so far the only multilateral instrument covering all aspects of the control of restrictive business practices. It calls upon governments to adopt, improve and effectively enforce appropriate competition legislation and to implement juridical and administrative procedures. The UNCTAD Set establishes principles and rules for enterprises, which advise them to refrain from anti-competitive behaviour among themselves, such as price-fixing, collusive tendering, market or customer allocation arrangements, allocation of production or sales by quotas, refusals to deal with or concerted refusals to supply potential importers, and collective denial of membership of an association crucial to competition. They also cover actions involving abuse or acquisition and abuse of a dominant position of market power, such as mergers or acquisitions, predatory behaviour to eliminate competition (such as below-cost pricing), unjustifiably discriminatory pricing, fixing the prices at which exported goods can be sold in importing countries, and restricting parallel imports to maintain artificially high prices. In its section dealing with measures at the international level, the Set provides for consultation procedures whereby a country may request a consultation with other countries concerning the control of such practices. However, the Set's principles are of a non-binding nature, and moreover its institutional machinery could not act as a tribunal or pass judgement on the activities or conduct of individual governments or of individual enterprises in connection with specific consultations.

GATT/WTO agreements focus on governmental measures and action and they do not regulate anti-competitive practices by firms. However, a number of these agreements are particularly relevant for competition policy, in as much as they deal with practices of enterprises that may distort or impede international trade and the actions that governments are allowed or required to take to regulate or remedy such practices.

So far, the most direct link between the provisions of GATT agreements and anti-competitive practices by firms is provided by Article VI, which permits states to apply duties against imports if they are sold below normal value (anti-dumping) and countervailing duties to offset subsidies in the country of export. Furthermore, several of the most recent WTO agreements address private practices:

- the Agreement on Technical Barriers to Trade (which relates not only to government rules but also to the standard-setting activities of non-governmental bodies);
- the Agreement on Government Procurement (which deals with practices of public enterprises);
- several provisions in the General Agreement on Trade in Services (for example the provisions on monopolies and exclusive service suppliers which require that these suppliers not abuse their monopoly position outside the scope of their monopoly), supplemented further by relevant provisions of the agreement on basic telecommunications services completed in 1997;
- the TRIMS Agreement (which deals with investment performance requirements that restrain trade and specifies that consideration be given to whether the Agreement should be complemented with provisions on investment policy and competition policy);
- the TRIPS Agreement (which discussed further below, requires members to cooperate on control of anti-competitive practices in contractual licences).

Competition Policies and International Investment Agreements

While there are numerous reasons why competition issues as they relate to FDI require international policy responses, as explained above, diverging approaches to the substantive standards for competition policy make the task of finding an appropriate policy response a difficult one. To an extent, this is the result of differences in the political and social objectives of countries. Developing countries, for example, tend to take account of development objectives, and in particular to foster enterprise development. Developed countries, in turn, take different approaches to competition so as to pursue particular national objectives, such as to promote techno- logical innovation by exempting R&D (research and development) alliances from competition rules. Most developed countries now take the view that economic efficiency and consumer welfare, rather than any particular social or economic objective, should be the paramount objective of competition law. Nevertheless, competition is inevitably viewed from the viewpoint of national rather than global economic efficiency and welfare. This can lead to conflicting perspectives, as seen for example in the action taken by the European Commission in levying large fines against US and other non-EU firms participating in the Wood Pulp cartel, which had received specific exemption under US export-promotion legislation.

Likewise, in the field of enforcement, competition laws often differ. For example, under US law violations can give rise to punitive damages and in some cases can be treated as criminal offences, but they are only civil-law infringements in the European Union. It has long been recognized that there is a need for international cooperation in the enforcement of compe- tition laws, partly due to conflicts and objections by some states to exer- cises of jurisdiction by others which they regard as excessive or 'extra-territorial'. The UNCTAD Set calls for the institution of improved procedures for obtaining information from enterprises and the establish- ment of appropriate mechanisms at the regional and subregional levels, to promote exchange of information on restrictive business practices and to assist each other in this area. The OECD has since 1967 operated a proce- dure for notification by a state of any action which may affect important interests of another state, which allows for consultation; and a number of bilateral agreements also exist (OECD, 1987). A significant step has been the 1991 Agreement between the US and the EU, which formally came into force in 1995, and envisages positive cooperation in enforcement especially in relation to mergers and acquisitions.

Overall, however, there are many gaps in competition regulation. Although there has been a growth in the number of countries adopting competition laws this decade (UNCTAD, 1997a: 189), few can be said to have strong, well-established and experienced competition authorities, and it is likely to be some time before they do (UNCTAD,1997a: 212).

In brief, a possible MFI would need to acknowledge the important inter-face between competition policy and FDI, both at the establishment phase and subsequently. Several methods could be used to manage this interface between FDI and competition law. They could range from cooperation and information-exchange schemes to common or integrated competition rules. Perhaps the most developed joint competition regime is that of the EU, based on articles 85–91 of the Treaty of Rome establishing supranational competition rules. Cooperation and coordination schemes are approaches more typically followed in bilateral agreements and in agreements such as NAFTA. However, competition rules are a notable absence in investment treaties.

TRANSFER OF TECHNOLOGY

Transfer of technology is another issue that is intrinsically linked to FDI and which will need to be addressed by a possible MFI. Here again, as in the case of competition policy, international policy responses might be called for, though their exact content would require further exploration. This section deals with these issues.

Developed countries are the major producers and suppliers of technology. It is estimated that over two-thirds of global R&D takes place in the United States, Japan and the European Union; developing countries account for only 6 per cent, or if China is excluded for probably less than 4 per cent. Firms investing large sums in R&D have naturally pressed for strong intellectual property laws, which provide them with exclusive rights under certain conditions, as a reward and incentive for innovation. These arguments have increasingly been accepted by developing countries, even though the vast majority of the holders of intellectual property rights in developing countries are non-residents. Advanced industrial countries are thus net exporters of technology to developing countries.

Transfer of technology is a commercial operation that takes place through firm-to-firm arrangements and involves flows of knowledge, be they embodied in goods (as in the sale of machinery and equipment) or in the form of ideas, technical information and skills (through licensing, franchising or distribution agreements). Technology transfer can take place either at arm's length, as in the case of the export of capital equipment or of licensing agreements between unaffiliated firms, or it can be internalized through the transfer of new production techniques within a TNC, between affiliated firms. These different forms of technology transfer have implications in terms of payments (royalties, fees), taxation and competition issues. They are also associated with the activities of international firms and FDI flows, which is one of the most important channels of transfer of technology to developing countries.

International rule-making has so far focused mainly on the protection of the proprietary rights of producers of technology and less on the terms and conditions of technology transfer. The issue of property rights has been dealt with in a number of conventions, beginning with the Paris Industrial Property Convention of 1883 and the Berne Copyright Convention of 1886. Most recently, a strong link has been established between these arrangements and the GATT regime for trade liberalization, in the WTO-TRIPS Agreement of 1994, which also lays down many important new provisions for international regulation of intellectual property rights.

Exclusive property rights – which is how intellectual property rights are generally conceived – could create opportunities for abuse, especially when such rights are overwhelmingly held by large international firms. Thus, many countries regulate not only the conditions of ownership of such rights, but the terms of their transfer, usually through licences. However, developed and developing countries have differed in their approach to this. Developed countries have generally sought to prevent the anti-competitive abuse of intellectual property rights through restrictive conditions in licences, such as exclusive grantback conditions. Developing countries, in many cases, have emphasized development criteria, such as the appropriateness of the technology to the level of development and its growth impact in terms of potential export opportunities or job creation. Largely due to these differences, international rule-making on matters that relate to the international market for technology and, more generally, the advantages to host countries derived from the transfer of technology, has not met with success. What lessons can be drawn from this past experience, and how could such issues be dealt with in the future?

The UNCTAD Draft Code

Negotiations on a draft code of conduct on the transfer of technology were carried out, under the auspices of UNCTAD, for almost ten years from 1976 without reaching completion (Bizec and Daudet, 1980; Fikentscher, 1980; Yusuf, 1984; Roffe, 1985). Among the main objectives of the draft code were

- the establishment of general and equitable standards for parties to transfer technology transactions;
- the need to build up mutual confidence between private parties and governments;

- the encouragement of transactions under conditions where the bargaining positions of the parties would be balanced in such a way as to avoid abuses of a stronger position;
- the growth of scientific and technological capabilities by means of the international transfer of technology;
- the enhancement of the contribution of technology to the identification and solution of social and economic problems;
- the formulation, adoption and implementation of national policies and laws in the field of transfer of technology.

The negotiations encountered numerous obstacles due to a wide divergence of views and attitudes on how to formulate international general principles on the transfer of technology. Industrialized countries, particularly major technology-producing nations, saw the code as an interventionist instrument, the perceived aim of which was to endorse bureaucratic structures that would hinder the transfer process instead of facilitating it.

The draft code was an attempt at legitimizing national regulation of transfer-of-technology transactions and the role governments could play in this area. A whole chapter of the draft code was devoted to this matter. The draft code stressed the regulatory aspects of contractual arrangements. Measures for international cooperation and special treatment for developing countries to facilitate an expanded flow of technology were important aspects of the draft code.

Chapter 4 of the draft code dealt with restrictive practices that parties should avoid in transfer-of-technology transactions. This chapter posed the most difficult problems in the negotiating process. In fact, several highly complex issues could not be settled, including the basic purpose of the chapter (the conceptual problem) and the treatment of technology transactions between affiliated enterprises. The failure to resolve these issues determined the fate of the negotiations. Some of these intractable conceptual issues were finally resolved in the Uruguay Round. The TRIPS Agreement essentially embodies the competition approach advocated by the developed countries as against the 'development test' advanced by the developing countries (see further below).

Recent Attempts at Dealing with Transfer-of-Technology Matters

There are a number of recent examples of transfer-of-technology commitments made by governments in the course of negotiations on trade and environmental agreements. The Energy Charter Treaty of 1994 calls upon its signatories 'to promote access to and transfer of energy technology on a commercial and non-discriminatory basis' and 'eliminate existing and create no new obstacles to the transfer of technology in the field of Energy Material and Products' (ECT, Article 8).

Likewise, the WTO-GATS states that 'developed country Members ... shall establish contact points ... to facilitate the access of developing country Members' service suppliers to information, related to their respective markets, concerning ... the availability of services technology' (GATS, Article IV.2c III). The TRIPS states that 'developed country Members shall provide incentives to enterprises and institutions in their territories for the purpose of promoting and encouraging technology transfer to least-developed country Members in order to enable them to create a sound and viable technological base' (Article 66.2) and 'shall provide ... technical and financial cooperation in favour of developing and least-developed country Members' (Article 67).

Similarly, all major treaties on environmental protection deal with the transfer of environmentally sound technologies to developing countries and with the financial and technical assistance necessary to realize the objectives of the agreements. For example, the Framework Convention on Climate Change states that

> The developed country Parties ... shall take all practicable steps to promote, facilitate and finance, as appropriate, the transfer of, or access to, environmentally sound technologies and know-how to the parties, to enable them to implement the provisions of the Convention. In this process, the developed country Parties should support the development and enhancement of endogenous capacities and technologies of developing country Parties ... (Article 4.5).

More recently (May 1998), the Commission on Sustainable Development recommended that

> the international community should promote, facilitate, and finance, as appropriate, access to and transfer of environmentally sound technologies and the corresponding know-how, in particular to developing countries, on favourable terms, including concessional and preferential terms, as mutually agreed, taking into account the need to protect intellectual property rights as well as the special needs of developing countries for the implementation of Agenda 21.

These recent commitments suggest that the home countries of TNCs should promote and facilitate the transfer of technology or, as in the case of TRIPS, provide incentives to enterprises and institutions to achieve such aims. TNCs are not formally recognized as legal persons under international law and, therefore, the parties to these commitments are their home countries. These statements are of a hortatory nature and thus difficult to implement in practical terms. The TRIPS Agreement deals with the issue of transfer of technology in very general terms, but it is much more specific on the protection and regulation of abuse of intellectual property rights.

The TRIPS Agreement and Competition

The TRIPS Agreement is based on the non-discrimination principles of the GATT (national and most-favoured-nation treatment), but it provides exemption for national measures to deal with abuse of intellectual property rights, in particular anti-competitive practices in licensing arrangements. It allows members to take, if needed, 'appropriate measures, provided that they are consistent with the provisions of this Agreement, ... to prevent the abuse of intellectual property rights by right-holders or the resort to practices which unreasonably restrain trade or adversely affect the international transfer of technology' (Article 8.2). The Agreement applies only to anti-competitive conduct related to intellectual property rights and not to anti-competitive conduct in general. In this respect, the TRIPS Agreement (Article 40) accepts the principle that some licensing practices or conditions which restrain competition may have adverse effects on trade and may impede the transfer and dissemination of technology. It further stipulates that 'nothing in this Agreement shall prevent Members from specifying in their legislation licensing practices or conditions that may in particular cases constitute an abuse of intellectual property rights having an adverse effect on competition in the relevant market' (Article 40.2). The Agreement allows member countries to adopt, consistently with the other provisions of this Agreement, appropriate measures to prevent or control such practices, which may include for example exclusive grant-back conditions, conditions preventing challenges to validity of property grants and coercive package licensing, in the light of the relevant laws and regulations of that member.

The TRIPS Agreement does not cover all the misuses of intellectual property rights. Restrictive practices or practices affecting technology transfer that occur outside a licensing context, such as delimitation agreements, assignments, intellectual property clauses in research and development contracts or in cooperation agreements, joint ventures and subcontracting arrangements, as well as all unilateral conduct by enterprises enjoying some sort of market power, are not subject to the provisions of the Agreement.

In brief, the TRIPS Agreement is generally open-ended in dealing with anti-competitive licensing practices. It adopts the so-called 'competition test' and the 'rule of reason' in the evaluation of when a practice should constitute an abuse. It also encourages consultations among nations to ensure compliance with the TRIPS Agreement and to settle disputes that might arise in case of violation of domestic laws dealing with anti-competitive practices. Based on these principles, the TRIPS Agreement enables countries to adopt domestic measures to control anti-competitive practices in contractual licences.

TRANSFER OF TECHNOLOGY ISSUES IN A POSSIBLE MFI: CONCLUDING REMARKS

Before identifying the key lessons which could be drawn from the history outlined above, it should be noted that, in the last two decades, there has been a significant change in the manner in which the process of technology transfer is perceived (UNCTAD, 1996b). In the past, the emphasis was placed on the international transfer of technology *per se* rather than on what happens to it once it has been transferred. Although the importance of domestic innovation was fully recognized, the focus of attention was predominantly on the acquisition of technology from abroad. It was not surprising, therefore, that much of the analysis at that time focused on the imperfections in the technology-transfer process and on the role played by TNCs. TNCs were accused, *inter alia*, of charging high prices for technology when already the marginal cost to them for supplying technology was zero or very low. The policy envisaged was primarily to adopt defensive measures to remedy defects in the international market for technology rather than positive actions designed to foster endogenous or local technological capability. Thus a number of countries established regulations governing technology imports with the intent of reducing some of the more undesirable effects for technology importers.

Today, transfer of technology is perceived differently. Defensive measures are less in vogue on the grounds that market imperfections are best addressed by measures aimed at improving the contestability of markets – hence the link between competition policy and transfer of technology – rather than by regulatory measures intended to forcibly modulate the conditions on which the transfer of technology takes place. Transfer of technology from abroad remains important, not as a substitute but rather as a complementary positive stimulus to domestic technological dynamics. Large international firms continue to be an important channel for transfer of technology, although in recent years, as a result of the globalization process, novel modes of transferring technology have emerged, such as investment in the form of joint ventures, production-sharing, subcontracting, franchising, Buy-Operate-and-Transfer arrangements and strategic alliances. Small and medium-sized firms both from developed and from emerging economies have also become suppliers of technology.

An important change in perception has also taken place as regards intellectual property rights. This is mainly due to the awareness that new technologies, particularly those associated with information and communication technologies, play a major role in the development of the so-called knowledge-based economy. A manifestation of this new perception is the announcement by the Indian government in August 1998 of its intention to accede to the Paris Convention and the Washington Patent Cooperation Treaty. The issues of technology development and diffusion and the protection of intellectual property rights have become more pressing to international firms partly because of the escalation in recent years of R&D costs (a phenomenon which is likely to increase international competition), the global exploitation of intellectual assets and the shortening of lead-time as new technologies become more quickly available (UNCTAD, 1996c).

Recent efforts to deal with the concerns of developing countries in this area have once more placed emphasis on the acquisition of foreign technology, but again through very general hortatory declarations. As in the past, the responsibility of facilitating the transfer of technology is being placed on home governments of TNCs. A number of questions could be asked. Who controls the technologies generated in supplier countries? If the technologies are controlled by firms producing them, as is often the case, then how can governments commit themselves to ensuring the transfer of assets over which they have no control? At the same time, TNCs, especially those with multiple national interests, do not necessarily respond to a single 'home' country government. Could 'home' country governments influence corporate decisions of firms operating in a particular 'host' country?

Bearing in mind these limitations, home countries can design policies and incentive structures that encourage outward FDI and the transfer of technology to developing countries – indeed, a number have instituted policies with this objective in mind. Such governments usually have facilities that provide information about foreign markets and legal and administrative frameworks abroad. Most home governments have instituted investment-insurance programmes for foreign investors. Some of these forms of assistance have already been multilateralized. For example, the World Bank Group's International Finance Corporation provides both equity and loan financing to foreign investors; and the Multilateral Investment Guarantee Agency (MIGA), also of the World Bank, insures foreign investors against political risks in countries that have become MIGA signatories.

But the development of domestic technical capabilities is the main responsibility of host countries and it is towards this end that multilateral efforts at rule-making should be directed. New agreements in the area of FDI should acknowledge the important link between FDI and transfer of technology so as to support domestic policies through international measures.

Countries differ in their strategies towards FDI and technology development. These strategies range from passive open-door policies, with no intervention to promote selectively industrial development (as in Hong Kong), to restrictive policies on FDI and maximization of 'external' forms of technology transfer in the context of policies to strengthen the manufacturing sector, promote local linkages and increase innovative capabilities (as in Republic of Korea, Taiwan Province of China and, previously, Japan). Each of these strategies has worked in one sense or another, and each reflects the economic position, judgement and capabilities of the countries concerned. However, with the growing liberalization of FDI policies and the internationalization of minimum standards of protection – as in the case of intellectual property – many of the strategies adopted in the past are no longer viable for developing host countries (UNCTAD, 1998a).

While countries rely mainly on domestic policy instruments to attain their development objectives with respect to FDI, international instruments can support their efforts. Bilateral efforts, including double taxation treaties as well as bilateral investment treaties, have been particularly useful. A new multilateral framework on investment could play a role in reinforcing domestic policy instruments. However, it may be doubted whether outright liberalization policies can adequately deal with the complex regulatory arrangements needed to ensure that markets are competitive and contestable.

It may perhaps be suggested that developing countries should place more emphasis on a new type of dialogue with developed countries, a dialogue that would foster the transfer of foreign technologies that are controlled by international firms whose collaboration is vital in order to transfer technology in an operational and effective manner.

The pursuit of such a new dialogue between developed and developing countries would be facilitated if a new agenda was designed in which the differences among host countries were clearly identified and addressed, as their needs and requirements normally differ depending *inter alia* on the level of economic development and of technological sophistication. It is also pertinent to distinguish between what is to be done by governments (host and home), institutions and the private actors involved. An important concept to be developed in this respect is the promotion of new partnerships for the development, sharing, use and diffusion of technologies based on mutuality of interests.

In this context, new initiatives aimed at strengthening human, entrepreneurial and institutional capacities in developing countries need to be considered as a means of addressing development-related issues arising from FDI and, consequently, enabling developing countries to participate more effectively in negotiations on a possible MFI and, eventually, benefit therefrom.

NOTES

1. The views expressed in this chapter do not necessarily reflect those of UNCTAD. The author acknowledges the valuable comments made by Fabio Fiallo, Tes Tesfachew and Jean Vanhoutte.
2. This section draws heavily on Chapter V of UNCTAD, 1997a.
3. See also the OECD Recommendation of the Council for Cooperation Between Member Countries in Areas of Potential Conflict Between Competition and Trade Policies of 1986, which calls on OECD countries to take into account competition considerations when implementing trade policies (OECD, 1987).
4. The same chapter commits members to establishing a working group to make recommendations on appropriate further work on the relationship between competition policy and trade in the NAFTA area, consult from time to time on the effectiveness of their competition policies and cooperate on issues such as notification and exchange of information.

REFERENCES

Bizec, François and Daudet Yves (1980) *Un code de conduite pour le transfert de technologie*. Economica, Paris.
Fikentscher, W. (1980) *The Draft International Code of Conduct on the Transfer of Technology*. Max Planck Institute, Munich.

OECD (1987) *Competition Policy and International Trade*. Organization for Economic Cooperation and Development, Paris.

Roffe, P. (1985) 'Transfer of Technology, UNCTAD's Draft International Code of Conduct', *International Lawyer,* vol. 19, 689–707.

Third World Network (1996) *The Effects of FDI, the Need for National Investment Policy and the Issue of a Multilateral Investment Framework*, Briefing Paper no. 4, 10 October.

UNCTAD (1996a) *World Investment Report 1996: Investment, Trade and International Policy Arrangements*. United Nations, Geneva.

UNCTAD (1996b) *Fostering Technological Dynamism: Evolution of Thought on Technological Development Process and Competitiveness: a Review of the Literature*. United Nations, Geneva.

UNCTAD (1996c) *The TRIPS Agreement and Developing Countries*. United Nations, Geneva.

UNCTAD (1997a) *World Investment Report 1997: Transnational Corporations, Market Structure and Competition Policy*. United Nations, Geneva.

UNCTAD (1997b) *Proceedings of the United Nations Conference on Trade and Development*. United Nations, Geneva.

UNCTAD (1998a) *Foreign Direct Investment and Development*. United Nations, Geneva.

UNCTAD (1998b) *Bilateral Investment Treaties in the Mid-1990s*. United Nations, Geneva.

Yusuf, A. (1984) 'L'élaboration d'un code international de conduite pour le transfert de technologie: Bilan et perspectives.' *Revue Générale de Droit International Publique*, vol. 88, 781–824.

9 Stabilizing Capital Flows to Developing Countries: the Role of Regulation

Stephany Griffith-Jones, with
Jenny Kimmis

The deep integration of developing countries into the global economy has many advantages and positive effects. In particular, capital flows to developing countries have clear and important benefits. For example, appropriate foreign direct investment can bring long-term benefits such as employment, technological know-how and access to markets. Other external flows may also have important positive micro-economic effects, such as lowering the cost of capital for creditworthy firms. At a macro-economic level, foreign capital flows can complement domestic savings, leading to higher investment and growth; this is very valuable for low-savings economies, but may be less helpful to high-savings economies like those of East Asia.

However, large surges of short-term and quickly reversible capital flows to developing countries can also have very negative effects. Firstly, they can push key macro-economic variables, such as exchange rates and prices of assets such as property and shares, away from their long-term equilibrium. Secondly, and more importantly, these flows pose the risk of very sharp reversals, which may lead to currency and financial crises resulting in very serious losses of output, investment and employment, as well as increases in poverty.

In the case of the Asian crisis, the reversal of private capital flows has been really dramatic. According to figures from the Institute of International Finance, the five East Asian countries hardest hit by the crisis (South Korea, Indonesia, Malaysia, Thailand and the Philippines) experienced in a single year a turnaround of US$105 billion, reaching more than 10 per cent of the combined GDP of these economies. The shift was from an inflow of capital of US$93 billion in 1996 to an estimated outflow of US$12 billion in 1997 (see Table 9.1) mostly from commercial bank lending.

This massive and sudden reversal of capital flows in itself caused a dramatic reduction in absorption, as well as currency crises. In Asia, violent devaluation and large increases in interest rates meant that the currency

Table 9.1　External Financing of Five Asian Economies
(US$bn)

	1996	1997	Change between 1996 and 1997
External financing, net	92.8	15.2	−77.6
Private flows, net	93.0	−12.1	−105.1
Equity investment:	19.1	−4.5	−23.6
Direct equity	7.0	7.2	+0.2
Portfolio equity	12.1	−11.6	−23.7
Private creditors:	74.0	−7.6	−81.6
Commercial banks	55.5	−21.3	−76.8
Non-bank private creditors	18.4	13.7	−4.7
Official flows, net	−0.2	27.2	+27.4

Source: Institute of International Finance 'Capital Flows to Emerging Economies', 29 January 1998, Washington DC.

crises interacted with banking crises, which led to a contraction of bank lending. It is notable that in developing countries (as with Mexico in 1994–5), currency crises can spill over into domestic financial crises and *vice versa*, whereas this does not happen very often in developed countries (Akyuz, 1998).

The combination of the reversal of capital flows, currency and domestic financial crises led in East Asia to a very severe economic crisis in countries that had been growing extremely rapidly for a very long period (see Table 9.2). A large decline in GDP or sharp slowdown in growth is now predicted for all the countries listed in Table 9.2, with the exception of Taiwan (compare with EIU Country Reports second/third quarter 1998); indeed GDP has already contracted in all of them in the year since the crisis (Indonesia's by as much as 15–20 per cent). The effects of this fall in growth will be socially uneven, and many families will be impoverished. There is therefore a growing consensus that important changes need to be made in the international monetary system as a whole – and in recipient country policies – to deal with the volatility of short-term capital flows, so as to avoid costly crises, as well as to manage them better if they do occur. Authoritative figures such as Alan Greenspan, Chairman of the US Federal Reserve (*Financial Times*, 28 Feb. 1998) and Joseph Stiglitz, Chief Economist of the World Bank (Stiglitz, 1998a and b) as well as economic analysts, have called for such changes.

This chapter attempts to contribute to the process of identifying possible changes, evaluating their potential and defining the necessary institutional elements for their implementation. It is not primarily concerned with the

Table 9.2   Real GDP Growth in Selected Asian Economies

	1993	1994	1995	1996	1997	1998*
Hong Kong	6.1	5.4	3.9	5.0	5.3	−2.0
Indonesia	7.3	7.5	8.2	8.0	4.6	−15.0
South Korea	5.8	8.6	8.7	7.3	5.5	−7.9
Malaysia	8.3	9.2	9.5	8.6	7.8	−5.6
Taiwan	6.3	6.5	6.0	5.7	6.8	4.7
Thailand	8.3	8.7	8.8	5.5	−0.4	−6.0
Singapore	10.4	10.5	8.7	6.9	7.8	−0.2

Note: *Forecasts.
Source: Economist Intelligence Unit (EIU) Country Reports 2nd/3rd quarter 1998.

MAI, but discusses a range of measures which might be considered appropriate, in the wake of the Mexican and Asian crises, to dampen the volatility of short-term capital flows. However, the MAI aimed to liberalize all capital flows including short-term bank and portfolio flows, and even speculative transactions. Hence, it has two important implications for the issues discussed in this chapter. First, there is the danger that the MAI could have provoked further disorderly and unsequenced liberalization without a prior improvement in the arrangements for prudential supervision, in home countries, host countries and internationally. Thus, the emphasis of the MAI on liberalization, and its lack of provisions for improving regulation or supervision, seem inappropriate at this time, to say the least. More seriously, the MAI provides only limited and defined exceptions to its basic obligations requiring freedom for all types of cross-national capital flows. In particular, the exception for controls on cross-border capital transactions allows only temporary measures to deal with serious balance-of-payments and external financial difficulties or exceptional circumstances creating serious threats to monetary and exchange rate policies. Several of the measures discussed in this chapter, for example the Chilean provisions which have been praised by eminent authorities such as Stiglitz (discussed below), would appear to be invalid under the MAI, as they are designed to be neither temporary nor exceptional.

CAUSES OF THE ASIAN CRISIS

A large literature is emerging emphasizing from different perspectives the domestic causes of the Asian crisis (for example Boorman, 1998; Corsetti,

Pesenti and Roubini, 1998; IMF, 1997; Radelet and Sachs, 1998; and Wade and Veneroso, 1998). It is beyond the scope of this chapter to examine in detail the varying domestic causes of the crisis. Three key points are, however, worth stressing (Stiglitz, 1997):

1. The current account deficits in East Asia were private-sector deficits.
2. The Asian crisis was a consequence of over-investment (some or much of it misallocated) and not of over-consumption.
3. The most important cause of the crisis was a sharp deterioration in confidence, not of macro-economic fundamentals, which were mostly extremely strong.

Indeed, what seems most disturbing about the Asian crisis is that it happened to countries which were widely considered to have been so successful for a long period, not just in terms of economic growth but also in terms of great dynamism in their exports, low rates of inflation, high rates of savings and rather equitable income distribution. Even though several of these countries had high balance-of-payments current-account deficits, this had been seen as acceptable for quite a long time both by analysts and markets alike, firstly because they were financing very high investment rates, and secondly because they did not originate in fiscal deficits – on the contrary, the Asian economies had fiscal surpluses – but were caused by private-sector deficits.

So what went wrong? Clearly there were problems in the Asian economies, including serious weaknesses in their domestic financial systems and in their governance (see below). However, another really important causal factor concerns the behaviour of international capital flows. This is due to imperfections of international capital markets, which are not new, but whose impact has increased due to technological developments which allow the wheels of international finance to turn far faster than before. Paradoxically, the negative effects of this can be strongest for the more successful economies. A successful economy – such as those of the so-called Asian Tigers – offers high yields and profits to international investors. Capital account liberalization can cause such investors to rush in, and the surge of capital inflows will affect key macro-economic variables. Exchange rates may become greatly over-valued; the prices of key assets – such as shares and land – tends to rise significantly and quickly. As a result there is both an increase in real income (as imported goods become cheaper) and an increase in perceived wealth (as asset prices become at least temporarily higher), as well as a perceived increase in future income. Banks can increase lending, lifting liquidity constraints.

As a result, individuals consume more, and private companies increase their investment.

The sum of these individual decisions has macro-economic implications. The current account of the balance of payments deteriorates, often quite rapidly, as both consumption and investment rise. Initially, this is not seen as a problem, as foreign lenders and investors are happy to continue lending/investing, given high profitability combined with the perception of low risk. Then, something changes. The change may be domestic or international. It may be economic or political. It may be an important change or a relatively small one. The key element is that this change *triggers a sharp modification in perceptions, leading to a large fall in confidence in the economy among internationally mobile investors;* these may be either foreign investors in the country or nationals able and willing to take their liquid assets out of the country. The change of perceptions tends to be both large and quick. A country that was perceived as a successful economy or a successful reformer, for which no amount of praise was sufficient, suddenly is seen as fragile, risky and crisis-prone. The change of perception tends to be far larger than the magnitude of the underlying change warrants. The frightening aspect is that there is a very strong element of self-fulfilling prophecy in the change of perception. Currency crises happen to a significant extent because lenders and investors fear they can happen. As they stop lending and investing and then pull out, they help to make their worst nightmares come true. As a result, there can be much overshooting. Exchange rates may collapse, as may stock-markets and property prices. Governments or central banks are forced to raise interest rates to defend the currency. As a result, banking systems become far more fragile than they were before, as previous weaknesses are magnified and new ones emerge.

An additional problem is contagion. Countries in the same region, or with weaknesses seen to be similar to those of the crisis country, can also suffer from a change of perception by investors. The crisis spreads even to other countries, including those with basically good economic fundamentals. They may suffer somewhat less, but may, if unlucky, be caught up in the whirlwind of deteriorating perceptions.

Elements of this pattern can be seen in the currency and banking crises in the Southern Cone of Latin America in the early 1980s, the Mexican *peso* crisis of 1994 and the Tequila effect, as well as the 1997 Asian crises, and the subsequent threats to other countries such as South Africa. Of course there are significant differences between these crises and the previous ones throughout the centuries (Kindleberger, 1984). But the boom-bust behaviour of short-term lenders and investors, driven not just by real trends (which they help shape), but by dramatic changes in perceptions is a common denominator to these different crises.

There is a relevant academic literature which explains why capital and financial markets are special, in that – though generally functioning well – they are prone to important imperfections. Factors such as asymmetric information and adverse selection play an important role in explaining these imperfections, given that financial markets are particularly informa-tion intensive (Stiglitz, 1994). Furthermore, as Keynes (1936) showed with his well-known metaphor of the beauty-contest, there are strong incentives to follow the herd in financial markets, as each individual short-term investor, lender or fund manager tries to choose the investment or loan that he/she thinks likeliest to be chosen by other investors or lenders, because the assessment of fellow investors will be a crucial element in determining short-term prices. An analysis of the Mexican *peso* crisis showed that the problems associated with market over-optimism (or 'irra-tional exuberance' as Greenspan calls it) followed by market over-pessimism, were more to do with the behaviour of fund managers than with the lack of information available (Griffith-Jones, 1996). Their incen-tive structure leads to herd behaviour, since their reputation will be dam-aged if they lose money while others make profits, but they will not suffer if they incur losses together with other market participants. Therefore, investors invariably base their decisions on the general perception of the market, rather than on a systematic analysis of economic fundamentals.

Also of relevance for understanding the Asian crisis is the concept of self-fulfilling attacks, that is crises arising without obvious current policy inconsistencies (Obstfeld, 1996; Griffith-Jones, 1998). In this model, spec-ulative attacks are actually caused not by bad fundamentals, but by future expected shifts of macro-economic policy, which will be *caused* by the attack itself. In these models, the attitude of speculators and investors is crucial to whether an attack occurs. This implies multiple equilibria for exchange rates. The existence of self-fulfilling attacks and multiple equi-libria means that good macro-economic fundamentals are a very important necessary-but-not-sufficient condition for avoiding currency crises. Stiglitz (1998) illustrates this clearly by comparing small open economies to row-ing boats on an open sea. Bad steering or leaky boats may make a disaster significantly more likely or even inevitable. However, the chances of being overturned are significant no matter how well the boats are constructed and steered.

There is at present limited understanding of what triggers self-fulfilling attacks (Wyplocz, 1998), so they are fundamentally unpredictable. It is interesting that the main explanations given by market actors for the various recent crises (for example Mexico and the various Asian countries) tend to be rather different ones. As a result, developing countries' policy-makers face the daunting task of 'playing to moving goal-posts' in order to avoid crises. Conditions of vulnerability may be identified, such as the ratio of short-term foreign-exchange debts plus the stock of assets that can easily leave the country divided by the level of foreign-exchange reserves; or high current-account deficits. But many countries have such high vulnerability indicators yet do not have a crisis. On the other hand, some of these indicators may be relatively low and/or improving (such as that the current-account deficit was relatively low and improving in South Korea in 1997) and the country may still have a crisis. These patterns confirm the multiple-equilibrium character of currency and other crises, where a triggering event can cause a dramatic change of perception, giving importance to these vulnerability indicators, and precipitating a major change of credit flows.

Further research is required into conditions of vulnerability and the nature of triggering events, to be able to predict risk of – and, above all, improve prevention of – currency crises. However, measures are also necessary to shelter developing countries from these volatile and unpredictable flows and their negative effects. Domestic macro-economic and financial-sector policies, and controls on short-term capital inflows can of course play an important role. However, they are difficult to implement perfectly. As a consequence, an international effort is also required to make costly currency crises in developing and transition countries less likely, and to manage them better if they do occur.

In the nineteenth century, the rapid development of private banking resulted in frequent national banking crises. The establishment and development of national regulatory bodies and of central banks with lender-of-last-resort facilities made such crises less frequent (Griffith-Jones and Lipton, 1987). Similarly, the rapid development of global capital and banking flows in the latter part of the twentieth century implies the need for new measures of global governance to regulate those flows. These will include better regulation of international credit and portfolio flows, as well as improvements of the lender-of-last-resort facility and possible development of international debt workout procedures. We now turn to some of these options.

CRISIS PREVENTION: THE IMF PROPOSALS

The Asian crisis has provoked considerable discussion and reflection in the international community. To reduce the probability of future crises, a number of interesting proposals are currently being discussed, both by the IMF and others. This section will summarize and then evaluate the three main proposals for crisis prevention being put forward by the IMF, showing that while each of them has a role to play in strengthening the international financial system, it is unlikely that these measures alone could prevent future crises.

Improving the Quality of Information

The Asian crisis has provoked calls for improvements to information disclosure, data dissemination and international surveillance. Similar demands were made in the wake of the Mexican *peso* crisis, when emphasis was placed on better information regarding national economic policy. The current emphasis is on improved data in other areas such as foreign exchange reserves, short-term foreign-currency-denominated debt, and the state of the financial system. The question of accurate information is made even more complex by the increased use of off-balance-sheet transactions such as forward contracts and other financial derivatives. The Asian crisis has highlighted this issue as the true foreign-exchange positions of some countries were hidden by central bank transactions and positions in derivatives. Therefore, improved information on derivatives would be particularly useful, and the role of the IMF in improving this information is very valuable.

1. The IMF has stated that countries must be encouraged to improve the quality of information that they make available to the fund and to the public (Camdessus, 1998a; Interim Committee, 1998). In order to encourage transparency it was proposed at the 1998 meeting of the IMF and the World Bank that the Fund could delay the completion of its annual Article IV health check of a country's economy if it is not satisfied with the information being disclosed. The IMF also wants to encourage more emerging market economies to make public the results of these consultations with the Fund through the issuance of Press Information Notices (PINS) on the IMF website.
2. IMF surveillance needs to be tighter and more far-reaching. In particular, the financial sector needs to be examined in more detail. The IMF and the World Bank have recently been building up their financial-sector surveillance capacity. At a recent G7 meeting in Washington, proposals to create new surveillance structures were made (discussed further below).
3. Efforts need to be made to improve transparency on the part of the IMF itself. The establishment of the Special Data Dissemination Standard

(SDDS) in 1996 and the Dissemination Standard Bulletin Board (DSBB) on the IMF website, indicate the Fund's commitment to improving data dissemination in the aftermath of the Mexican *peso* crisis, and these could be broadened and strengthened (Interim Committee, 1998). The Asian crisis has led to requests that the IMF be obliged to inform the markets when it thinks a country is heading for a crisis. The dangers are clear: it could compromise the Fund's position as confidential adviser to member countries, and a public warning may provoke the very crisis that it is trying to prevent. However, the Interim Committee has proposed developing a 'tiered response' whereby the Fund would give increasingly strong, and ultimately public, warnings to countries which it believed were heading for trouble (Interim Committee, 1998).

While all commentators on the Asian crisis are agreed that improved information disclosure and tighter surveillance would be helpful, these changes are not sufficient to prevent future crises. In the first place, the attempts to implement greater transparency in the aftermath of the Mexican crisis have revealed the difficulties involved. Yet getting data on public finances is much easier than obtaining information on private capital flows (Stiglitz, 1998: 8). Moreover, even if information and transparency were to be greatly improved, it is doubtful that this would necessarily lead to better investment decisions and the removal of the threat of market over-reactions. It has been shown that in the lead-up to the Asian crisis, investors and lenders were well aware of some of the problems the worst-hit countries were experiencing (Wade and Veneroso, 1998; Stiglitz, 1998b; World Bank, 1998), yet they did not adjust their lending and investment until the crisis hit. As discussed above, this apparent anomaly can be put down to the herd behaviour of market participants.

Strengthening Domestic Financial Systems

Problems in the domestic financial systems of the worst-affected countries are central to the IMF analysis of the Asian crisis (IMF, 1997; Fischer, 1998). The main problems are believed to be: weak financial institutions; inadequate bank regulation and supervision; and the relations between government, banks and corporations (referred to as 'crony capitalism'). Strengthening domestic financial supervisory systems is a core element of the IMF strategy for crisis prevention (IMF, 1997: 45), including adoption of systems based on the Core Principles of the Basle Committee on Banking Supervision, and the 'best practices' of the International Organization of Securities Commissions (IOSCO) (IMF, 1998). The IMF has begun to build a role for itself in assessing financial-sector regulation as part of the Fund's surveillance of its members (IMF, 1998). This focuses on the banking system, due to the Fund's primary role as financial intermediary in many member countries and the limits of staff expertise. The role of the IMF in the surveillance of domestic financial systems is still under consideration. Limitations of staff resources and expertise mean that IMF surveillance in this area would normally focus on identifying weaknesses in the financial systems of member countries which could have a significant impact on the macro-economic situation. The Fund, as it stands, cannot oversee the regulatory and supervisory authorities in each country, or address problems in other areas of the financial system (IMF, 1998: 1). However, at the G7 meeting in April 1998, Canada and Britain proposed establishing a joint surveillance unit from the IMF and the World Bank, to be responsible for designing financial-sector reform strategies in crisis situations and for carrying out surveillance of national financial regimes in non-crisis countries.

However, establishing effective risk management and sound regulatory and supervisory systems in all IMF member countries would be a huge task. As Rodrik notes (1998: 7):

> Putting in place an adequate set of prudential and regulatory controls to prevent moral hazard and excessive risk-taking in the domestic banking system is a lot easier said than done. Even the most advanced countries fall considerably short of the ideal, as their bank regulators will readily tell you.

Stiglitz echoes these concerns (Stiglitz, 1998b: 8):

> The reform of the domestic financial sector in the Asian countries and elsewhere will, therefore, be lengthy and complex. Furthermore, the current emphasis of the IMF, for reasons cited above, is on regulation and supervision of the banking sector, yet in the Asian crisis, much of the foreign borrowing was by the non-bank private sector [see Table 9.1, and Aykuz, 1998: 3]. However, it would be extremely difficult to control the foreign borrowing of private companies (Stiglitz, 1998b: 3).

Prudent Capital Account Liberalization

The third strand in the IMF crisis-prevention strategy concerns encouraging countries to liberalize capital flows in 'a prudent and properly sequenced way' (IMF, 1998: 4). Camdessus states that capital-account liberalization should be 'bold in its vision, cautious in its implementation' (Camdessus, 1998: 4). He outlines the basic necessary conditions as being: a sound macro-economic policy framework; reforms to the financial system; a phased opening of the capital account to take account of the country's macro-economic situation and the state of domestic reforms; and timely and accurate information disclosure.

McKinnon and others have stated that full capital-account liberalization should be the last step, after the consolidation of other liberalizing measures and the strengthening of the domestic financial system (McKinnon, 1991). Countries should also be able to reverse liberalization measures if a change in the macro-economic situation calls for it. In particular, countries should be able to use market-based measures to discourage excessive surges of short-term flows as has been the case in Chile (see below).

The IMF's three main proposals examined here would all contribute to strengthening the international financial system. Shaping an effective crisis prevention strategy, however, will require sharper tools.

REGULATING CAPITAL INFLOWS

National Measures

A number of countries, such as Chile and Colombia, have implemented measures, such as taxes and non-remunerated reserve requirements on flows during a fixed period, to discourage excessive surges of short-term capital flows. Their aim has been threefold:

1. To change the structure of capital inflows in order to increase the share within total capital flows of foreign direct investment and long-term loans, and above all to discourage short-term and potentially reversible flows, and hence make the country less vulnerable to currency crises.
2. To increase the autonomy of domestic monetary policy, since measures such as non-remunerated reserve requirements allow the recipient country to maintain higher national interest rates than the international ones; this is useful for controlling inflation and curbing excessive growth of aggregate demand, without attracting excessive capital inflows.
3. To curb large over-valuation of the exchange rate, caused by a surge, which discourages growth of exports and poses the risk of growing and unsustainable current-account deficits.

Several studies in the mid-1990s (Ffrench-Davis and Griffith-Jones, 1995; Khan and Rheinhart, 1995) showed how such measures to discourage inflows have been a contributory factor to a relatively more successful management of capital inflows. Furthermore, these measures are widely seen as one of several reasons (with prudent macro-economic management being perhaps the main one) why Chile and Colombia were amongst the few countries in Latin America to be relatively unaffected by the *tequila* crisis in 1994–5 and by the 1997–8 Asian crisis. In the case of Chile, there is econometric and other evidence that the disincentives to short-term inflows have contributed fairly significantly to reduce the inflow of short-term, interest-arbitraging funds, and their proportion of total inflows (Agosin, 1996; Budnevich and Le Fort, 1997). Also, Chilean policymakers saw it as important that, at a time of declining US interest rates in the early 1990s and a booming economy in Chile, the central bank should be able to increase rather than lower interest rates in order to maintain macro-economic equilibrium.[1] There is also evidence that total capital flows to Chile were lower than they would otherwise have been (though a clear counterfactual is always difficult) and that as a consequence the resulting strengthening of the currency has been less.

Two of the attractive features of the Chilean measures are that they are market-based, rather than quantitative (Fischer, 1997), and that they apply to practically all short-term flows, thus simplifying administrative procedures and reducing possibilities of evasion, even though some evasion is naturally inevitable. Colombia has a similar, though more complex, approach to Chile's. Its measures are also broadly seen as successful, particularly in discouraging short-term flows and improving the term structure of total capital flows. It is interesting that the IMF (1995), the World Bank (1997) and the BIS (1995), that is, all the major international financial institutions, now explicitly recognize that – though having some limitations and minor micro-economic disadvantages – market measures taken by recipient governments to discourage short-term capital flows do play a positive role, if they are part of a package of policy measures that include sound macro-economic management as well as a well-regulated domestic financial system. This support for measures by recipient countries to discourage short-term flows has grown since the Asian crisis (Stiglitz, 1998; Wolf, 1998; Rodrik, 1998; Radelet and Sachs, 1998).

International Regulatory Measures

However, measures by recipient countries may not be enough to deal with the problem of capital surges and the risk of their reversal. There seem to be at least three compelling reasons making complementary action by source countries necessary.

1. Not all major recipient countries will be willing to discourage short-term capital inflows, and some may even encourage them. For example, the tax and regulatory measures taken in Thailand to establish the Bangkok International Banking Facility actually encouraged short-term borrowing (Boorman, 1998).
2. Even those recipient countries, such as Chile, Colombia and Malaysia, which have deployed a battery of measures to discourage short-term capital inflows, have on occasion found these measures insufficient to stem very massive inflows.
3. If countries experience attacks on their currencies, which also create difficulties for them to service their debt, it is now far more probable that they will be forced to seek official funding to allow them to continue servicing their foreign exchange obligations in full, rather than being able – as in the past – to restructure such obligations. As the IMF (1995) has pointed out, one important reason for this is the difficulty of restructuring securitized exposures owned by a diversity of investors. Because international official funding plays such a large role in providing finance during such crises, to avoid moral hazard there is a clear need for international and/or source country regulation that will discourage excessive reversible short-term capital inflows, contributing to a costly currency crisis. Without such international and/or source country regulation, international private investors and creditors will continue to assume excessive risks, in the knowledge that they will be bailed out if the situation becomes critical. This is the classical moral hazard problem.

Hence, it is important to complete and improve international prudential supervision and regulation, in order to adapt it to the new scale and nature of private flows. As Martin Wolf (1998) wrote in the *Financial Times*: 'After the crisis, the question can no longer be whether these flows should be regulated in some way. It can only be how.' In the same spirit, the G-24, in their April 1998 statement, called for the creation of a Task Force that, amongst other aspects, would examine: 'more effective surveillance of the policies of major industrialized countries affecting key international monetary and financial variables, including capital flows.' Soros (1998) has argued forcefully that international capital and credit flows need to be regulated.

There are two types of flows to emerging markets for which additional regulation and supervision seems particularly necessary: (a) short-term bank loans, and (b) easily reversible portfolio flows. Short-term bank loans played a particularly important role before and during the Asian currency crises, especially in some countries, such as South Korea. In principle, bank loans (including short-term ones) are already regulated by bank supervisors in the industrial countries, coordinated by the Basle Committee. Such regulations include requirements for provisioning against potential future losses on lending to emerging countries (for which the Bank of England has developed a particularly detailed provisioning matrix) and capital-adequacy requirements. However, existing regulations were not enough to discourage excessive short-term bank lending to several of the Asian countries. A key reason was that until just before the crisis most of these Asian countries (and particularly South Korea, which was admitted to the OECD in 1996) were seen by everybody, including regulators, as creditworthy (Radelet and Sachs, 1998). This was caused not just by asymmetries of information and disaster myopia (Griffith-Jones, 1998) but also by the excellent record of the East Asian countries described above. Another, perhaps somewhat secondary, but also important, reason seems to have been current regulatory standards.[2] These specify that for non-OECD countries (which included South Korea until recently) loans of residual maturity of up to one year have a weighting of only 20 per cent for capital-adequacy purposes, whilst loans over one year have a weighting of 100 per cent. As a result, short-term lending is more profitable for international banks. This adds a regulatory bias to banks' economic preference for lending short-term, especially in situations of perceived increased risk when they prefer to keep their assets more liquid. The capital-adequacy weighting differential appears too large in favour of short-term loans for non-OECD countries, resulting in excessive incentives for short-term lending. A narrowing of this differential may therefore be desirable. Further measures to discourage excessive surges of short-term bank loans to emerging markets as suggested by Witteveen (1998) also require further study. However, care must be taken that any measures adopted to discourage excessive short-term loans do not directly or indirectly affect essential trade credit.

As regards portfolio flows to emerging markets, there is at present no regulatory framework, in source countries or internationally, for taking account of market or credit risks on flows originating in institutional investors, such as mutual funds, or indeed more broadly for flows originating in any non-bank institutions. This is an important regulatory gap that urgently needs to be filled, both to protect retail investors in developed countries and to protect developing countries from the negative effects of excessively large and potentially volatile portfolio flows. Retail investors from developed countries need protection in addition to important efforts being made to improve information by the regulatory authorities, especially in the US (d'Arista and Griffith-Jones, 1998). The key reason is that it is practically impossible to improve information and disclosure sufficiently for retail investors on risk/return for their investments in emerging markets, because of the conceptual complexities involved, and especially since the problems of asymmetric information and principal agency are particularly large for this category of investments (Mishkin, 1996).

For emerging market countries, the Asian crisis confirms what was already clearly visible in the Mexican *peso* crisis. Institutional investors such as mutual funds, given the very liquid nature of their investments, may significantly contribute to currency crises. This regulatory gap could perhaps best be filled by risk-weighted cash requirements for institutional investors, to be placed as interest-bearing deposits in commercial banks. This proposal is in the mainstream of current regulatory thinking, which sees risk-weighting as the key element in regulation (for an authoritative statement from the US Federal Reserve Board, see Phillips, 1998).

Such risk-weighted cash requirement for mutual funds (and perhaps other institutional investors) would require standards established by the home country's regulatory authorities, for instance in the United States the Securities and Exchange Commission in consultation with the Federal Reserve Board and the Treasury, and in the UK the Financial Services Authority in conjunction with the Bank of England and the Treasury. Weight should be given to the views of market analysts such as credit-rating agencies, as well as particularly to the views of international agencies such as the IMF and BIS, which have a long expertise in assessing countries' macro-economic performance. This would provide guidelines for defining macro-economic risk and for its measurement in determining the appropriate level of cash reserves. Thus, cash reserves would vary according to the macro-economic risks of different countries. The guidelines for macro-economic risk (which would determine the cash requirements) would take into account such variables as the ratio of a country's current-account deficit (or surplus) to GDP, the level of its external debt to GDP, the maturity structure of that debt, the fragility of the banking system, and other risk factors specific to each country. Factors such as custody-related risks (which already greatly concern securities regulators) could be included where relevant. It is important that quite sophisticated analysis is used, to avoid simplistic criteria stigmatizing countries unnecessarily and arbitrarily. The views of the central bank, the Treasury, the IMF and the BIS should be helpful in this respect, especially given the long experience of foreign-exchange crises and their causes that the international community has acquired.

Since the level of required cash reserves would vary with the level of perceived 'macro-economic risk', it would be relatively more profitable to invest in countries with good fundamentals. If macro-economic or financial-sector fundamentals in a particular country deteriorate, investment in it would decline *gradually*, which hopefully would force an early correction of macro-economic policy, and, once this happened, a resumption of flows would take place; this smoothing of flows would hopefully discourage the massive and sudden reversals of flows that sparked off the Mexican *peso* and Asian currency crises, making such costly crises less likely. Though the requirement for cash reserves on mutual funds' assets invested in emerging markets could increase somewhat the cost of raising foreign capital for them, this would be compensated for by the benefit of a more stable supply of funds, at a more stable cost. Similarly, retail investors in developed countries might receive slightly lower yields, but would be assured of lower risks and lower volatility. Given the dominant role and rapid growth of institutional investors in the US and UK, this proposal could be adopted first in these two countries without creating significant competitive disadvantages. However, once implemented in the major countries, harmonization of such measures internationally would be important, via IOSCO, to prevent investments by mutual funds being channelled through off-shore intermediaries that did not impose these cash requirements. This could follow a similar process to the adoption of regulations on provisioning and capital adequacy for bank loans, which were coordinated through the Basle Committee. The mechanism would be based on the same principles, adapted to suit the institutional features of mutual funds, where shareholder capital backs 100 per cent of invested assets.

Finally, it is important to stress that new regulation of investments by mutual funds should be in line with that affecting other institutions such as banks and their potentially volatile short-term credits. An extension of regulation to institutional investors is necessary because they are clearly under-regulated, in comparison with other financial institutions, principally because their growth is so recent, especially in emerging market investments.

It is also important to stress that, given the evolution of the markets, past strategies, such as prohibiting investment in certain markets, are clearly no longer appropriate. Such prescriptive rules could have potentially negative effects on investors (who might lose profitable opportunities) and on some emerging market economies, as their access to portfolio flows might be curtailed either in general, or – even worse – abruptly in times of macro-economic difficulties. The central proposals made here, of a risk-weighted capital-charge cash requirement, would have the advantage that changes in cash requirements could be gradual, thus contributing to smooth flows, which is the desired objective for the developing economy, and which would also give greater protection to investors from developed countries. Furthermore, risk-weighted cash requirements for institutional investors are consistent with modern mainstream regulatory thinking which sees risk-weighting as the key element in regulation.

These proposals have certain important similarities (especially in their objectives) with Soros' interesting proposal (Soros, 1998). This appears more radical because it implies setting up and funding a new institution, the International Credit Insurance Corporation (ICIC), which would guarantee international loans for a modest fee. On the basis of detailed data on countries' total borrowing, and an analysis of the macro-economic conditions in the countries concerned, this authority would set a ceiling on the amounts it would insure. Up to those amounts the countries concerned would be able to access international capital markets at prime rates. Beyond these, 'the creditors would have to beware' (Soros, 1998) as there would be no cover. Soros' idea would fulfil the same aim, in that it would tend to cap excessive surges of capital flows while encouraging moderate flows, since the ICIC would not just perform an insurance, but also a signalling role. The proposal as made seems to refer more to international loans, but it could also possibly be extended to other flows, such as portfolio investments. The key problem of Soros' proposal may be a serious moral hazard, unless the fee charged is high enough to cover risks of non-payment, which are of course hard to estimate *ex-ante*. However, the Soros proposal would smooth flows by encouraging them up to a 'reasonable' level, and discouraging them beyond that. It is also of interest because it explicitly tries to tackle imperfections in international credit markets, in particular herd behaviour.

The Tobin Tax

Such additional regulation to improve and complete international prudential supervision for credit and capital markets should be complemented by appropriate international taxation measures. In particular, James Tobin's proposal to levy an international uniform tax on spot transactions in foreign exchange, initially made in 1972, has received renewed attention following turbulence on foreign-exchange markets, both in Europe (1992) and in the emerging markets (ul-Haq, Kaul and Grunberg, 1996). Kenen (1996) in particular has shown the practical feasibility of such a very low tax on all currency transactions. The aim would be to slow down speculative, short-term capital movements, which would be more affected as they more frequently involve foreign-exchange transactions, while having only a marginal effect on long-term flows. This would achieve two objectives:

1. It would increase the autonomy of national authorities for monetary and macro-economic policy, giving them more independence from the effects of international money markets. This would be particularly valuable for LDCs, to the extent that their economies adapt less easily to external shocks, and because their thinner financial markets are more vulnerable to the impact of external capital flows.
2. The tax (Tobin, 1996) would make exchange rates more reflective of long-run fundamentals rather than of short-range expectations and risk. This would reduce volatility and the likelihood of currency crises.

This proposal is perhaps more radical than those considered above. However, there is a widespread feeling, even in private circles, that financial liberalization may have proceeded too far or at least too fast, and that if carried to the extreme may risk damaging the far more important trade liberalization whose benefits are far more universally recognized. Furthermore, a new tax with potentially high yields would be attractive to fiscally constrained governments. Part of the proceeds could also fund public goods such as poverty alleviation and the costs of environmental protection, especially in poorer countries. Therefore, a small tax on financial flows – which particularly discourages short-term flows – might be a welcome development. It could initially be introduced on a temporary basis, for example five years, to be consistent with the fairly widespread perception that financial fragility and systematic risk are particularly high in the current stage of 'transition' to more internationally integrated financial markets.

CONCLUSIONS

The international community has been reflecting on lessons emerging from the Asian crisis, with the IMF playing a central role in proposals for strengthening 'the architecture of the international financial system'. While these ideas of the IMF are valuable, many now believe that more far-reaching reforms to the international financial system are necessary. While proposals to improve information and surveillance represent necessary steps toward a stronger international financial system, they would not be sufficient to prevent future crises, in view of the herd-like behaviour of market participants and the inevitably long-term nature of improvements in financial-sector supervision in emerging market countries. Furthermore, while more prudent capital-account liberalization in emerging market countries would undoubtedly be welcome, many now believe that relatively small and open economies need to be protected from the full force of international financial flows. This could be done by one or several measures that better regulate or tax short-term capital flows, nationally and/or internationally.

At a national level, prudent monetary and fiscal policies and a well supervised domestic financial system can be accompanied by measures such as the Chilean system of non-remunerated reserve requirements on inflows up to one year, which seem to work particularly well, even though they have some micro-economic costs. Internationally, desirable modifications to arrangements for prudential regulation of short-term capital flows include amendments to capital requirements to remove regulatory incentives towards short-term loans, and the introduction of parallel regulation of portfolio flows from non-bank institutions. Risk-weighted cash requirements for institutional investors in source countries, varying with macro-economic evolution in developing countries, may be an appropriate way to smooth such flows, which would be beneficial for developing countries. An alternative mechanism is the creation of a guarantee institution, that for a fee would guarantee flows to emerging markets, up to a limit. Another idea worth considering is that of a very small international tax on all foreign-exchange transactions (known as the Tobin tax), that would also help discourage short-term flows without having any major effect on desirable long-term flows.

The policy debate in these areas needs to lead urgently to new policy measures and mechanisms, so as to avoid costly currency crises. Given the complexity of the issues involved, the policy debate and actions need to be underpinned by improved knowledge. Further work is required to improve our understanding of how international credit markets work and the factors affecting decisions by the main players. Policy measures, including those outlined above, should receive more detailed study, taking account of their costs and benefits and (crucially) problems of implementation. Finally, important questions remain about which international institutions are best suited to perform which tasks, and how coordination can be improved, among those institutions, as well as between them and national authorities on the one hand, and the important private-sector parties on the other.

NOTES

1. Personal communication with Ricardo Ffrench-Davis, then Chief Economist at the Central Bank.
2. Communication from Colin Miles, Bank of England.

REFERENCES

Agosin, M. (1996) 'El retorno de los capitales extranjeros a Chile', *El Trimestre Economico*, Mexico.

Akyuz, Y. (1998) *The East Asian Financial Crisis: Back to the Future?* UNCTAD Working Paper, available at http://www.unicc.org/unctad/en/pressref/prasia98. htm.

Bank for International Settlements (BIS) (1995) *65th Annual Report*. BIS, Basle.

Boorman, J. (1998) *Reflections on the Asian Crisis: Causes, Culprits, and Consequences*, paper prepared for the FONDAD conference on 'Coping with Financial Crises in Developing and Transition Countries: Regulatory and Supervisory Challenges in a New Era of Global Finance', March.

Budnevich, C. and Le Fort, G. (1997) 'Capital Account Regulations and Macroeconomic Policy: Two Latin American Experiences'. Banco Central de Chile, March. *Documento de Trabajo 06*. Santiago, Chile.

Camdessus, M. (1998a) *Is the Asian Crisis Over?* Address by Michel Camdessus at the National Press Club, 2 April 1988, Washington DC. Available from http://www.imf.org/external/np/speeches/1998/040298.HTM.

Camdessus, M. (1998b) *Capital Account Liberalization and the Role of the Fund*. Remarks by Michel Camdessus at the IMF Seminar on Capital Account Liberalization, 9 March 1998, Washington DC. Available from http://www.imf.org/external/np/speeches/1998/030998.HTM.

Chote, R. (1998) 'Crystal Balls in Washington', *Financial Times*, 17 April, 19.

Corsetti, Giancarlo, Pesenti, Paolo and Roubini, Nouriel (1998) 'What Caused the Asian Currency and Financial Crisis?', *Asian Crisis Homepage*, March 1998, at http://www.stern.nyu.edu/~nroubini/asia/AsianCrisis.pdf.

D'Arista, J. and Griffith-Jones, S. (1998) *The Boom of Portfolio Flows to 'Emerging Markets' and its Regulatory Implications*, mimeo IDS, Sussex.

Feldstein, Martin (1998) 'Refocusing the IMF', *Foreign Affairs*, vol. 77(2), 20–33.

Ffrench-Davis, R. and Griffith-Jones, S. (eds) (1995) *Surges in Capital Flows to Latin America*. Lynne Reinner, Boulder.

Fischer, Stanley (1997) 'Capital Account Liberalization and the Role of the IMF', 19 September, at http://www.imf.org/external/np/apd/asia/FISCHER. HTM.

Fischer, S. (1998) 'The IMF and the Asian Crisis', 20 March, Los Angeles, at http://www.imf.org/external/np/speeches/1998/032098.HTM.

Greenspan, Alan (1998) *Financial Times*, 28 February.

Griffith-Jones, S. (1999) *Global Capital Flows: Should They be Regulated?* Macmillan, Basingstoke.

Griffith-Jones, S. (1996) 'How Can Future Currency Crises Be Prevented or Better Managed?' in Jan Joost Teunissen (ed.) *Can Currency Crises Be Prevented or Better Managed?* FONDAD, the Hague.

Griffith-Jones, S. and Lipton, M. (1987) 'International Lender of Last Resort: Are Changes required?' in Z. Ros and S. Motamen (eds) *International Debt and Central Banking in the 1980s*. Macmillan, Basingstoke.

IMF (1995) *International Capital Markets: Developments, Proespects and Key Policy Issues*. International Monetary Fund, Washington DC.

IMF (1997) *World Economic Outlook: Interim Assessment, December 1997*. International Monetary Fund, Washington DC.

IMF (1998) *Toward a Framework for Financial Stability*, prepared by a staff team led by David Folkerts-Landau and Carl-Johan Lindgren. International Monetary Fund, Washington DC.

Interim Committee of the Board of Governors of the IMF (1998) *Communiqué, 16 April 1998*, at http://www.imf.org/external/np/cm/1998/041698a.HTM.

Kenen, P. (1996) 'The Feasibility of Taxing Foreign Exchange Transations', in ul Haq *et al.* (eds) *The Tobin Tax: Coping with Financial Volatility*. Oxford University Press, New York.

Keynes, John M. (1936) *The General Theory of Employment, Interest and Money*. Cambridge University Press, Cambridge.

Khan, M. and Reinhart, C. (1995) 'Macro-economic Management in APEC Economies; the Response to Capital Flows', in M. Khan and C. Reinhart (eds) *Capital Flows in the APEC Region*. Occasional paper 122, IMF, Washington DC.

Mishkin, Frederik (1996) 'Understanding Financial Crises: a Developing Country Perspective', in *Proceedings of the World Bank Annual Conference on Development Economics*, 29–77.

McKinnon, R. (1991) *The Order of Economic Liberalization: Financial Control in the Transition to a Market Economy*. Johns Hopkins University Press, Baltimore.

Obstfeld, M. (1995) *International Currency Experience: New Lessons and Lessons Relearned*. Brookings Papers on Economic Activity, no. 2, 119–220.

Phillips, S. (1998) 'Risk Weighted Regulation'. Paper presented at FONDAD Conference, Holland, March.

Radelet, Steven and Sachs, Jeffrey (1998) 'The Onset of the East Asian Financial Crisis'. Draft paper, 10 February.

Rodrik, Dani (1998) 'Who Needs Capital Account Convertibility?' University of Harvard, http://www.nber.org/~drodrik/essay.PDF.

Soros, George (1997) 'Avoiding a Breakdown', *Financial Times*, 31 December, 12.

Stiglitz, Joseph (1994) 'The Role of the State in Financial Markets' in *Proceedings of the World Bank Annual Conference on Development Economics*, IBRD, Washington DC, 19–61.

Stiglitz, Joseph (1997) 'Statement to the Meeting of Finance Ministers of ASEAN *plus* 6 with the IMF and the World Bank, Kuala Lumpur', 1 December, http://www.worldbank.org/html/extdr/extme/jssp120197.HTM.

Stiglitz, Joseph (1998a) 'Boats, Planes and Capital Flows'. Personal View in the *Financial Times*, 25 March, 32.

Stiglitz, Joseph (1998b) *The Role of International Financial Institutions in the Current Global Economy*. Address to the Chicago Council on Foreign Relations, 27 February, Chicago, http://www.worldbank.org/html/extdr/extme/ jssp022798.HTM.

Strauss-Kahn, D. (1998) 'A Fix, not a Fudge'. Personal View in the *Financial Times*, 17 April.

Ul Haq, M., Grunberg I. and Kaul, M. (eds) (1996) *The Tobin Tax: Coping with Financial Volatility*. Oxford University Press, New York.

Wade, R. and Veneroso, F. (1998) *The Asian Financial Crisis: the Unrecognized Risk of the IMF's Asia Package*. Draft manuscript, Russell Sage Foundation, 1 February.

Wolf, Martin (1998) 'Flows and Blows', *Financial Times*, 3 March, 22.

World Bank (1997) *Private Capital Flows to Developing Countries*. IBRD, Washington DC.

Witteveen, H., (1998) 'Economic Globalisation in a Broader, Long-term Perspective: Some Serious Concerns' in J. J. Teunissen (ed.) *The Policy Challenges of Global Financial Regulation*. FONDAD, the Hague.

Wyplosz, C. (1998) *Globalized Financial Markets and Financial Crises*. CEPR, London.

10 Labour Regulation in Internationalized Markets
Bob Hepple

INTERNATIONALIZATION OF LABOUR MARKETS

This chapter is primarily concerned with one of the main ways in which the new market imperialism (as defined by Picciotto, 1998) affects labour standards.[1] There has been a progressive removal of barriers to trade and investment, which the MAI aims to consolidate further. On the other hand, labour has remained relatively immobile, and barriers to economic migration have even been increased. As a result firms, especially large Transnational Corporations (TNCs), are able to dominate international labour markets. This raises the question of whether and how international regulatory arrangements should encourage the ratcheting of labour standards upwards rather than downwards.

Global Commodity Chains and Transnational Corporations

A great many consumer goods and other products are now produced through global commodity chains. Workplaces in different countries are connected by contractual or ownership links between enterprises that form a transnational 'chain' of production and distribution. For example, in 1961 only 4 per cent of the clothes sold in the United States were imported; today imports account for over 60 per cent. Although often labelled as products of United States TNCs, these clothes are mainly produced in developing countries either by a subsidiary of the TNC or by an outside contractor. The market is dominated by a few large retailers who set not only the price but also the design and quality of the goods, and this, in turn affects the wages and conditions of workers who produce them (Howard, 1997).

On the one hand, these global commodity chains enable TNCs to dominate international markets – TNCs directly employ 73 million people world wide, produce 25 per cent of manufactured goods and account for two-thirds of world trade, half of which takes place through subsidiaries of the same TNC (UNCTAD, 1994: 168). On the other hand, these very links provide new opportunities for solidarity between workers in different countries, and between workers and consumers. This provides a social basis for new forms of labour regulation which are examined in this chapter. The legal bases for such regulation are to be found in the mechanisms for interpreting and enforcing contracts between enterprises in different countries.

This type of production entails a distinct form of internationalized labour market, dominated by TNCs. These corporate giants can choose where to locate their sources of supply, as well as opting between using outside contractors or setting up subsidiaries in which the TNC has an ownership stake. In both cases the different producers operate under various national systems of labour law. Even if the central management of a TNC lays down employment rules or codes of conduct, these have to be interpreted and enforced under the multiple national systems in which the TNC or its contractual suppliers operate. Thus, if a TNC decides to observe multinational codes of conduct, it will have to find managerial means of ensuring compliance with these labour standards within the affiliates of the TNC, and contractual means in relation to its suppliers (discussed by Fridd and Sainsbury, in Chapter 12 of this volume). However, in both cases, it has no means of influencing entirely independent enterprises in the same country.

These enforcement gaps within national labour-law regimes are compounded by the fragmentation of international networks of labour regulation. The following are the main international provisions affecting labour standards and rights:

- *ILO*: 181 international labour conventions and 188 recommendations, the Tripartite Declaration on Multinational Enterprises and Social Policy (1977), and the Declaration of Fundamental Principles and Rights at Work (1998);
- *OECD*: the Employment and Industrial Relations chapter of the Guidelines for Multinational Enterprises (1976);
- *EU and European Economic Area (EEA)*: employment and social legislation (Bercusson, 1996);
- *NAFTA*: cross-border monitoring of domestic labour laws under the North American Agreement on Labour Cooperation (NAALC) which is a side accord to NAFTA;
- *MERCOSUR*: the proposed Charter of Labour Rights.

This chapter will assess some of these emerging methods of transnational labour regulation.

Economic Migrants and Posted Workers

Two other important aspects of the internationalization of labour markets should be noted, although they cannot be examined within the confines of this chapter. The first is the migration of workers from poor countries into more advanced ones. These workers tend to be disproportionately employed in low-level jobs, and where they enter or remain in the country clandestinely they work outside the protection of national labour laws. These underground labour markets not only lead to the exploitation of migrant workers but also threaten the integrity of national regulation.

Secondly, TNCs sometimes appoint workers from their home state to jobs in host states in which the TNC operates. Questions then arise as to the labour-law regime which should apply: that of the home state or the host state? If the laws and practices of the home state are inferior to those of the host state, this may be seen as a threat to standards in the host state.

This problem has received particular attention in the EU. The European Court of Justice has recognized the right of member states to extend their national legislation or collective labour agreements to any person who is employed, even temporarily, within their territory, no matter in which country the employer is established (*Rush Portuguesa*, 1990: para. 18). This confirmed the lawfulness of measures taken by host states to apply their domestic labour standards to workers seconded by out-of-state service providers. Subsequently, the European Council passed the Posted Workers Directive (97/71/EC), which requires member states to ensure that whatever the law applicable to the employment relationship, workers posted for a limited period to work in another member state enjoy a hard core of protective rules laid down in the law, administrative provisions and certain collective agreements in the state where the work is carried out. Although the stated purpose of the Directive is to remove obstacles to the free movement of services, its underlying policy is to ensure that temporary workers receive the protection of national labour-law systems (Davies, 1997: 585–91).

LIBERALIZATION AND SOCIAL DUMPING

All these forms of internationalized labour markets raise theoretical questions about the role of labour regulation. A basic tenet of the theory of liberalization is that the gains from international trade and foreign direct investment (FDI) derive from the differences among nations, so that they can make use of comparative advantage. Countries with low labour costs are able to attract investment. This in turn may lead to greater demand for labour, higher real wages and improved living and working conditions in those countries (Grossmann and Koopmann, 1996: 123).

The Industrialized Countries

However, some argue that when labour costs rise in this way, companies will be tempted to relocate to countries where social protection and the costs of labour are lower, and regulations are thought to be more 'flexible'. This leads to downward pressures on wage costs and labour standards in other countries. Some, at least, of the workers in the richer countries may be forced to accept reduced wages and labour standards in order to compete with workers who have inferior standards in poorer countries. According to this view, the dilemma which FDI poses for nation states is that the more comprehensive and effective labour legislation is, the more likely it is that TNCs will wish to relocate, with the result that the very jobs which national labour law is designed to protect risk destruction (Stone, 1996: 445). This is the familiar 'race to the bottom' in which firms adopt short-term cost-cutting strategies rather than productivity improvements. While workers in the richer North have a head start in this race, they can stay ahead only if their employers improve investment in their workplaces, rather than using the possibility of relocation to reduce their living standards.

The conclusion that some draw from this is that liberalization creates a threat to the higher social and labour standards of developed countries. The neo-liberal response to this is to argue that regulations governing labour standards and other social conditions are in any case an impediment to the free working of markets, and should be removed to allow free markets and comparative advantage to operate. Others argue that less developed countries should be forced to accept minimum labour standards as a condition of access to world markets. However, the empirical evidence for the perceived threats to countries with high labour standards is remarkably weak. The balance of evidence seems to suggest that trade and investment flows are only minor factors in the rise in unemployment and wage inequality in the industrialized countries, and that these countries enjoy vast benefits from increased exports of skill-intensive goods and services (Lee, 1996: 485). Moreover, high labour standards appear to be conducive to high levels of labour productivity and hence long-term competitive advantage (Deakin and Wilkinson, 1994: 307–9).

The Developing Countries

There is a different perspective from the poorer developing countries. These states are under immense pressure to compete among themselves for FDI and access to world markets. This is evidenced, in particular, in those export zones in which labour standards have been abandoned, and basic labour rights to freedom of association and effective collective bargaining are denied. In some cases (for example Myanmar, Sudan) there has been brutal repression.

However, most developing countries want to enhance and improve living and working conditions; in particular they are paying increasing attention to workers in the vast, heterogeneous, and still growing informal sector. The ILO's *World Labour Report 1997–98* notes that this 'constitutes an important, if not central, aspect of the economic and social dynamics' of these countries (ILO, 1997: 176). The informal sector includes a wide variety of activities ranging from petty trade, service repairs and domestic work to transport, construction and manufacturing. It rarely involves a clear-cut employer-employee relationship. The diversity of jobs and employment status make it difficult for informal-sector workers to organize themselves into unions; moreover, patriarchal family and ethnic loyalties may count for more than solidarity between workers. The ILO report points out that informal-sector units 'operate on the fringe, if not outside, the legal and administrative framework', with many ignoring or paying scant attention to regulations concerning safety, health and working conditions.

In the past few years a number of trade unions and NGOs around the world have supported initiatives to help informal-sector workers. Furthermore, the ILO report concludes that 'the State has a major role to play in helping informal sector workers overcome their disadvantages'. This makes it a priority of national policy to establish and enforce a regulatory framework in which 'the right of informal sector workers to join or create representative associations of their choosing, as well as state recognition of their role as interlocutors and/or partners in policy-making or programme implementation are ... key enabling factors'.

The threat to these essential national policies comes from the neo-liberal creed espoused by, among others, the IMF, World Bank and other sources of capital, who make loans and assistance dependent upon the creation of so-called 'flexible' and 'deregulated' labour markets. Their aim is to ease the movement of capital, and at the same time restrict those kinds of solidarity between states, communities and workers which might increase their bargaining power with investors. The international financial institutions sometimes make their funding conditional on the recipient revising its labour laws. This gives rise to a perception of 'social imperialism' – developing countries believe that they are being denied their sovereign right to determine their own labour standards (Anderson, 1996: 452). The familiar story is that a developing country seeking World Bank or IMF support is asked to produce what amounts to paper evidence that the country is observing basic labour standards. This leads to the employment of an 'expert' who rapidly drafts a labour code for the state in question. The IMF or World Bank aid then flows, but the labour code remains unenforced. Behind the paper tigers of laws and codes of conduct is the thriving jungle of market imperialism.

'Social Dumping': in Search of a Definition

Attempts to establish a new international regulatory framework usually begin with the difficult question of how to define 'social dumping'. The aim is to distinguish legitimate comparative advantage from destructive competition based on a race to the bottom. Article XX of the GATT provides exemptions allowing states to defend their domestic markets against products with features which may be regarded as undesirable. Thus, Article XX's provisions essentially embody internationally agreed rules on practices considered unfair in international trade. It does not refer to 'social dumping' as such, but does permit quantitative restrictions on imports or other discrimination in relation to the products of prison labour, or if necessary to protect 'public morals' or to protect 'human, animal, or plant life or health'. A more general definition of 'social dumping' is suggested by Grossmann and Koopmann (1996: 116):

> Unlike conventional dumping which means selling abroad below cost or at lower prices than charged in the home market, 'social dumping' refers to costs that are for their part depressed below a 'natural' level by means of 'social oppression' facilitating unfair pricing strategies against foreign competitors. Remedial action would either consist of the offending firms consenting to raise their prices accordingly or failing that, imposing equivalent import restrictions.

This approach depends on identifying those measures of 'social oppression' which cause wage costs and labour standards to be unfairly depressed.

Put in economic terms, the 'social dumping' case for international labour regulation is that it is necessary to remove those distortions on competition which are not related to productivity. Such distortions occur when firms are able to utilize undervalued labour. By undervaluation is meant paying workers with comparable skills and productivity different wages simply by shifting demand for labour to a more disadvantaged group of workers who are unable to resist. Firms that can undervalue labour in this way can avoid more radical solutions to their competitive problems, such as restructuring or investment in new technologies. Indeed, the availability of undervalued labour discourages innovation, and firms which are innovative face unfair competition from firms which are inefficient technically and managerially but are able to be profitable in the short term by employing undervalued labour.

This argument was the justification given for including in the Treaty of Rome (1957) a provision (Article 119) requiring equal remuneration for men and women doing the same work. It was said by a group of experts that

> countries in which there are wage differentials by sex will pay relatively low wages in industries employing a large proportion of female labour and these industries will enjoy what might be called a special advantage over their competitors abroad where differentials according to sex are smaller or non-existent.
>
> (Ohlin, 1956: 107)

There are obviously greater opportunities for using undervalued labour in a system which discriminates on grounds of sex, race or any other arbitrary basis. A similar argument justifies measures against other forms of social oppression such as forced and child labour. Equally, the denial of freedom of association and the right to collective bargaining can also be regarded as a rejection of basic human rights.

Limits of the 'Social Dumping' Approach

It is doubtful, however, whether the social dumping approach is adequate in itself to form the theoretical basis for a new approach to international labour regulation. First, this approach over-emphasizes the role of labour costs in decisions about relocation. Enterprises are not likely to relocate to another state with lower *nominal* labour costs if those costs simply reflect lower productivity of workers in that state. This would mean that there is no net difference in unit labour costs. The basic point is that what matters is not the *nominal* level of wage costs in a firm or industry but the net unit labour costs – the costs of labour for each unit of production after taking productivity into account (Deakin, 1997: 66). If labour costs do not reflect the relative productivity in a particular state, and enterprises do relocate to that state, the result would be to increase demand for labour, with the likelihood of rising wage levels. This would, in due course, cancel out the advantages of a relocation which was based purely on low labour costs. The *World Investment Report 1994* concluded that

> despite a few notable cases, TNCs do not often close down, on account of low labour cost considerations alone, production facilities in one country to re-establish them in another country ... Broader and more important macroeconomic and cyclical factors, technological change and labour market inflexibilities are the principal influences on the growth and distribution of employment.
>
> (UNCTAD, 1994: xxvii)

Secondly, there is no reason to believe that comparative advantage does in fact flow from social dumping, whether this is through the violation of core labour standards or simply because of the comparative advantage of cheap labour (Chinn, 1998: 43). An OECD study in 1996 argued persuasively that patterns of specialization are mainly determined by relative factor endowments, technology and economies of scale. The study pointed to empirical research which indicates that there is no correlation between aggregate real wage growth and the level of observance of core labour rights, such as freedom of association. Moreover, aggregate data on FDI suggests that the presence or absence of core labour standards are not important determinants. Host states which observe core standards are not significantly worse in attracting FDI than those which systematically abuse these standards. On the contrary, raising labour standards may raise productivity and so encourage FDI (OECD, 1996). A similar conclusion was reached by a report on labour standards in the Asia-Pacific region (Commonwealth of Australia, 1996). This is not to say that there are no abuses of labour standards linked to export sectors (such as Export Processing Zones) but the worst abuses are usually found in domestic, non-trade sectors which do not rely on FDI.

This critique of the social dumping approach leads one to reject it as inadequate, and ultimately illusory. In any event, the denial of market access on the basis of allegations of social dumping would be extremely difficult to apply, because the GATT requires that any restriction must be applied in a manner which would not constitute arbitrary or unjustified discrimination between countries where the same conditions prevail. So a 'social clause' in the GATT, which sought to penalize social dumping, would require the importing country to base it on an evaluation of the labour-standards record of all states with which it trades, and assumes criteria for such an evaluation. Moreover, the derogation from free trade would have to satisfy the test of proportionality, for example all imports could not be banned in order to prevent some products of child labour (Hepple, 1997: 361).

Developing a Race to the Top

An alternative approach to international labour regulation is to encourage the development of those processes *within* the kinds of market activity identified at the beginning of this chapter, which favour the raising of labour standards, that is a 'race to the top' (Barenberg, 1998). This has been called an 'instrumental' approach (Chinn, 1998: 47). The internal labour markets of TNCs usually provide better wages, conditions of work and social security benefits than those prevailing in domestic firms, due to the fact that they tend to be concentrated in industries which utilize high skills, are capital-intensive, and have superior managerial and organizational techniques. Indirectly, there may be a spillover of the best practices of these TNCs to domestic firms (UNCTAD, 1994: 196–7).

The global commodity chains dominated by TNCs generate employment through various linkages with enterprises in home and host countries. The *World Investment Report 1994* reported that 'as a general rule, for each job directly generated by a TNC, one or two may result indirectly from backward and forward linkages' (UNCTAD-DTCI, 1994: 192). Lall points out:

> The attraction of developing countries is no longer the presence of large protected markets, cheap unskilled labour and exploitable natural resources. Increasingly, FDI flows into competitive and higher technology activities which require disciplined and productive labour, high skill levels, world-class infrastructure and a supportive network of suppliers.
>
> (Lall, 1995: 421)

Whether or not the quality of employment is raised throughout the global chain of production and distribution depends largely on corporate integration strategies. In the emerging model of complex integration – that is, regionally or globally integrated production and distribution networks within function, product or process specialization – there is likely to be a degree of convergence in the employment conditions of parent and foreign affiliates in order to maximize the global efficiency of the TNC. The TNC will increasingly rely on workforce quality in the host country, and this can be encouraged in order to generate positive effects on labour conditions throughout the global commodity chain, and hopefully also into the informal sector.

The task, therefore, is to create an international regulatory framework which encourages and develops the potential of TNCs to raise the labour standards of economically and socially disadvantaged groups of workers and producers, particularly in the informal sector. At national level, the application and elaboration of this framework has to take account of specific local cultural, social and economic features. We must, therefore, turn to the emerging methods of international labour regulation, to evaluate their potential for the dissemination of 'best practices'. This will involve an examination both of the substantive principles which they uphold, and also their enforcement mechanisms.

EMERGING METHODS OF INTERNATIONAL LABOUR REGULATION

International Labour Organization

The Preamble to Part XIII of the Treaty of Versailles (the ILO Constitution) declared that 'the failure of any nation to adopt humane conditions of labour is an obstacle in the way of other nations which desire to improve the conditions in their own countries.' Over the past eight decades the International Labour Conference has adopted 181 Conventions and 188 Recommendations. These form the essential backdrop of international standards against which all current debates on 'social clauses' in trade and investment agreements must be judged.

In the 1980s and early 1990s there was a general slow-down in the process of ratification of ILO Conventions and serious abuses of standards occurred in several countries, including industrialized nations in the grip of neo-liberalism such as the United Kingdom (Hepple, 1997: 357). The dominant feature of ILO standards from the 1944 Declaration of Philadelphia until the 1970s was their promotion of freedom of association, collective bargaining and tripartism. These pro-collective standards have had to fight for survival in an increasingly individualistic, deregulatory climate. The 1977 ILO Tripartite Declaration of Principles Concerning Multinational Enterprises and Social Policy has been ineffective. The ILO has certainly been greatly hampered by its lack of effective sanctions in securing compliance with its standards, even by countries which ratify them. Although about two-thirds of governments submit triennial reports on their observance of the Declaration, less than half of these consult the social partners in preparing their replies (Gunter and Bailey, 1992: para. 90). The disputes procedure is aimed purely at interpretation, has no teeth to secure compliance and has been rarely invoked.

Whatever the merits of the arguments for a 'social clause' in the WTO, however, it has certainly created pressure on the ILO to show greater effectiveness. In his report to the 81st session (1994) of the International Labour Conference, the Director-General of the ILO put forward several proposals to revitalize international labour standards. These included the suggestion that the liberalization of trade and investment could be reconciled with adherence to international standards by selectively concentrating on 'fundamental' human rights in the workplace, as defined in seven 'core' Conventions: freedom of association and collective bargaining (1948 no. 87 and 1949 no. 98), forced labour (1930 no. 29 and 1957 no. 105), non-discrimination (1951 no. 100 and 1958 no. 111) and the minimum age for employment (1973 no. 138).

These seven Conventions do not in themselves provide a unique and comprehensive set of definitions for the selected 'core' standards. For example, Convention no. 138 provides for a minimum employment age but remains silent on other aspects of the exploitation of child labour. To remedy this, proposals are being prepared for the International Labour Conference in 1999 to outlaw the worst forms of child labour, including hazardous work, debt bondage, forced labour and slave-like conditions, prostitution, pornography and drug-trafficking, while recognizing the need for positive projects to improve the health and education of children and their families. A campaign to encourage states which have not already done so to ratify the seven core Conventions brought the total number of ratifications by 31 December 1997 to 853, still requiring 356 ratifications before there would be universal coverage.

A boost to the ILO's activities was given in the declaration of ministers at the WTO Conference in Singapore in December 1996 stating that the ILO, and not the WTO, was the competent body to set and deal with core labour standards. There were several reasons for regarding the ILO as the more appropriate body. First, the WTO is a specialized organization on trade where trade ministers serve as representatives, while the strength of the ILO, which has nearly 80 years' experience of setting labour standards, lies in its tripartite composition (governments, employers and unions). Secondly, decision-making in the WTO requires consensus, while the International Labour Conference can act by majority decision. Thirdly, for reasons mentioned earlier, it would be difficult to utilize WTO sanctions against imports from defaulting countries.

These considerations led to the adoption at the June 1998 session of the International Labour Conference of a Declaration of Fundamental Principles and Rights at Work. All 174 members, whether or not they have ratified the Convention in question, now have an obligation arising from the very fact of membership of the ILO to 'respect, to promote and to realize' the principles underlying the fundamental rights in the seven core Conventions, namely

- freedom of association and the effective recognition of the right to collective bargaining;
- the elimination of all forms of forced and compulsory labour;
- the effective abolition of child labour;
- the elimination of discrimination in respect of employment and occupation.

The weaknesses of the Declaration lie in its 'promotional' follow-up mechanism. It is no more than a political statement of a non-binding character. It does not impose any obligation to observe the detailed requirements of any Convention, nor is there an obligation to ratify the seven core Conventions. It is purely promotion (requiring annual national reports and a triennial global report), and not complaints-based. There are no sanctions for non-compliance. Moreover, in order to meet the concerns of some developing countries, paragraph 5 of the Declaration:

> stresses that labour standards should not be used for protectionist purposes, and that nothing in this Declaration and its follow-up shall be invoked or otherwise used for such purposes; in addition the comparative advantage of any country should in no way be called into question by the Declaration and its follow-up.

Many of the developing countries also remain strongly opposed to using the Declaration as a condition for technical assistance by other international institutions.

The Organization for Economic Cooperation and Development

In 1976, the OECD Ministerial Council adopted a Declaration on International Investment and Multinational Enterprises, which included Guidelines for Multinational Enterprises and a commitment to the National Treatment principle. The content of the Guidelines and the 1977 ILO Declaration are similar. Both uphold the principle of state sovereignty by recognizing that TNCs must observe national laws and practices. They both spell out collective rights in some detail, in particular the right of workers in TNCs to have representatives of their own choosing. Both instruments encourage collective bargaining, requiring TNCs to adopt a positive approach to trade unions and other *bona fide* workers' organizations, and to engage in constructive negotiation. Of particular importance is the statement in the 1977 ILO Declaration (para. 53), echoed in the OECD Guidelines (para. 8) that TNCs

> should not threaten to utilize a capacity to transfer the whole or part of an operating unit from the country concerned nor transfer employees from the enterprise's component entities in other countries in order to influence unfairly those negotiations or to hinder the exercise of a right to organize.

The OECD Guidelines expect the parent company to take the necessary organizational steps to enable subsidiaries to observe the Guidelines, *inter alia*, by providing adequate and timely information and ensuring that the enterprise's local representatives are duly authorized to take decisions on the matters under negotiation (Employment and Industrial Relations chapter, para. 9). Reasonable notice must be given of major changes in operations (para. 6).

The Guidelines are rich in principle, but weak in enforcement. They are not mandatory or legally enforceable. National Contact Points (NCPs) in each country are supposed to promote the Guidelines, collect information, handle enquiries and assist in solving problems which may arise between business and labour in matters covered by the Guidelines. In individual cases, where NCPs have been unable to resolve the matter, OECD member governments or the Business and Industry Advisory Committee (BIAC) or the Trade Union Advisory Committee (TUAC) may request clarification of the Guidelines by the Committee for International Investment and Multinational Enterprises (CIIME). About 30 cases have been brought to CIIME's attention. These procedures have been criticized by trade unions, on the grounds that NCPs have almost ceased to exist in some countries, and that CIIME has generally been unwilling to interpret the vague text so as to favour trade union positions. There has been no evaluation as to whether or not the Guidelines have had an impact on the observance of core labour standards in developing countries.

The Guidelines, and in particular the Employment and Industrial Relations chapter, are of considerable relevance to FDI, and could become

increasingly important should the MAI be adopted. In the course of negotiations for the MAI, a majority of governments appear to have accepted
the following approach:

1. There would be an affirmation in the preamble of their support for
   internationally recognized core labour standards, and their belief that
   the ILO is the competent body to deal with these standards.
2. The OECD Guidelines could be annexed to the MAI text, without
   changing their non-binding character.
3. There would be a binding obligation on member states not to waive or
   derogate from their domestic health, safety, environmental or labour
   measures in relation to an individual investment or investor (but this
   would not prevent governments from adjusting these measures for public policy reasons other than attracting a particular foreign investment).[2]

Unilateral, Bilateral and Multilateral Trade and Investment Instruments

Article 7 of the proposed Havana Charter of the International Trade
Organization (1947) required members to take action to eliminate unfair
labour conditions, particularly in production for export, within their own
territory. This influenced multilateral commodity agreements, such as the
International Sugar Agreement (1953), and agreements in the tin, cocoa
and rubber industries, all of which encouraged domestic standards in the
exporting country comparable to those in the importing country, and permitted anti-dumping or countervailing duties in order to achieve harmonization of conditions (Charnovitz, 1987: 568).

Another approach has been to impose quantitative restrictions on
imports. Specific legislation in various countries has restricted imports of
goods produced by prison, forced or child labour or in conditions endan-
gering the health of workers in the country of manufacture. The United
States Trade and Competitiveness Act 1988 classifies the denial of certain
worker rights in foreign countries as 'unreasonable' trade practices,
against which sanctions may be imposed. However, the trading partner's
overall level of development and progress in achieving these rights must
be taken into account.

A third approach has been the use of preferential (as distinct from most-
favoured-nation) trade policies. The United States insisted on 'reasonable
workplace conditions' and 'the right to organize and bargain collectively'
as conditions for allowing duty-free access to the US market granted in the
Caribbean Basin Initiative (CBI) of 1983. The 1984 US Generalized

System of Preferences (GSP) required that, to benefit from such preferences, countries must be 'taking steps' to achieve certain standards. This has been used against countries such as Nicaragua, Paraguay and Romania. Investment insurance had been withheld from several countries by the United States' Overseas Private Investment Insurance Corporation for failing to adopt and implement internationally recognized workers' rights. Some recently negotiated bilateral US investment agreements also require respect for such rights, and for the enforcement of domestic laws protecting workers.

The system of preferences has also been used by the European Union, but it has gone beyond the American approach of the 'stick' of withdrawing trade preferences to the use of the 'carrot' of positive incentives to encourage social development. Since 1 January 1998, additional preferences may be awarded to countries which can demonstrate compliance with ILO Conventions nos 87 and 98 on freedom of association and the right to collective bargaining, and no. 138 on child labour. These additional preferences are viewed as compensation for the improved costs of social regulation. However, they are of little use in the case of the 'least developed countries' (LDCs) which in any case have no tariffs levied on their exports, in order to facilitate development. There have been serious abuses of union rights in some of these LDCs. This has led to the suggestion by the European Trade Union Confederation (ETUC) that these countries should be given additional EU Cooperation funding for social development programmes if they can demonstrate compliance with core labour rights.

The mechanism for implementing the EU's GSP programme gives an opportunity to trade unions and NGOs to provide relevant information to the European Commission, providing a useful political platform for exposing violations of human rights standards. Bilateral cooperation agreements made by the EU specifically refer to the need to safeguard workers' rights, and since 1992 all agreements between the EU and third countries have been required to incorporate a clause defining human rights, including social rights, as a basic element of the agreement.

NAFTA and the MERCOSUR

The North American Agreement on Labor Cooperation (NAALC), a side accord to NAFTA, came into operation in September 1993. This relies on cross-border monitoring in order to ensure that Canada, Mexico and the United States observe their own domestic labour laws. The NAALC came into existence against the political background of strong opposition by organized labour to NAFTA because of the fear of 'social dumping'. Even though Mexican law specifies labour standards superior in some respects to those in the United States and Canada (for example job security), it was alleged that the Mexican standards are poorly enforced (Adams and Singh, 1997: 161).

The NAALC commits each party to promote 11 basic principles, in accordance with their own laws, customs and history. The agreement is administered by the Commission for Labor Cooperation, and contains a dispute resolution process. If a dispute relating to the enforcement of labour laws cannot be resolved, nothing further can be done under the NAALC unless it relates to health and safety, child labour or minimum wages. In respect of those three issues a complaint may be presented to an arbitral tribunal. A panel finding in favour of the complainant may result in penalties including fines and suspension from NAFTA's benefits. A study of the first four cases decided under the NAALC concludes that 'despite the scepticism of critics, the NAALC and the institutions that it has spawned have had modest successes in labour's favour' (Adams and Singh, 1997: 180–1).

A weaker version of the NAFTA approach seems to be emerging in MERCOSUR. The Treaty of Asuncion (April 1991) between Argentina, Brazil, Uruguay and Paraguay establishing MERCOSUR referred to social issues only in its preamble. All four states have constitutional guarantees of labour and social rights, but in the face of movements for greater labour market flexibility, the trade unions have been pressing for the adoption of a Charter of Social Rights, and for the imposition of sanctions against states breaking their domestic legislation. These attempts have so far failed, although in May 1998 the Heads of State and Government agreed on the exchange of information on labour legislation and the promotion of core labour standards, recognizing the ILO as the competent body to deal with these standards.

The European Union

The growth of the 'social dimension' of the EC and EEA since 1957 is in many ways an outstanding model of the advantages and pitfalls of transnational labour regulation in the face of free movement of capital, goods, services and workers (Barnard, 1995: 51–105). The history of the EC has been dominated by the conflict between free market and social market ideologies. Since 1989 the latter have gained ascendancy, against the neoliberals led by the UK's Thatcher and Major governments, first with the adoption in 1989 by 11 of the then 12 member states of the Community Charter of Fundamental Rights of Workers, and then, with the concurrence of the UK's new Labour Government in 1997, of the Treaty of Amsterdam which integrates the Social Chapter into the EC Treaty and includes a commitment to the European Social Charter (1961) of the Council of Europe, as well as the Community Charter, as the inspiration of Community policies.

However, the Social Chapter still falls far short of being a comprehensive statement of directly enforceable labour rights. Indeed Article 137(6) of the amended EC Treaty expressly excludes from the procedures for enacting Community law any measures on pay, the right of association, the right to strike or to impose lock-outs. These matters remain within the exclusive legislative competence of the member states. Although the important European Works Council Directive 94/45/EC requires large TNCs operating in more than one member state to set up and consult a transnational Works Council, Community measures do not cover the fundamental rights to freedom of association and collective bargaining.

SOME CONCLUSIONS

The argument of this chapter has been that, from the perspective of both industrialized and developing countries, the 'social dumping' thesis, constructed within the framework of a theory of liberalization, provides an inadequate basis on which to develop a new international regulatory framework. It leads to simplistic and ultimately illusory measures such as the withdrawal of access for developing countries to markets or investment. It contains more than a whiff of social imperialism, especially if it takes the form of subjective determinations imposed unilaterally by industrialized countries on former colonies whose economic and social development was for generations held back or distorted so that imperial nations could benefit from cheap low-wage imports of raw materials.

The alternative strategy proposed depends on a close analysis of the actual development of global commodity chains and the internal labour markets of TNCs. The aim should be to encourage existing processes within those production and distribution chains and internal labour markets which favour a 'race to the top' in labour standards.

Each of the emerging methods of international labour regulation through the ILO, OECD, NAFTA and the EU has serious weaknesses both of principle and enforcement. However, we can detect a dynamic moving towards the construction of *social* markets on an international scale. The criterion by which these methods must be judged is whether they enable the economically and socially most advanced, within and between national states, to raise up the labour standards of the more disadvantaged groups of workers and also producers in the informal sector.

First, there is now an international consensus on 'core' labour rights based on the 1998 ILO Declaration. All are important, but perhaps of the greatest significance for the future is the explicit recognition of the freedom of association and the right to effective bargaining. The OECD Guidelines and 1977 ILO Declaration usefully elaborate these fundamental principles. Secondly, the emerging mechanisms recognize a number of ways of disseminating 'best practices'. These include:

- requirements for disclosure of information and consultation and other forms of participation;
- the mutual monitoring of domestic labour laws and international sanctions for their non-enforcement;
- compensation through additional preferences, structural funds and the like, for social measures which aid development;
- the strengthening of collective complaints-based procedures for the enforcement of agreed standards.

None of these developments has occurred spontaneously. Their future evolution will depend upon how effectively the emerging mechanisms can be used and strengthened by activists in order to mobilize consumers and workers and to influence policy-makers.

NOTES

1. The concept of 'labour standards' is used here both in a descriptive sense, that is the 'actual terms of employment, quality of work and well-being of workers in a particular location and point in time', and also in a normative or prescriptive way, namely 'rights, such as the right to form associations of workers and employers, and the right to bargain collectively' (Sengenberger, 1994: 3). The normative standards may be either substantive, stipulating specified levels of minimum rights in the employment relationship (e.g. minimum wages, maximum working time) or procedural (the process by which substantive norms are established and disputes resolved). Substantive standards may be compulsory, meaning that individual workers cannot contract out of these standards, or they may be optional.
2. MAI Negotiating Text, 24 April 1998, Annex to chairman's proposal on environment and related matter and labour, para. 4 on 'not lowering measures'.

REFERENCES

Adams, R. and Singh, P. (1997) 'Early Experience with NAFTA's Labor Side Accord', *Comparative Labor Law Journal*, vol. 18, 161–81.

Anderson, K. (1996) 'The Intrusion of Environmental and Labor Standards into Trade Policy' in W. Martin and A. Winter (eds) *The Uruguay Round and Developing Countries.* Cambridge University Press, Cambridge.

Barenberg, M. (1998) 'Globalization and Labor Law: Legal and Extra-Legal Norms Across Multiple Regimes' (unpublished paper).

Barnard, C. (1995) *EC Employment Law.* John Wiley and Sons, Chichester.

Bercusson, B. (1996) *European Labour Law.* Butterworth, London.

Charnovitz, S. (1987) 'The Influence of International Labour Standards in the World Trading System: a Historical Review', *International Labour Review,* vol. 126, 565–84.

Chinn, D. (1998) *A Social Clause for Labour's Cause: Global Trade and Labour Standards – a Challenge for the New Millennium.* Institute of Employment Rights, London.

Commonwealth of Australia (1996) *Report on Labour Standards in the Asia-Pacific Region,* Tripartite Working Party on Labour Standards (Chair: Michael Duffy), AGPS, Canberra.

Davies, P. (1997) 'Posted Workers: Single Market or Protection of National Labour Law Systems?' *Common Market Law Review,* vol. 34, 571–91.

Deakin, S. (1997) 'Labour Law as Market Regulation: the Economic Foundations of European Social Policy' in P. Davies, S. Sciarra and S. Simitis (eds) *European Community Labour Law.* Oxford University Press, Oxford.

Deakin, S. and Wilkinson, F. (1994) 'Rights vs Efficiency? The Economic Case for Transnational Labour Standards', *Industrial Law Journal,* vol. 23, 289–310.

Grossmann, H. and Koopmann, G. (1996) 'Social Standards in International Trade' in H. Sander and A. Inotai (eds) *World Trade After the Uruguay Round.* Routledge, London.

Hepple, B. (1997) 'New Approaches to International Labour Regulation', *Industrial Law Journal,* vol. 26, 353–66.

Howard, A. (1997) 'Labour, History, and Sweatshops in the New Global Economy' in A. Ross (ed.) *No Sweat – Fashion, Free Trade and the Rights of Garment Workers.* Verso, London.

ILO (International Labour Organization) (1997) *World Labour Report: Industrial Relations, Democracy and Social Stability, 1997–98.* International Labour Office, Geneva.

Lall, S. (1995) 'Employment and Foreign Investment: Policy Options for Developing Countries', *International Labour Review,* vol. 134, 521–39.

Lee, E. (1996) 'Globalization and Employment: Is Anxiety Justified?' *International Labour Review,* vol. 135, 485–97.

OECD (Organization for Economic Co-Operation and Development) (1996) *Trade, Employment and Labour Standards – a Study of Core Workers' Rights and International Trade.* OECD, Paris.

Ohlin, B. [ILO Committee of Experts] (1956) 'Social Aspects of European Economic Cooperation', *International Labour Review,* vol. 74, 99–120.

Picciotto, S. (1998) 'Globalization, Liberalization, Regulation'. Paper given to conference on Globalization and the Law, Cumberland Lodge, April 1998.

Rush Portuguesa Lda v Office National d'Immigration [1990] *European Court Reports* I-1417, Case C-113/89.

Sengenberger, W. (1994) 'Labour Standards: an Institutional Framework for Restructuring and Development' in W. Sengenberger and D. Campbell (eds)

Creating Economic Opportunities: the Role of Labour Standards in Industrial Restructuring. International Institute for Labour Studies, Geneva.

Stone, K. (1996) 'Labour in the Global Economy: Four Approaches to Transnational Labor Regulation' in W. Bratton, J. McCahery, S. Picciotto and C. Scott (eds) *International Regulatory Competition and Co-ordination*. Clarendon Press, Oxford.

UNCTD (United Nations Conference on Trade and Development, Division on Transnational Corporations and Development UNCTAD-DTCI) (1994) *World Investment Report 1994: Transnational Corporations, Employment and the Workplace*. United Nations, New York.

Part III
The Interaction of Formal and Informal Regulation

11 Corporate Codes of Conduct: the Privatized Application of Labour Standards

Neil Kearney

ABUSES OF WORKERS AND THEIR RIGHTS

The scandal about sweatshop conditions in certain manufacturing sectors, including garments and shoes, is nothing new, but has taken on much greater intensity in the past few years. And no wonder!

Carmen Rosario is a small, frail teenager, working in the Dominican Republic's garment industry. She started work at 13 and endured some horrendous conditions until, together with colleagues, she could stand it no longer and began to organize a union. Her employers embarked on a campaign of intimidation and harassment, culminating in late 1997 in an attack by hired thugs, using baseball bats with nails driven through them. Carmen suffered multiple injuries, including a broken arm. Her co-worker, Ingrid Bastardo, who was seven months pregnant, was beaten and punched and kicked in the stomach. Around the same time a young man in a Chinese shoe factory, wrongly accused of a petty theft, was fired and forced to crawl on his hands and knees out of the factory through the entire workforce. Asked why he didn't just walk out, he explained that he would have been beaten by the security guards if he had done so.

In Mexico, young women workers are subjected to compulsory pregnancy tests monthly, while one factory even insists that they bring their soiled sanitary towels to prove that they are not pregnant. In a Guatemala City plant, a supervisor routinely punched young women workers in the stomach every fortnight to weed out those who might be pregnant. The same supervisor was accused of forcing sexual favours from the workforce in return for a pass permitting them to use the bathroom.

Nor are abuses limited to developing countries. At the same time as Haitian workers were reported to be producing top brand-name products in appalling conditions, including compulsory overtime in dirty and dangerous factories, immigrant garment workers were found in virtual slavery in an illegal factory compound in California.

Among the most exploited, most abused and most helpless groups of workers across the world are children. This army of child slaves, 250 million of them according to the ILO, in every continent, do every job imaginable and for the lowest pay and in the worst conditions. Children as young as five years old work up to 20 hours a day making shirts in Karanigonj in Bangladesh. Children glue shoes in Italy. They weave carpets in Nepal. They stitch footballs in Pakistan. They knit sweaters in Portugal. They assemble toys in Thailand. They pack garments in the heart of Manhattan in New York. Half will never go to school. Many will die before the age of 12 from overwork and horrendous working conditions.

Some of the production carried out by these youngsters is for export. And while most of the children involved are working for medium- or smaller-sized manufacturing units, the goods they make are marketed and sold by leading multinational merchandisers and retailers. A good example is the stitching of footballs in Sialkot in Pakistan, involving large numbers of children, for leading brand names in Europe and North America. Indeed, it is the constant pressure of the multinationals forcing down their purchasing price that causes local companies to use the cheaper labour of children. Cut-throat competition and constant reduction of lead times worsens the situation because every order is a 'rush order' necessitating long working hours to meet deadlines.

In the Philippines, children from the age of four work 11 hours a day stitching dresses for the dolls of children of the same age in industrialized countries. These youngsters earn barely enough to enable them to eat. They suffer from back pains and hand cramps. They are stopped from going to the toilet. They are beaten when they make mistakes.

These are only some of the thousands of victims of the unrelenting quest for profit by multinational manufacturers, merchandisers and retailers. In some industries, certainly, labour costs are not always a key sourcing criterion for companies, which need to take into account other factors such as access to markets, a skilled labour force and a good local infrastructure. However, they are important in the textile, clothing and leather sectors, and in recent years such companies have scoured the world, searching out the cheapest sources of production. Recently, subcontracting is being used as a means of further reducing labour costs. It is here that some of the very worst abuses of workers' rights occur. Most of the recent exposures of multinational merchandiser and retailer sourcing involving exploitation have involved subcontractors. A good example was the linking by trade unions in Turkey of child labour and Italian-based retailer Benetton. Many multinationals try to give the impression that local exploitation has nothing to do with them, but it is increasingly impossible to sustain such arguments, given the strong contractual relationships demanded by such companies and the regular presence of production and quality controllers.

Governments, desperate to attract inward investment, are also under pressure to offer incentives to potential employers. These increasingly involve the establishment of export processing zones, giving investors tax-free status and freedom from domestic legislation, particularly that relating to wages and working conditions. Some companies take full advantage of this freedom, leading to gross violations of internationally recognized labour standards. And when workers object and attempt to establish trade unions to defend their interests employers often respond brutally. Bangladesh, for example, now has a number of export processing zones where workers are precluded by law from organizing and bargaining with their employers. When women workers established an independent garment workers' federation to fight exploitation in the export industries they were subjected to a campaign of harassment and intimidation culminating in an arson attack on the union offices by paid thugs who poured petrol on the union lawyer and attempted to set her alight.

Elsewhere governments have promised inward investors that they will not be bothered by difficult workers or by trade unions and have conscripted the local police and military to uphold that promise. Workers in Indonesia, Lesotho and across Central America have suffered the consequences. Potential investors in El Salvador were once told that they could forget their worries about militant trade unions as a military unit was billeted within the zone who could be on call within three minutes. In Swaziland, a former industry minister advised Taiwanese businessmen coming to establish a garment plant in the country not to pay local employees too much as they wouldn't know how to spend the money.

Hundreds of export processing zones now exist, and in every continent. Most sustain assembly industries which in general provide low-paid and exploitative, insecure jobs. In the textiles, garment and shoe industries export producing zones exist in 160 countries, producing mainly for export to 30 countries. Competition is intense. And with most production costs fixed and not greatly variable from country to country, it is labour costs which are most under attack, putting them on an ever-downward spiral. For example, the wage costs involved in the production of a shirt which retails for US$60 are no more than 10 cents. Similarly, the labour costs involved in producing a pair of US$180 sports shoes have been driven down below US$2.

CORPORATE CODES OF CONDUCT

Fortunately, the globalization of production has been accompanied by a revolution in communications. Abuses which in the past might have taken months or even years to come to light are now often carried in worldwide news broadcasts the day they happen. This has put very considerable pressure on multinational retailers and merchandisers who spend huge amounts on building their image and brand names. Bad publicity in the form of stories of worker exploitation, particularly child labour, will undo, at a stroke, much of the benefit accruing from saturation advertising, with a subsequent impact on market share. In addition, recent research suggests that such publicity also has an adverse impact on stock value, where image and reputation may account for as much as 30 per cent of such value.

In reality, such companies dislike bad publicity. They do not want it, but they cannot stop it, given the transparency of the current appalling conditions in manufacturing. That is why many have been forced to make public statements to the effect that they will respect domestic labour legislation and some international labour standards, both in their own operations and in those of their suppliers. Such statements have become popularly known as 'corporate codes of conduct'. Hundreds are now in existence, with the greatest proliferation being in the textile, clothing and leather sectors, particularly originating in US retailing and merchandising.

Corporate codes of conduct, in effect, have privatized the implementation of national labour legislation and the application of international labour standards. Their proliferation is a reflection of the failure of governments to implement effective labour legislation and of intergovernmental institutions, such as the International Labour Organization, to enforce internationally agreed basic minimum labour standards around the world. They also reflect the obsession of many governments in recent years, particularly in the industrialized world, with deregulation. Rather than legislate to eliminate exploitation at home and abroad, many administrations, including that of the United States, preferred to encourage multinational companies to adopt voluntary undertakings on responsibility for the labour standards of their suppliers and business partners.

Corporate codes of conduct are, however, no substitute for national legislation enacted and effectively implemented by governments or for international labour standards enforced around the world; neither can they be a substitute for the right of workers to organize and to bargain collectively with their employers; nor are they shortcuts to more equitable wages and better working conditions. Indeed, unless properly handled, codes of conduct may work to the disadvantage of those they were intended to help.

For example, one sports shoe producer in Indonesia recently claimed that as it had accepted a merchandiser's code of conduct there was no need to continue the collective agreement negotiated with the local trade union. Elsewhere, so-called monitoring systems involving NGOs have been put in place which effectively negate the role of the democratically elected union structures in the plants concerned.

In spite of these drawbacks, corporate codes of conduct, if they continue to grow in number and impact, may be the catalyst that will force governments to examine new mechanisms for the enforcement of workers' rights, regardless of the location of employment. Unfortunately, to date the great majority of corporate codes have been little more than public relations exercises – fig leaves for exploitation – the latest in a long line of efforts by firms to escape responsibility for the production conditions from which they profit. Only recently, one major European retailer exposed for dealing with suppliers using grossly exploitative practices, including child labour, proclaimed total ignorance of conditions at each of the plants, expressed regret for what had been exposed, and said all would soon be well since the company would now adopt a code of conduct. At the very same time, the company's buyers were telling suppliers that they must cut their prices by 30 per cent on last year's figures – prices which had spurred exploitation in the first place! Such companies cannot have it both ways – on the one hand demanding certain standards from their suppliers while on the other remaining unwilling to pay a price for merchandise that will enable the standards to be upheld.

Corporate codes of conduct are, in effect, written statements of principles a corporation will follow regarding working conditions. Despite pressure from unions and NGOs that codes of conduct contain, at a minimum, the core ILO standards, most codes introduced unilaterally by companies are often less than what is demanded by national law and international labour standards, but typically will include references to the non-use of forced labour and child labour and to the implementation of reasonable health and safety standards. Some include a reference to the payment of minimum wage levels, but, to date, very few have included a commitment to recognizing the right of workers to organize and to bargain collectively. Until recently no company code made a commitment to the payment of a living wage.

Company codes had their origin in the early 1990s when several companies, including Levi Strauss, Sears and Toys'R'Us were the subject of scrutiny following allegations that prison labour had been used in the production of their Chinese imports. Pressure continued as attention focused on the use of child labour in export industries, particularly in Bangladesh.

Initially many of the companies concerned claimed that working conditions in their suppliers' plants had nothing to do with them. However, so great were the stories of gross exploitation that very soon most such companies were forced to accept accountability for the conditions in factories making their brand-name or own-label products, whether or not they owned the factories.

A major factor in forcing companies to change tack was growing consumer awareness and disgust at the conditions in which expensive goods were made. Numerous surveys confirmed growing consumer disquiet and a willingness even to pay more in return for guarantees that exploitation, and particularly the exploitation of children, was not part of the production process. In addition, as many as 80 per cent claimed that they were willing to change brands in search of 'clean' produce. Such strength of feeling sent companies rushing headlong for a safety net and codes of conduct were conveniently handy.

Levi Strauss became one of the first companies to adopt a corporate code of conduct for all its operations in 1992, after the China disclosures and following criticism of its contractors' practices in Saipan in the Pacific. The Levi's Code is still regarded as one of the best of the unilaterally adopted codes. Those companies that followed tended to try to avoid over-explicit commitments, and many subsequent company codes were so general as to be almost useless as instruments that would uphold or advance workers' rights. This has been borne out in research which indicates that only a handful of the codes in existence contain mechanisms for implementation. Still fewer are the subject of ongoing monitoring by the company responsible. Independent verification is almost unknown. Yet monitoring and verification are vital for code compliance. A 1997 study of garment-manufacturing plants in San Francisco found that compliance with local labour legislation including wage and overtime laws was 20 per cent higher when the plants were monitored by the retailers that bought their goods.

Such has been the scale of exploitation in sectors such as garments in every part of the world that corporations have continually been the subject of campaigns of embarrassment. In the United States, the Department of Labour launched an anti-sweatshop campaign aimed at cleaning up the estimated 28 000 production units in the domestic fashion industry. In 1995, the Department created a Trendsetter List of companies that had established a process for monitoring labour conditions in their various contractors. Companies could apply to be placed on the list but could be removed if found not to be implementing their codes. To date only one removal from the list has been effected. The jeans' company Guess? was kicked off the list following the discovery of numerous labour violations at its supplier plants in California.

Under continuous pressure such as this, a number of corporations have responded by changing their practices and modifying their codes, leading to some improvement in content and implementation. The US retailer, GAP, was one such. Publicly charged with taking supplies from an El Salvador-based contractor engaged in abusive labour practices, including the use of child labour and unsafe working conditions, GAP initially indicated it would cancel the contract and cease sourcing in El Salvador. The campaign rapidly changed course, demanding that rather than cut and run GAP remain in El Salvador and force its contractor to comply with its code. Following a US-wide pre-Christmas campaign GAP agreed to do just that and also indicated that it would permit and partially fund an independent verification of its code in El Salvador – the first company to make such a concession.

However, in spite of modifications, most codes of conduct still fall well short of the requirements of the core Conventions of the ILO, and virtually none commit the companies concerned to insisting on the payment of a living wage for all workers which would eliminate many of the abuses so prevalent today. As far as workers are concerned, corporate codes of conduct are probably only, at best, a handle that can be used by themselves and by their trade unions to help enforce their rights. A code would probably not have prevented Carmen Rosario's arm being broken but, properly applied, it could help secure trade union recognition at her factory. It bears repeating that, on their own and without proper implementation, codes are likely to be largely ineffective, but can be extremely useful when combined with trade-related and corporate pressure.

Effective and Equitable Codes

A number of elements are required to make a code work equitably and effectively:

- The content of the code and the process by which it is determined and implemented must involve and empower the workers covered by it.
- The code must reflect the local needs of workers and as an absolute minimum guarantee the core standards of the ILO and provide for the payment of a living wage.
- The company adopting the code must be genuinely committed to its full implementation and provide the resources, training, monitoring and reporting mechanisms to make it work.

- The company's behaviour towards its employees and those of its suppliers, subcontractors and so on must be transparent and adherence to the code be subject to independent verification by qualified and certified assessors.

Codes which unilaterally impose conditions and stifle worker participation and negotiation are counter-productive and harmful. So, too, are those which are vague or ignore international standards, those adopted purely for public relations purposes and those closed to independent verification.

In reality, such codes can only be truly effective if they include the key elements of ILO Conventions and, in particular, the Right to Organize and to Bargain Collectively (No. 98) and if they are fully implemented by the company concerned, are rigorously monitored internally and include a mechanism for the independent verification of their application and effectiveness. The ILO Conventions concerned are Nos. 29 and 105 prohibiting the use of forced, including bonded or prison labour; No. 111 forbidding discrimination; No. 138 relating to the minimum age for employment and Nos. 87 and 98, which provide for freedom of association and the right to collective bargaining. Here, it is not just sufficient for companies to say that they will not inhibit trade union organization. Instead, there should be a requirement to recognize legitimate trade union organizations in an enterprise and to bargain with them in regard to wages and working conditions. In addition, workers' representatives in plants should not be the subject of discrimination and should have access to all workplaces necessary to enable them to carry out their representation functions in accordance with ILO Convention No. 135.

In addition to including the areas covered by the core Conventions of the ILO mentioned above, codes should provide for the payment of a living wage, restrict working hours in line with international standards, provide for a safe and healthy working environment and ensure that workers have an established employment relationship and that company obligations under labour or social security laws are not avoided through labour-only contracting arrangements or other temporary contract forms.

Codes of conduct are not of very much use in authoritarian countries such as China or Burma. In both countries independent workers' organizations are forbidden. This makes it nearly impossible to secure the rights afforded by the UN Declaration on Human Rights and by the core Conventions of the ILO. Companies doing business in such situations need to insist that their suppliers facilitate parallel means of workers' organization along the lines of the Sullivan Principles for South Africa under the apartheid system. The employer would not establish such mechanisms but would provide the workforce with the opportunity to do so in the form of elected consultative committees on productivity, health and safety and other relevant issues. The Sullivan Principles were created in the 1970s to justify the continued presence in South Africa of American firms, and to guide their behaviour within a regime which mandated, even required, the exploitation of workers. The statement of principles for US corporations operating in South Africa, drawn up in 1977 by the Reverend Leon H. Sullivan, a Director of General Motors, are regarded by some as a good model for corporate codes of conduct in restrictive and repressive situations. The final version of the Principles is notable for the range of duties placed on companies operating in South Africa and the forceful language in which these were expressed. A positive obligation was placed on companies requiring them to 'secure rights of black workers to freedom of association and assure protection against victimization, while pursuing and after it attaining these rights'. They also called for a substantial role for companies in supporting legal change.

Corporations really wanting to ensure universal respect for workers' rights need to adopt country guidelines alongside their code of conduct spelling out how they and their suppliers must conduct themselves in order to avoid supporting government repression. One company which has done just that is Levi Strauss. As a result, they discontinued sourcing in Burma and China, though they have since re-established operations in the latter, claiming improvements in human rights there.

IMPLEMENTATION

In the early stages of code development discussion centred almost entirely on code content. Today, however, attention is focused on the implementation of codes, how they should be monitored and what systems of independent verification are needed to give them legitimacy. The role of trade unions and NGOs in these processes is also the subject of lively debate. Trade unions believe it is vitally important that a uniform approach to code content and implementation be adopted, that adherents to a code regularly conduct internal monitoring of its operation and that there is always a viable and independent external system of verification.

Responsibility for implementation should lie with management, in the same way as responsibility for financial control, productivity and quality maintenance. A clearly defined management policy is needed, with commitment from the top and instructions to all staff to implement it. Assessments of individual staff performance should include response to implementation of the code. All adherents to a code need to have a system of formal internal monitoring with regular examination of the application of the code. Such monitoring should be carried out by staff, specifically designated for that purpose, working in much the same way as internal financial auditors or quality-control specialists. Those responsible for breaches of the code should be subject to disciplinary action.

Effective application and monitoring of a code require that all involved know its content and understand its implications. Copies, in the local language, must be prominently posted throughout the workplace. Additionally, every worker should be provided with a copy and given a verbal explanation of its contents. To ensure that the intent of the code is fully understood will require training of all personnel and the involvement of trade union representatives at unit, plant and company level. The internal monitoring system should cover all products manufactured, supplied or distributed by the company concerned.

The monitoring methods should be transparent, documented and effectively communicated to management, workforce and shareholders. Detailed descriptions of monitoring methods, including spot-checks, interview and sampling techniques and progress reports should be made available to all. Once the monitoring system is in place, results should be disclosed to key stakeholders in a way that allows performance to be measured. The monitoring system should provide feedback into management decisions to ensure a process of continuous improvement.

Any corporate code of conduct should be beneficial to both the company and those it employs. Stringent application of the code should help to eradicate exploitation and this in turn should benefit the company through improved performance, productivity, quality and image. But, to deliver such benefits, a code must be credible, both to those employed and to outside observers. Indeed, that credibility is all important. Without it, the code is probably not worth the paper it is written on.

Independent Monitoring

Self-assessment, no matter how well applied, will not deliver credibility. And while self-assessment is central, indeed, vital to code application, only independent verification will confer legitimacy and credibility. In reality, companies cannot police and judge themselves when they themselves are the potential offenders. So who should provide independent verification and how?

Not Trade Unions

Trade unions should not provide such verification, unless the code is the subject of a collective agreement between the union or unions concerned and the company! Trade unions are not in business to carry out management functions. The task of a union is to monitor every workplace where it has members in the interests of those members, and not in the interests of ensuring a company complies with its management guidelines. Nor is it the role of a trade union in one country to come in and decide the fate of workers in another. Where a code is the subject of a collective agreement, any trade union verification must be carried out in close collaboration with all workers concerned and with their unions. But, while unions should not themselves carry out the monitoring function, they should be actively involved in the independent verification process, and consulted by the verification agents before, during and after the verification exercise.

Not NGOs!

Workplace practices are complex affairs. Few NGOs have the capacity to conduct an effective assessment of the often complicated supplier relationships established by multinational merchandisers and retailers and to verify whether each of the elements of a code is being implemented throughout that relationship. Witness the Goodworks debacle at Nike. A high-profile visit by the Reverend Andrew Young to plants producing Nike sports shoes in Vietnam, Indonesia and China resulted in his declaring the production units to be modern, well-run and with generally acceptable working conditions, in spite of a huge amount of public evidence to the contrary. This clearly showed that a few hours' visit to a plant by outsiders, however well intentioned, cannot deliver a professional assessment of whether or not the terms of a code are being implemented.

Some unaccountable groups would no doubt welcome the opportunity to try to supplant existing workplace representation. Indeed, this has already occurred with the NGOs concerned becoming involved in conflict with newly established trade union structures and, in effect, becoming little more than paid consultants to the company. This has worsened, not improved, industrial relations. In general, NGOs should remain *ad hoc* watchdogs campaigning to right abuses.

Not Academics!

Witness the hash Dartmouth College made of their Nike study. Academics can provide a good overview and can analyse verification findings but they are ill-placed to conduct the verification exercises, not having the necessary in-plant experience or skills.

Here, the certainty ends. This is a relatively new field and thinking on the verification process is developing all the time. What is clear is that most corporate codes will primarily be the property of industrialized world multinationals, merchandisers and retailers. The verification process must be such that it meets the needs of both the company with half a dozen production points in different countries and an US retailer like Nordstrom which sources from 13 000 different suppliers, each with on average five subcontractors – a total of 78 000 production points.

Views differ, even within trade unions, on how this can best be done. However, many now believe that responsibility for workplace conditions rests with the employer directly concerned. Those sourcing from that employer should ensure that this responsibility is respected. With that in mind the most effective means of ensuring code compliance would be to make it a contractual obligation on suppliers to provide evidence that they are adhering to the code. In short, suppliers would have to provide a certificate of code compliance in much the same way that they often have to provide a banker's certificate confirming their financial ability to fulfil the contract.

That certification should be carried out by professionals working to clearly defined independent verification standards and trained in skills incorporating factory inspection, accountancy, health and safety, as well as detection. A detailed knowledge of national labour legislation and international labour standards as well as a good understanding of the complexities of each workplace would also be essential. The ILO is well-placed to develop and conduct some of the necessary initial specialist training required by such practitioners. In an ideal world, the ILO would be in a position to establish procedures for the determination of core competences for labour auditors or assessors, and a uniform process for their accreditation at national and international levels. It should also develop and maintain a register of accredited auditors or assessors of the application of approved codes. Finally, it should work towards the establishment of a standardized code applicable to every enterprise and every sector, regardless of location, pending the strengthening of its own instruments and their being made mandatory. Unfortunately, we do not live in an ideal world and it may some time before the tripartite structure of the ILO is sufficiently in tune to meet the challenges posed by globalization.

Working to closely defined standards and rules, practitioners would cease to be recognized if their work was inadequate or if they were corrupted. Thus, their ability to continue to work credibly would be dependent on their carrying out high quality verifications. The verification system would cover all operations of the company concerned, its contractors and subcontractors, and including homeworkers. Those carrying out the verification would have to have access to all parts of the production chain and to all company records. The verification process would include discussion with management, trade unions and workforce, examination of company data and observation of the plant. This would be preceded by a familiarization exercise involving discussion of local issues with trade unions, NGOs, community groups and so on. That discussion would be renewed at the conclusion of the verification exercise.

As with monitoring, the verification process should be transparent, documented and effectively communicated. Verification methods, including spot-checks, interview and sampling techniques and progress reports should be made public in a way that does not breach the legitimate need for commercial confidentiality in some cases. A certificate confirming compliance with the code in question should be issued at the end of a successful verification exercise.

Any certificate granted would be for a limited period and subject to withdrawal for breaches of the code or as the result of upheld complaints. Accordingly, the verification process would need to incorporate an appeals and complaints procedure, providing a confidential means for workers, their unions and other interested parties to oppose certification or to lodge complaints against the company concerned. Arrangements for local access to these procedures enabling confidential representations would need to be set in place.

The whole purpose of corporate codes of conduct is to improve performance. Accordingly, a systematic approach to righting faults would need to be part of the verification process. Verification might be carried out by specialist social auditing firms, by accounting firms which have established special units for the purpose and (in spite of reservations expressed earlier) perhaps also by trade unions and NGOs which again have established specialist units. However, such units should operate separately from the general trade union or NGO activity and work entirely on code verification.

Probably the best way of promoting effective independent verification is to create a certification agency or foundation with the active participation of business, labour and human rights' groups which would establish independent monitoring standards and accredit suitably qualified certification firms or units. The agency would oversee the performance and review the activities of such firms or agents on a regular basis. It would also coordinate the appeal and complaints' procedures.

Though many now believe that it is not for trade unions or NGOs to carry out the verification process, there is a major role for both to play in that process. They should be actively involved in briefing the verifiers, in monitoring their work and in raising complaints which have not been resolved through normal industrial relations' practice. Both also have a major role to play in communicating code content and implications to workers and developing awareness of how a code can be used to affect change.

Trade unions and NGOs should also be actively involved in assisting and encouraging companies to make the adjustments needed to secure certification. And, where certification is refused, both should highlight how the company's failure to meet its social obligations is affecting its commercial viability.

RECENT INITIATIVES

A number of initiatives have been undertaken to try to meet these requirements. One that has progressed furthest is an effort by the New York-based Council on Economic Priorities to create an international factory accreditation apparatus similar to the ISO9000 and ISO14000 operated by the International Standards Organization. An accreditation agency has been established and a set of standards, known as SA8000, has been developed. These draw heavily on the core conventions of the ILO and include the right to organize and to bargain collectively. SA8000 also outlaws forced labour, child labour and discrimination. It provides for the payment of a living wage and sets out stringent health and safety criteria. In addition, it outlines the remedial measures to be taken when child labour is discovered, to avoid the situation where such children are simply dumped on the streets, leaving them even worse off.

SA8000 may be adopted by manufacturers, merchandisers or retailers and is equally applicable in each case. Typically, a retailer or merchandiser would adopt the standard and then make it a contractual obligation on all suppliers to abide by it. Confirmation of this would be provided in certificate form, issued following a stringent verification process by agents accredited for that purpose. Thus, in time every supplier would be the subject of regular inspections to ensure their continued adherence to the standard. Though professional auditing companies which already do work under the ISO system are likely to be the main certification agents, other organizations, including unions and NGOs, could also be agents provided they establish specialist teams for that purpose.

The SA8000 approach has a number of advantages. Audits would be standardized and would measure all factories against the same standard.

Consumers would have a fairly good guarantee that goods made in certified factories meet a clearly defined public standard. Supplier companies would only have to deal with a single standard, unlike the plethora of codes they must now follow or pretend to follow. The cosmetics group Avon has become the first multinational to adopt SA8000 and seek its application in their own plants and in those of their suppliers. Some 20 other companies are now following the Avon example.

SA8000 follows on from a number of other initiatives aimed at getting away from the multilateral approach by individual companies. The earliest such code was one negotiated by FIFA, the International Federation of Football Associations, the International Confederation of Free Trade Unions, the International Textile Garment and Leather Workers Federation (ITGLWF) and FIET, the commercial workers' international federation. The impetus for this arose from revelations of widespread use of child labour in the manufacture of footballs in Pakistan. The code which was negotiated concentrated on the core Conventions of the ILO and later gave rise to the publication of a model code by the international Trade Union Movement. This model has been considerably influential and forms the basis of a Clean Clothes Campaign code now widely adopted in Europe as well as providing the core elements of SA8000. The base code adopted by the UK-based Ethical Trading Initiative also relies heavily on the terms of the International Trade Union Movement's model code.

Before the code negotiated with FIFA, less comprehensive agreements had been developed in some commercial and industrial contexts. Initially, most of these concentrated on the non-use of child labour in the production of goods and provision of services. FIET negotiated such a code with Euro-Commerce and the European Regional Organization of the ITGLWF with the European Footwear Employers. A later agreement between Eurotex, the European Textile and Garment Employers and the ITGLWF's European Region was more comprehensive, covering issues such as the right to organize and to bargain collectively. None of these agreements provided for a detailed monitoring and verification process, though outline proposals were developed and are subject to ongoing discussion and negotiation.

With the new emphasis on the implementation of codes, monitoring or verification processes are either now in operation or under consideration in a number of fora. Some coordination of all these efforts is going to be needed to ensure a common approach which will not lead to undue confusion on the part of producers. A small manufacturer in Bangladesh, supplying six different retailers, having six different codes of conduct and monitoring and verification systems, might well be forgiven for trying to cut corners. However, this would undermine the whole credibility of the corporate code concept; and without creditability this whole process is nothing.

CONCLUSION

It cannot be over-emphasized that corporate codes of conduct do not automatically lead to improvements in working conditions, nor are they a permanent solution to worker exploitation. Only workers themselves through trade union organization can, in the medium and longer term, protect their own interests. Wrongly used, the implementation, monitoring and verification of codes could become a permanent obstacle to worker organization and a permanent hindrance to any real improvement in working conditions.

The next few years will show whether or not the corporate world is serious about eliminating abuses of workers rights and paying a living wage to all those involved in the manufacturing and distribution process. And it must show that it is serious, because if conditions such as those in parts of India are allowed to continue, the corporate world will suffer serious damage to its public image. In india, slavery in different export sectors such as carpet weaving begins from the age of four, and children are bought and sold like cattle. One ten year old was hung upside down from the ceiling when he was too ill to work. Another, wanting time off to go to a family funeral, had paraffin poured over him and was set alight. Many of these children are speechless from their trauma.

It is inhuman abuse such as this that is forcing change. Change is now inevitable! If the corporate sector fails to respond voluntarily, governments will be forced to act. And even if companies generally embrace codes of conduct and insist that they be observed, governments are also likely to become much more involved as the most repressive regimes cry 'foul' and attempt to classify such action as non-tariff barriers to trade.

The day this issue is raised at the World Trade Organization will be the day that the worth of corporate codes of conduct is proved, as it is likely to be the beginning of the process that will highlight the link between trade and worker rights. Any examination of this issue will indicate how globalization has worsened production conditions. And having created the problem, why shouldn't globalization be used to right it?

12 The Role of Voluntary Codes of Conduct and Regulation – a Retailer's View

Petrina Fridd and Jessica Sainsbury

During 1997–8, a team at Sainsbury's developed a *Code of Practice for Socially Responsible Trading* (see Appendix, pages 228–34) for the J. Sainsbury group – which incorporates Sainsbury's Supermarkets, Homebase, Savacentre and the wholly owned subsidiary in the US – Shaw's, a chain of supermarkets on the east coast of the USA. The code was developed because Sainsbury's has long recognized a social responsibility to improve employment conditions. Furthermore, we wanted to address concerns about ethical accountability raised by interested parties such as consumers, NGOs and staff. In addition, drawing up a code enabled us to set out the principles by which we want to underpin our trading relationships with our own-label suppliers. These will be strengthened through the code and will enable us to work with those suppliers who share the same values and who are committed to being socially responsible.

As a large retailer, it will be an enormous task to ensure that all our own-label suppliers comply with our code of practice. Nearly half of Sainsbury's lines are own label (approximately 14 000), and these are sourced from five continents, through more than 4000 suppliers (not counting individual farms and factories).

Fortunately, we already try to have long-term partnerships with suppliers. Before starting production, each supplier provides detailed technical specifications for each product, and their product quality and production facilities are then regularly monitored by Sainsbury's technical staff. However, we do recognize that applying the principles of our code to local circumstances will require sensitivity and understanding, and will be a long and on-going process.

The Code of Practice

Our code of practice was drawn up along the lines of the relevant ILO Conventions and Recommendations, and with the advice of various

NGOs, including the Fairtrade Foundation. It was published in March 1998, and has been sent to all our suppliers of own-label products for their information, and to gain their commitment to work towards its principles.

The principles were developed to spell out Sainsbury's understanding of the responsibility it shares with its suppliers for certain social matters. Although they have general application, they have been drafted with particular reference to our trade with suppliers in developing countries. They are not intended to be contractual but to form an expression of the social values shared by Sainsbury's and its suppliers. However, they will form part of the negotiations with new suppliers, and those who are not committed to them, or are not willing to work towards them, will not be given contracts.

The Principles

The Principles begin with a general statement that we will deal openly and fairly with suppliers, adhere to contract terms and avoid the exercise of undue pressure. The provisions on protection of children take as their standard the ILO Conventions on child employment. This means that child labour (under the age of 15) will only be accepted where national laws or regulations permit the employment or work of persons aged 13–15 on light work, so long as it is proven that it is not likely to be harmful to their health or development and not such as to prejudice their attendance at school.

Although other companies have adopted a policy of 'no children' in their codes of conduct, we did not want to create a similar effect to the 'Harkin Bill'. This proposal, sponsored by US Senator Tom Harkin in 1993, for a Child Labour Deterrence Bill had an incredible effect on child labourers in Bangladesh, although it was not even law. Employers dismissed children to avoid trade penalties which they imagined would be forthcoming with the bill. Many of these children ended up being even more poorly paid in unregulated informal industries. Where we identify children working in suppliers' factories or plantations, we do not want to cease trading with them instantly, or force them to discharge their child employees immediately. Instead we want to work with suppliers to ensure that if children aged 13–15 are employed, they receive a full education, their health and safety is not jeopardized, and they are provided with proper training that will be useful to them when they finish school. Of course, in a few years' time, we hope that suppliers will not need to employ children at all.

The provisions on health and safety reflect a clear awareness of obvious hazards and a general regard for the well-being of employees. The code of practice applies to factories, farms and plantations as well as accommodation, and covers all aspects including sanitation, fire, electrical, mechanical and structural safety. The principles encourage the development of equal opportunities in employment, while recognizing the need to be sensitive to cultural differences.

Employees are expected to be free to join lawful associations, and forced labour or coercion at work is regarded as unacceptable. Where unions are banned by law, we would expect suppliers to have an alternative workers' organization which liaises with their employers. Pay should not be lower than that required by local law, or in the absence of law that paid generally within the industry. It will also have regard to what is needed to maintain family life above subsistence level.

Monitoring and Compliance

The issues of monitoring, enforcement and independent verification are also addressed in the code. With the Fairtrade Foundation, we devised a social evaluation questionnaire that could be used by technologists during their quality audits. We tested this in the field through a number of pilot studies covering areas as diverse as tea in India, power tools in China and canned fruit in South Africa. As a result of these studies, we modified the questionnaire to include all the main points of our code of practice, and also hints on what to look for and what to ask when evaluating compliance against each principle (as well as acceptable norms for that industry and country).

Sainsbury's own technologists, having been trained in social awareness, will conduct a basic evaluation as part of their regular quality audit. They will make monitoring against socially responsible principles part of normal/routine inspections. If they discover breaches of our code, or if we are aware of concerns raised by local NGOs or trade unions, it is anticipated that an independent third-party auditing team would then carry out a full social audit. It is likely that these teams would include a commercial auditor, NGO experts, health-and-safety experts, and officials from trade unions/worker associations, as appropriate, from the region.

Initially suppliers will be expected to work with Sainsbury's representatives towards making improvements over an agreed period of time. This will be done in a spirit of partnership, but Sainsbury's would not expect to continue doing long-term business with companies that are unwilling to work towards such improvements – this provides the ultimate sanction, and it is set out in the code.

Collaboration and Partnership

Outside of Sainsbury's, there have been plenty of other initiatives recently about socially responsible trading, with many retailers drawing up their own codes. There is now a growing momentum, along with challenges from consumers and NGOs, and a general willingness by retailers to address these concerns, and wherever possible, work together.

Over the last few years, there have been several collaborative initiatives, including those of the Ethical Trading Initiative (ETI) and the Council of Economic Priorities (CEP). Sainsbury's has been actively involved in both. In collaboration with the Department for International Development, 20 of the UK's best known companies, including Sainsbury's, together with NGOs, and trade unions started working together through the ETI to develop and encourage the use of a widely endorsed set of standards in codes of conduct. The ETI is also evaluating various monitoring and auditing methods which will enable companies to work together with other organizations outside the corporate sector to improve labour conditions around the world. Through the ETI, Sainsbury's is taking part in a series of pilot audits on wine in South Africa, and horticulture in Zimbabwe, to test some of these auditing methods.

The CEP, a US-based group, has drawn up a global standard for social accountability, SA8000. This common standard sets out specific, auditable provisions regarding child labour, forced labour, health and safety, compensation and working hours, together with the management systems needed to deliver them. Sainsbury's is a member of this organization and sits on the advisory board. Through the ETI, Sainsbury's is examining this standard along with other possibilities as a way forward to promote socially responsible trading.

A Common Code?

Although many retailers have drawn up comparable codes, based on the same ILO Conventions, a common code could present an alternative method of 'levelling the playing field'. A single code would ensure that we all request our suppliers (whom we quite often share) to work towards one set of guidelines and standards, equivalent to ISO 9000 standards in the quality sector.

A common code could offer several benefits: suppliers would not have to cope with complying to a myriad of different codes, nor would they have to receive multiple monitoring visits from each retailer. Such a code would obviously also benefit the retailers, by sharing the costs and reducing the duplication of independent monitoring. However, since many company codes cover comparable principles, a collaborative process such as the ETI could reap some of the benefits of a common code (such as shared monitoring), without actually setting one up. This would also preserve individual companies' flexibility with dealing with suppliers' non-compliance.

Another alternative way forward could be through voluntary industry codes. These could be established in countries where there are many suppliers within one industry. The benefits of these are that they would enable suppliers' to be in control of the process of working towards socially responsible trading. They could also save retailers and consumers money, because as long as industry codes are independently monitored and verified, retailers would not have to pay for their own monitoring and verification. Industry codes are already being developed. For example, certain tea producers are in the process of creating their own tea code, and a common code is being developed within the Kenyan flower industry. Ultimately these may be able to create universal industry standards, acceptable to all stakeholders.

Is Formal Regulation Needed?

Voluntary company codes are only one way of improving labour standards around the world. Since supplying companies are all situated in countries with their own employment legislation, government regulation can and should play a critical role in supporting socially responsible trading. However, this role is dependent on their laws being relevant, up-to-date and enforced by adequately funded and staffed government agencies.

At this stage, there would be a problem in relying solely on government legislation to promote socially responsible trading, since in many countries, employment and factory laws are ineffectively implemented and enforced. However, governments do have the prime responsibility of protecting and improving the employment conditions of their citizens. To further these, governments need to provide a legislative environment which obliges companies to operate in a socially responsible way. They also need to ensure that the complete body of their legislation promotes socially responsible trading. In some cases, national employment laws are undermined by inconsistencies created by special laws established for free trade zones, which for example may ban the establishment of trade unions.

If voluntary codes of conduct do not succeed in promoting socially responsible trading, there should be government regulation, but only as a last resort. Regulation could be used to oblige importing companies to operate according to certain standards. However, at this stage, such regulation would probably be counter-productive, since all companies are still learning how to promote socially responsible trading. As there is still not a great deal of experience of monitoring and verifying codes of conduct, it would be more useful to enable companies to experiment (through forums such as the ETI) on how to implement and monitor their codes effectively and sustainably, especially since these forums enable companies to benefit from the experience and partnerships of others – NGOs, trade unions and the government, as well as each other – in order to develop 'best practice'. If companies were forced to trade according to certain standards, the benefits of this partnership would be lost and firms would have to develop systems for ensuring their compliance with government regulations on their own.

A further problem of using government regulation rather than voluntary codes of conduct to promote socially responsible trading is that government regulation may be more difficult to devise than securing the cooperation and partnerships needed to implement and monitor voluntary codes of conduct in the first place. This is because decisions would have to be based on agreement on which standards to use as the basis for the legislation, how it would be enforced across a range of countries, and whether it should be established at national, EU or international level.

However, if in the future companies were not willing to work together, or if other importing companies were willing to free-ride the process and jeopardize the validity of voluntary codes of conduct, formal regulation could present an option to oblige companies to act. But this would be at the cost of learning about best practice through non-competitive partnership, and the involvement of NGOs and trade unions.

The Costs of Socially Responsible Trading

Part of the concern firms have about complying with and implementing socially responsible trading, either through voluntary codes or through regulation, is its associated cost. However, compliance does not always have to cost more. A common code or industry code will save on monitoring costs, and there are examples where 'good practice' improves working conditions whilst maintaining or even decreasing costs; some methods of addressing environmental concerns have done just this. Over a number of years, Sainsbury's has been working with produce suppliers on Integrated Crop Management Systems (ICMS) to reduce pesticide use. It is now obligatory for Sainsbury's produce suppliers to implement ICMS, and it is part of their contract's terms of reference. ICMS is about the responsible use of pesticides and promotes the use of biological and natural methods for the selective control of pests and diseases. Pesticide use is minimized through forecasting and other monitoring techniques; by using crop rotation with disease and pest-resistant varieties, and by training staff. Pesticides are used only when necessary and are targeted against specific pests or diseases, with localized treatments where possible. It was found that although initially ICMS did result in a considerable increase in management time, it was worth while, as the reduction in pesticide use produced both cost savings and environmental benefits.

These kinds of benefits might also be seen from an improvement in health and safety conditions. For example, a reduction in environmental dust within a factory would improve the health of workers and the quality of the product, as well as probably increasing profit margins. Benefits like these could result in increased investment in the North and South, in the form of training, such as in the use of pesticides and quality systems, or an increased awareness of new technologies (technology transfer) for health and safety, for example to improve ventilation.

The costs of improvement will need to be examined in each case, but in general they will have to be shared between retailers, suppliers and consumers – the balance will vary depending on the sector and country. It is important for suppliers to know that what is perceived as good by the consumer provides competitive advantage.

Conclusion

Socially responsible trading will be best achieved through the combined efforts of governments, companies, NGOs and trade unions. It is not enough to rely on either voluntary codes or government regulation in isolation. A combined approach, which acknowledges the need for experimentation and learning, will be most useful at this stage.

National governments do have the responsibility of providing a legislative environment which protects and enhances working conditions and living standards for both domestic and export producers in their country. However, government regulation cannot be a solution in itself unless it provides realistic goals, covers loopholes and is effectively implemented. Most countries where we source our own-label products do have detailed labour and factory laws, which if enforced, would make our code of practice almost redundant. Socially responsible trading needs governments to enforce their laws and regulations to create an environment where codes of practice are not necessary. But until they do, and as an additional check,

Regulating International Business

independently monitored and verified voluntary codes of conduct are needed to provide the guarantee that labour and factory standards comply with internationally acceptable standards.

Voluntary codes of conduct, established by companies in collaboration and partnership with governments, trade unions and NGOs (such as the ETI) do offer a way of promoting socially responsible trading. Voluntary codes, so long as they are based on common internationally recognized standards, enable companies, together with NGOs and trade unions, to develop effective and sustainable methods for independent monitoring and verification. In addition, voluntary codes permit a degree of flexibility in dealing with non-compliance of suppliers, which government regulation may not. This flexibility enables companies to work with suppliers to improve conditions, rather than dropping them if breaches are discovered. This flexibility, so long as it is not abused, will help safeguard and improve jobs in the long term, rather than jeopardize them.

At this stage, whilst companies are still cooperating and learning how best to implement their codes of conduct, there is no need for government regulation. However, should these collaborative processes fail, as a last resort, governments may need to provide legislation to oblige importing companies to operate by government standards. But the establishment of legislation would not be an easy process, and would take time. At this stage, governments will be more effective if they concentrate on encouraging and establishing experimental forums such as the ETI. This kind of partnership approach enables companies to work towards socially responsible trading in a cooperative and not a competitive way, and also enables NGOs and trade unions to be part of the process of developing acceptable codes and monitoring and verification methods, a role they might not be able to play if companies were individually obliged to comply with government-devised standards.

APPENDIX: CODE OF PRACTICE FOR SOCIALLY
RESPONSIBLE TRADING

**Principles for Socially Responsible Trading for the Purchase of
Own Label and Solus Products**

Introduction from the Chief Executives

Sainsbury's Supermarkets and Homebase are international businesses.
Whilst our stores operate in the United Kingdom, our buyers search the
world to find new sources of supply to satisfy the needs of our customers.
About half of our goods are sold under our own brand names for which we
lay down detailed technical specifications and monitor product quality and
production facilities. We aim to build long term partnerships with suppliers by offering commercial and technical help in a variety of ways.

As we broaden our supplier base, especially towards suppliers in developing countries, we have become more conscious of the need to take some
share of responsibility for social development and for the welfare of
employees who produce the goods we sell.

Together with a number of non-governmental organizations and other
organizations interested in international development, we have helped to
establish the Ethical Trading Initiative to promote directly the links
between commercial involvement and social progress.

At the same time we decided to set out clearly certain Principles which
underpin our trading relationships. In building partnerships with suppliers,
we shall seek to work with companies who share our values and who are
prepared to commit themselves to these Principles.

Applying these Principles to local circumstances will take time and will
require sensitivity and understanding. Our desire is to see the Principles
adopted as the normal way of working and not as an alternative option. We
shall also work for continuous improvement and review in the light of our
experience.

The Principles are accompanied by a Code of Practice which includes a
declaration of our intention to do business on fair terms, without exercis-
ing undue pressure, and describes the monitoring process that will be
undertaken to ensure that the Principles are being applied in practice.

We believe that by adopting and communicating these Principles we will take a practical step towards improving social conditions in the developing world.

Dino Adriano	David Bremner
Chief Executive	Chief Executive
UK Food Retailing Businesses	Homebase and US Businesses

The Principles

These Principles have been developed by Sainsbury's Supermarkets and Homebase to set out clearly our understanding of the responsibility we share with suppliers for certain social matters. Whilst they have general application the Principles have been drafted with particular reference to our trade with companies in developing countries. Supported by the Code of Practice, they are an expression of the social values we share with our partner companies and provide a basis for our trading relationship.

Fair Trading

In the conduct of its business Sainsbury's Supermarkets and Homebase will deal openly and fairly with suppliers, adhere to contract terms and avoid the exercise of undue pressure.

Protection of Children

Children may only be employed in circumstances which fully safeguard them from potential exploitation, which protect them from moral or physical hazard and long term damage to health and which do not disrupt their education.

Health and Safety

Policies and procedures for health and safety will be established which are appropriate to the industry. In the absence of legal requirements these will reflect a clear awareness of obvious hazards and a general regard for the well-being of employees. Such policies and procedures will apply also to any living accommodation provided in association with employment.

Equal Opportunities

Whilst being sensitive to cultural differences we expect the development of equal opportunities in employment without discrimination on race, religion and gender or other arbitrary basis.

Freedom of Association

Employees shall be free to join lawful associations; forced labour or coercion at work is unacceptable.

Remuneration

Pay will not be lower than that required by local law or, in the absence of law, that paid generally within the industry. It will also have regard to what is needed to maintain family life above subsistence level.

Code of Practice

Application and Monitoring

This Code of Practice sets out how the Principles, which of necessity are described in general terms, are to be applied in the ordinary course of business by Sainsbury's Supermarkets, Homebase and their suppliers.

Sainsbury's representatives will be looking to work positively with suppliers towards a general compliance with the Principles as amplified by the Code of Practice. Monitoring of performance will be incorporated into the normal monitoring and inspection process carried out by the staff of Sainsbury's Supermarkets and Homebase and their representatives. Availability of records and full access to premises and staff will be important in demonstrating compliance. Suppliers who employ agents or subcontractors will be expected to take responsibility for these aspects of performance as they do for any other aspect of contract compliance.

Specific lapses in performance will be taken up as part of the normal control arrangements. Where it becomes apparent that the Principles and Code of Practice are not being achieved in substance, suppliers will be expected to work with Sainsbury's representatives to achieve an agreed standard. This will be done in a spirit of partnership but Sainsbury's would not expect to continue doing business with companies that are unwilling to work towards such improvements.

Fair Trading

Clear terms and conditions will be agreed at the commencement of each contract. These will include product specification and payment terms.

Suppliers will have to respond to the highly competitive environments in which Sainsbury's and Homebase trade. Sainsbury's and Homebase will not make undue use of their size to bring unfair pressure on suppliers.

The importance of complying with product safety standards must be understood.

Protection of Children

Special care is needed in the employment of children. Where children are employed due consideration must be given to their age, the hours worked, rates of pay, safety and impact on education. The ILO Conventions on child employment should be the standard.

Establishing a child's age may be difficult where there is no legal system of verification; the employer has a responsibility to make proper enquiry into the child's age and to maintain a record.

Where children are employed the employer must comply with all applicable child labour law including those relating to schooling, hiring, wages, hours worked, overtime and working conditions.

It is expected that the employer will encourage eligible younger workers to attend classes or participate in work study or other government sponsored educational programmes.

Where it is traditional for whole families to work the nature of the work undertaken by children must be clearly understood and appropriate to their age.

Children should not be allowed to work at night.

Health & Safety & Working Conditions

General   Employers are expected to provide a safe working place and ensure that the local laws relating to health and safety in the workplace are adhered to. If living accommodation and facilities are provided health and safety requirements apply equally to these. Furthermore, employee representatives should be involved in the development of standards appropriate to the workplace.

Factories, Farms and Plantations   These must comply with all relevant national laws relating to working conditions including health and safety, sanitation, fire safety and electrical, mechanical and structural safety.

There must be sufficient ventilation and light. This could include windows, fans, air conditioners or heaters, as appropriate, in order to provide adequate ventilation, circulation and temperate control to all areas.

Machinery should be well maintained, inspected and equipped with operational safety devices.

Employees should be trained in the use of personal safety equipment; essential equipment should be available free of charge.

Fire safety: attention should be given to the following:-

- Fitting fire alarms to each floor with emergency lighting above exits and stairways.
- Accessibility of aisles and clearly marked emergency exits which should be unlocked during working hours and free from debris.
- Ready availability of fire extinguishers and other appropriate fire fighting equipment which should be easily accessible and regularly maintained.
- Evidence that evacuation drills are conducted.
- Hazardous and combustible materials must be stored securely, in well ventilated areas and disposed of in a safe and legal manner.

Health   Employees should have reasonable access to potable water throughout the day.

Every factory floor should be provided with one well-stocked first aid kit. Procedures to deal with serious injuries requiring medical attention must be in place.

Sufficient clean and sanitary toilet areas, with no unreasonable restrictions on their use, must be in place.

Accommodation (if applicable) Accommodation or dormitory facilities provided for staff must be kept clean and safe, maintained in a good condition and meet all relevant health and safety regulations and the local industry standard.

- There should be sufficient space for sleeping and toilets to allow segregation by gender or family group.
- Potable water should be provided or facilities to boil water should be accessible.
- Mats and beds and personal storage areas for clothing and personal possessions should be available for each employee.
- Facilities must have adequate lighting, be well ventilated and, as appropriate, have windows to the outside, air conditioners and/or heaters in all sleeping areas to provide adequate circulation, ventilation and temperature control; there will be proper fire precautions.
- Dormitory residents must have freedom of movement during their off-work hours (subject to limitations imposed for their safety and comfort).

Equal Opportunities   In applying the general principle full account must be taken of cultural and other factors in the country concerned.

- People with similar skills should receive equal treatment.
- There should be no discrimination in relation to access to jobs or training.

Freedom of Association

Employees must be free within the law to join unions or associations of their choosing without fear of intimidation or discrimination.

Employers should not use any forced labour.

Employers shall not engage in or permit physical acts to punish or coerce employees, neither will the employer allow psychological coercion or any other form of non-physical abuse.

Remuneration

Hours of Work and Wages   Working hours, wages, overtime pay and holiday entitlements should be set in compliance with all applicable laws pertaining, not only to the country, but also to each industry sector.

- Normal working hours should not exceed those recommended by International Labour Organization standards (a maximum of 48 hours per week with up to 12 hours of occasional overtime).
- Wages should be paid promptly in cash, cheque or direct to the worker's bank or other mutually agreed method which does not use company tokens.
- The employer should provide employees with an understandable statement of their remuneration and keep records of payment.
- Employers should not avoid their legal obligations to employees through the unjustified use of temporary contracts or insistence on self-employed status.

Overtime   It is accepted that overtime is often required in a variety of industry sectors. Overtime should not be excessive; where it is necessary the rate of pay or incentive rates must meet all legal requirements or higher local industry standard.

Time-Off/Holiday Entitlement   Employees should have on average at least one day off in seven. Employers should provide paid annual leave and holidays as required by law or higher local industry standard.

13 Regulating TNCs: the Role of Voluntary and Governmental Approaches

Ruth Mayne

An increasing proportion of the world's labour force is engaged in activities that are linked to international trade and capital flows (World Bank, 1995). Because labour is the key asset of the poor this means that the livelihoods of many of the world's poorest people are affected by the activities of international firms and investors. Yet international trade and investment can either enhance the employment opportunities, living standards and quality of life of people, or undermine them. In particular, the impact of foreign direct investment, which is the focus of this chapter, depends on many factors including the nature and quality of investment, the control and distribution of production and marketing, and the terms on which countries receive investments, among other things. These factors are in turn conditioned by the institutional and regulatory framework which governs foreign investment and trade.

Grassroots experience from Oxfam and other NGOs suggests that although foreign direct investment can make a positive contribution to increased growth and employment, as for example in the early experience of the East Asian tiger economies, in other cases its impact is negative. In parts of Africa and Latin America, where foreign investment is often capital intensive and/or in extractive industries, it can displace local livelihoods and do substantial environmental and cultural harm without creating adequate new jobs. Additionally, if international firms and investors are allowed to exploit weak regulatory structures, for example in free trade zones, or make extensive use of subcontracting, as a means of undercutting labour standards, the social benefits of foreign investment will be reduced. Foreign investment may also have a negative effect on a country's balance of payments, if the local affiliate is highly dependent on foreign loans and intermediate goods inputs, resulting in large foreign exchange outflows.

Consequently, effective institutional and regulatory frameworks are needed to allow governments to maximize the positive development benefits from foreign investment, and minimize its negative impact. This chapter examines the advantages and limits of voluntary corporate codes as a means of regulating foreign investors and firms, in particular to ensure that they adhere to certain fundamental workers' rights. It makes the case that although voluntary codes can play a valuable role if properly implemented and monitored, they should not be a substitute for binding forms of government and intergovernmental regulation. NGOs, trade unions and others need to improve their understanding of the relationship between voluntary codes and binding government regulation, to ensure that they are mutually enhancing and complementary. While many aspects of labour market regulation should remain at the local and national level, the chapter argues that there is an increasing need for multilaterally agreed inter-governmental regulation of certain minimum or core labour standards. However, it should be emphasized that the unilateral imposition of subjectively chosen standards by more powerful countries on weaker ones is not acceptable.

PROMOTING EMPLOYMENT RIGHTS AND OPPORTUNITIES: THE NEW POLICY PRIORITIES

As the figures below illustrate, the recent phase of accelerated globalization is associated with widespread unemployment and underemployment, growing job insecurity and increasing income inequality. This not only entails high human, social and economic costs, but is also contributing to social instability and growing opposition to the multilateral trading system. The scale of the problem suggests that existing employment policies and regulations are not functioning adequately and that improved measures are needed at the international level.

The Human and Social Imperative

The human and social arguments for protecting and promoting workers' rights are painfully evident. Paid employment is an important source of livelihood not just for workers in industrialized countries but also for the poor in many parts of Latin America, Asia and Africa. It is estimated that by the year 2025, 57 per cent of the population in developing countries will be living in urban areas (de Haan, 1997), many of them dependent on wage labour for their livelihoods.

At the same time unemployment and underemployment are rife, resulting in great economic insecurity and hardship. The 1998 ILO *World Employment Report* estimated, for example, that by the end of 1998, one billion workers – a third of the world's workforce – was either without work or underemployed. Even these figures may be an under-estimate as a considerable number of workers categorized as 'discouraged' are not included in official labour market statistics. Many of them have given up hope of work and are living on the streets or in family networks (ILO, 1998).

While many workers, notably in East Asia, experienced impressive gains in jobs and wages during the 1980s, a significant number in Latin America and Africa suffered an erosion of real wages or growing wage inequality. Increased rates of economic growth in Latin America in the 1990s have not been matched by improved employment opportunities. Workers in many of the transition economies have suffered dramatic and painful declines in employment and incomes in recent years (ILO, 1998). Meanwhile OECD countries have experienced high levels of unemployment, three times the level of the 1950s and 1960s, and wage differentials have widened in many countries (OECD, 1994). More recently even the employment gains in East Asia are being reversed by the economic crisis sparked off in 1997.

In addition, there is evidence of a shift towards more insecure, irregular and non-unionized forms of work in the formal sector of some countries. Whereas paid employment in the formal sector used to guarantee an escape from poverty, a growing number of workers earn poverty wages (ILO, 1995, 1996). In some Latin American countries, for example, more than 40 per cent of wage-earners live below the poverty line (ECLA, 1997).

These irregular forms of paid employment are associated with a growth in free trade zones, the deregulation of labour market by governments, and the spread of 'flexible' forms of work in the formal sector, such as temporary employment and subcontracting. They are also linked to the growth of informal sector employment which has occurred in many countries, where a growing proportion of the so-called 'self-employed' are in fact linked to the formal sector through subcontracting (ILO, 1995).

Flexible working arrangements offer certain advantages. They can help companies maintain competitiveness in the face of intensified global competition and as such help safeguard jobs. They can also offer significant advantages to some workers, for example they may help women balance employment with family responsibilities. However, in practice they are often used by companies as a way of denying 'flexible' workers the rights enjoyed by permanent workers. Unskilled subcontracted workers such as homeworkers are often classed as 'self-employed' or not registered at all, which allows companies to bypass many labour regulations and trade union agreements. As a result these arrangements often entail poverty wages, insecure jobs and poor working conditions.

This proliferation of exploitative working practices has been highlighted by organizations active at the grass roots. The International Confederation of Free Trade Unions (ICFTU), for example, has reported a continuing, and in many countries growing, abuse of workers rights and repressive government action against organized labour; it links this to the effects of neo-liberal policies and pressures from globalization (ICFTU, 1998). Recent campaigns by Oxfam and other NGOs have pointed to examples of manufacturers effectively denying workers the right to form and join trade unions in the free trade zones of countries such as the Dominican Republic. They have also found that certain large retailers or manufacturers in labour-intensive industries, such as clothing, shoes and toys, are making extensive use of subcontracting, often from sweatshop or home-based workers both at home and overseas, as a way of keeping down costs.

Such issues have also been spotlighted by high-profile campaigns targeting Northern-based companies. Notably, Nike has been accused by unions and NGOs of paying workers in Indonesia £1.40 per day, compared to an estimated £2.50 needed to meet subsistence needs. Meanwhile the $20 million per year which Michael Jordan earns to promote Nike trainers has been estimated as enough to raise all of Nike's Indonesian workers out of poverty (International Centre for Trade Union Rights, 1997).

The Commercial and Economic Arguments

Commercial interest reinforces the importance of protecting basic worker rights. As the ILO has pointed out, poor wages and standards may bring short-term competitive gains but in the longer term lead to inefficiency through low staff commitment and morale, poor health, high turnover and low productivity (ILO, 1995). They also leave companies susceptible to consumer campaigns, and evidence from a number of company surveys suggests these can negatively affect brand image and shareholder value. Conversely, good employment practices can be good for business. For example, a recent comprehensive study of 100 German companies in ten industrial sectors showed that companies which place workers at the core of their strategies also produce higher long-term returns to shareholders than their industry peers, outperform their competitors and create more jobs (Bilmes, Wetzker and Xhonneux, 1997). Likewise, a recent study of 42 British manufacturing companies showed a strong positive link between worker satisfaction, productivity and corporate profits (Patterson and West, 1998). Such findings have found new backing in the literature on social capital which emphasises the economic benefits of mutually respectful and trustful relationships at work (Szreter, 1999).

There are also broader economic benefits from higher working standards. Low wages may lead to stagnant demand, and can contribute to a downward spiral of investment and employment in individual countries (World Bank, 1994). Moreover poor standards and insecurity may foster defensive responses by workers to economic restructuring (ILO, 1995). Perhaps most importantly, low labour standards do not generate long-term competitive advantage (OECD, 1996) which ultimately relies on increasing productivity through investment in technology, skills and education. However, further evidence will be needed to convince governments, companies and the international financial institutions of the commercial and economic merits of improving worker protection.

THE ADVANTAGES OF VOLUNTARY CORPORATE CODES OF CONDUCT

NGOs have traditionally sought to improve company behaviour through both statutory and voluntary means. One of the most high-profile cases which embraced both strategies was the campaign against the marketing of breast-milk substitutes in developing countries. This achieved a high profile through a public boycott directed at the Swiss-based transnational food company Nestlé, and the campaign succeeded in obtaining the adoption of a World Health Organization (WHO) and UNICEF code of Marketing of Breast Milk Substitutes at the World Health Assembly in 1981 (Chetley, 1986). The code essentially constitutes a set of good practice requirements aimed primarily at governments and companies. Following its adoption, the campaign focused on getting governments and companies to implement the code, and then on monitoring compliance with it around the world, through a well-organized and financed NGO network (IBFAN, 1997).

The Proliferation of Corporate Codes of Conduct Campaigns

The free-market climate of the 1980s tended to shift the focus of NGO corporate campaigns towards voluntary approaches. This was in part a pragmatic response to both the perceived failure of governments to protect labour rights adequately in the past, and the growing hostility of governments and business to statutory forms of regulation. Because the voluntary approach seeks to inform consumers without encroaching on their freedom of choice, it was seen as more compatible with the free-market thinking of governments and companies, and as such more likely to garner their support.

The shift can also be seen as a response to the growing power of the corporate sector, which had benefited from the liberalization of international trade and investment in the 1980s. Because foreign direct investment was outstripping official aid as a source of external finance for some poorer countries, it also began to acquire a new importance as a potential motor of development. As a result, NGOs began to see companies not just as a source of problems, but also increasingly as a source of possible solutions.

The unwillingness or inability of governments to develop binding international rules setting standards for TNCs also enhanced the role of NGOs in calling attention to commercial abuse or injustice. For example, the failure of governments to agree the proposed UN Code of Conduct for TNCs and the closure of the United Nations Centre for Transnational Corporations in the early 1990s sent strong negative signals to NGOs about the possibility of achieving an effective international regulatory system for TNCs.

Consequently, many of the new NGO campaigns in the UK in the early 1990s were aimed at getting companies or industries to adopt voluntary codes of conduct, many of them aimed at securing adherence to certain fundamental labour standards. The strategy was to galvanize consumer power to persuade industry to accept responsibility for improving labour practices, within each corporate group and through their subcontracting and franchising chains. This was seen by many campaigners as a quicker, more direct, and more effective way of engaging the public and achieving change than by lobbying for governmental or intergovernmental regulation, or through union action alone.

Two of the best-known campaigns internationally have been the consumer campaigns targeting GAP and Nike. However, there has also been a range of other campaigns with varied impact. The Oxfam Clothes Code Campaign, for example, has contributed to the top five UK clothing retailers accepting responsibility for the conditions of workers in supplier factories. They all have developed, or are developing, codes of conduct. Nevertheless, not all of the codes fully meet the standards implied by the core ILO conventions which are advocated by Oxfam and others (discussed by Bob Hepple and Neil Kearney, in this volume).The most common missing element, crucially, is the right to freedom of association and collective bargaining. Moreover, not all the companies have committed themselves to establishing independent monitoring, and it remains to be seen how effective this can be (see further Chapter 11 in this volume, by Kearney).

Long-Term Engagement and Continuous Improvement

A common feature of many of the code-of-conduct campaigns in the early 1990s was that, rather than utilizing the more confrontational tactic of consumer boycotts, an increasing number began to promote a strategy of long-term positive engagement aimed at winning continuous improvement in company practice. The principles underlying the Oxfam Clothes Code Campaign, for example, stated that

> every effort should be made by companies to enter into a strategy of positive engagement with their suppliers, and work with them to reach the standards of this code (as a minimum), rather than take the simpler (but less effective) route of immediately withdrawing their business. However, where a particular supplier is unwilling to make progress towards meeting these standards, particularly where equivalent suppliers do, this should be a major factor in deciding whether a trading relationship should continue.

Although this approach still ultimately relies on the threat of public exposure to secure improved standards, and so was often initially perceived as hostile by the companies concerned, many have gradually realised that the adoption of voluntary codes could offer significant commercial advantages. By promoting a responsible image to consumers, voluntary codes can help companies maintain or increase sales. They may also help to prevent media exposés, and increase competitiveness by improving staff morale, commitment and productivity. Indeed, company surveys have shown that one of the main motivations for companies to adopt voluntary codes is the need to maintain and attract staff, many of whom do not want to be associated with a company engaging in unethical behaviour.

One of the reasons that NGOs stressed the need for a strategy of positive engagement and continuous improvement was because of their concern about the potentially high human costs of consumer boycotts. Although boycotts may help raise labour standards in the longer term, in the short term they may impose unacceptably high social costs by throwing workers out of jobs, especially in labour-intensive industries. Charitable or development-oriented NGOs, in particular, with their mandate of poverty alleviation, were unable or unwilling to ignore such effects.

A positive example of the strategy of positive engagement is the GAP campaign (discussed in Chapter 11). When the company was initially charged by campaigners with sourcing from El Salvador-based suppliers engaged in abusive labour practices they threatened to pull out. However, when campaigners argued that this was unacceptable and threatened further negative publicity, GAP agreed to stay and force its contractors to comply with its code.

Unfortunately, whatever their codes may say, immediately cutting links with contractors will continue to offer one of the quickest and most expedient ways for companies to reduce unwelcome media attention when abuses are revealed. Preventing this requires effective systems of independent monitoring. It also requires good reactive networking by NGOs, and by unions. This has been greatly facilitated by the increasing use of the Internet which means that company abuses can be very quickly publicized, and world-wide campaigns more easily coordinated.

The Treatment of Child Labour

One frequently cited example of the power and potentially damaging effects of trade boycotts was the effect of the proposed US Harkin Bill. In 1993, in response to consumer and public concerns, US Senator Tom Harkin tabled a Bill proposing the prohibition of imports into the US of any products made with child labour. In Bangladesh the immediate effect was dramatic: as many as 40 000 children were promptly thrown out of factories and many more have been forced to leave since. Studies by UNICEF and others indicate that many of them were forced to find work in more dangerous occupations under even harsher conditions: breaking bricks all day in the glaring sun, for example, or prostitution (Oxfam, 1996).

This example illustrates the potentially blunt and negative effects of consumer or trade boycotts when trying to deal with complex issues such as child labour. Many forms of child labour are a consequence of general poverty, rather than merely competitive pressures or exploitation by companies. Indeed the majority of child labour is found in family businesses and farms, rather than the export sector. Moreover, the inadequacy of many education systems means that one cannot assume that children will automatically go to school if banned from working. The international community is seeking to address this problem by developing a new ILO Convention which distinguishes more clearly between the most exploitative and abusive forms of child labour which should be immediately banned, and other forms which should be progressively eliminated. But because of its link with poverty, it is vital that any attempt to eliminate child labour must be complemented by broad measures aimed at alleviating poverty and improving education.

In contrast to the potentially damaging effects of boycotts, continuous improvement through voluntary codes can allow a more discriminating approach to child labour to be adopted. While many codes specify that companies and suppliers should immediately stop employing any child labour which is hazardous or harmful, or involves children below a certain age limit, some NGOs suggest a more flexible approach to other forms of child labour. For example, some NGO-promoted codes state that part-time work for older children may be allowed if it does not occur during school time and does not exceed a certain number of hours per day. In both cases many codes specify that companies and suppliers should implement a transitional strategy aimed at phasing out undesirable child labour, including the provision of necessary economic assistance to enable them to attend quality schooling.

An example of this approach is the joint programme implemented in Sialkot, Pakistan, by the ILO, UNICEF, Sialkot Chamber of Commerce and Industry (SCCI), Save the Children-UK and local NGOs, which aims to eliminate child labour in the manufacture of footballs. The project not only entails an external monitoring system to identify and phase out child labour in the football industry but also has a wide range of activities to provide alternatives to the working children and their families affected by the programme. These include the establishment of Village Education and Action Centres which provide rehabilitation services, including non-formal education, skills training, income-generation activities for adults in the family, credit/loan/savings facilities and raising of awareness. Half of the local manufacturers (70 per cent of the production) have joined the project, and over 2000 children are now registered in the rehabilitation centres.

Despite such examples, it is worth pointing out that little is yet known about the development impact of voluntary codes of conduct. While the clear expectation is that codes will improve standards and therefore workers' welfare, there may be some unintended negative consequences for workers and the wider community. Some NGOs and unions fear that companies will not be prepared to pay a higher price for goods supplied under ethical conditions, so causing many small suppliers to go out of business. Some companies predict that the introduction of codes will result in a restructuring of production to larger firms, away from small sweatshops or home based units. The need to ensure effective monitoring of child labour in the Sialkot project, for example, has meant that the stitchers have been regrouped away from their homes into special centres. This may result in a substitution of male for female workers and could possibly reduce overall employment. Others argue that voluntary codes will just force the bad practices further underground. Certainly, the employment effects of implementing core ILO standards are still imperfectly understood. Independent research is urgently needed to assess the wider development and social impact of voluntary codes.

Alliance Building

Another feature of the new generation of voluntary corporate campaigns is that they are encouraging alliances between development NGOs, trade unions, human rights organizations, fair trade and consumer groups. Although there have been conflicts over some issues, this ultimately means that the different groups have to learn from each other's experiences, thereby hopefully helping to guarantee the relevance of the standards finally proposed.

NGOs have for example brought a more developmentally sensitive approach to the treatment of child labour. At the same time, the greater experience of trade unions has proved essential in helping NGOs clarify campaign analysis and strategy. For example, unions have played an essential role in helping ensure that companies do not use voluntary codes as a substitute for collective bargaining at the national or international level, and that NGOs do not let themselves become substitutes for trade unions (as stressed by Neil Kearney, in Chapter 11 of this volume). The ICFTU has therefore consistently stressed that the primary role of such codes should be to foster the conditions under which collective bargaining can occur.

Developing a Common Approach

Another feature of some of the recent code of conduct campaigns is the willingness of some NGOs and trade unions to engage with companies in helping develop common approaches to the content and enforcement of labour standards in codes of conduct. In so doing, difficult decisions and policy trade-offs concerning the desired content and monitoring of labour codes have to be debated and decided directly between these groups rather than by policy makers in distant government or intergovernmental fora. As Petrina Fridd and Jessica Sainsbury point out in Chapter 12, this may help increase compliance in the long run.

The decision by NGOs to work with companies in order to develop a common approach is, for example, an important element of the UK-based Ethical Trading Initiative (ETI). The ETI is an attempt to coordinate the efforts of a group of around 15 major UK-based retailers, as part of which many of the UK development and human rights agencies are promoting voluntary codes of conduct, along with relevant national and international unions. The idea of the initiative is to develop a common approach to codes of conduct, and establish independent monitoring based on pilot projects between companies, workers and NGOs, which can then be applied more widely. The initiative is backed and funded by the UK government's Department for International Development, which is keen to promote ethical trading and to engage the business sector in helping eradicate poverty overseas.

Another practical example of how the new campaigns can help develop consensus and a common approach between the different parties is illustrated by Oxfam's Clothes Code Campaign in the Dominican Republic. Although both the constitution and the labour code in the Dominican Republic enshrine the right to freedom of association and collective bargaining, in practice companies in the free trade zones have resorted to a variety of tactics to deter unionization, including temporary recruitment, black-listing, intimidation, and the promotion of solidarity associations as substitutes for trade unions. According to a local NGO, CIPAF (Research Centre for Feminist Action), this problem was traditionally tackled in a confrontational manner, with workers organizations denouncing company violations, and employers disputing the allegations and threatening to move their operations to other countries. The effect was to prevent the government from taking any action due to the fear of losing much-needed jobs to other countries.

CIPAF and the local Oxfam office launched an international campaign in August 1996 under the slogan 'Work Yes, but with Dignity' aimed at fostering awareness of the poor working and living conditions of female workers in the free trade zones, and sensitizing the public and business to the need to adopt codes of conduct to improve labour practices. The international exposure resulting from the campaign prompted the executive director of the Dominican Association of Free Trade Zones (ADOZONA) Employers' Association to announce the willingness of the member companies to develop strategies for improving labour practices by adopting codes of conduct. This has opened the door for workers, NGOs, companies and subcontractors in the Dominican Republic to work together to produce a joint definition of the content of codes of conduct. Hopefully, it will also help them develop a coherent and consistent approach which takes into account local priorities as well as universal standards, rather than having a plethora of different codes foisted on them by Northern companies. If this is achieved it could help the Dominican Republic attract better-quality investors with a commitment to ethical practices and a long-term interest in the country.

From the NGO perspective, the international publicity generated by the campaign has provided them with an important tool to increase pressure for workers' rights, in line with national legislation, in particular allowing them to insist that unless the company codes include core ILO conventions, especially those requiring Freedom of Association and Right to Collective Bargaining, they will cut no ice abroad.

However, the common approach is not without its potential pitfalls and indeed still has its opponents within the NGO movement, who perceive a danger that NGOs may risk being co-opted in the process, thereby losing their freedom to expose and campaign against company malpractice, and ultimately resulting in weaker standards and enforcement systems. The NGOs participating in the ETI have sought to institute clear guidelines which guarantee their freedom to campaign publicly against any of the participating companies if necessary. However, the effects of the consensual approach may be more insidious, limiting NGO willingness, rather than their ability, to campaign publicly.

THE LIMITS OF VOLUNTARY CODES OF CONDUCT

While the examples above suggest that voluntary corporate or industry-wide codes of conduct can offer a valuable means of helping improve company practice, they also have their limits. Perhaps the most important point to bear in mind is that governments have the basic responsibility for promoting and protecting human rights and the rule of law. However imperfectly they perform this role in practice, most of them are at least formally accountable to their citizens and as such are the body best suited in each country to mediate between the different interest groups in society when setting and enforcing standards.

In contrast, companies are primarily accountable to their own shareholders. Hence, while there should be a clear expectation on companies to comply with the human rights standards specified in international conventions and national law, care should be taken to prevent the undue transfer of responsibility from governments to companies in the setting and monitoring of standards, and an over-reliance on self regulation. Not only may this result in an unbalanced approach, it may also allow governments to renege on their responsibilities to set and enforce labour standards, and allow companies to fend off demands for binding regulation at the national and international level.

Moreover, tipping the responsibility for setting and monitoring of standards too far in favour of market-based mechanisms will tend to promote undemocratic outcomes. The fact that companies adopt voluntary codes of conduct is in part due to the threat or actual use of consumer action. As the ILO has pointed out (ILO, 1997) this involves an arbitrary approach which singles out certain companies, mainly those with a brand name to promote in international markets. It also lets other companies free-ride, thereby undermining the efforts of 'ethical' employers, and has led some TNCs to argue in favour of an internationally agreed base-set of core workers' rights which would be binding on all international firms (or firms over a certain size). The voluntary approach also means that improved standards may be restricted to workers operating in, or connected through subcontracting relations to, the export sector. Government regulation, in contrast, would also cover domestic and informal sector workers (unless specifically exempted). Voluntary codes also tend to reflect existing inequalities of market power in which Northern consumers have far greater sway over production decisions than Southern consumers.

Moreover, the power of consumers to influence production decisions should not be overstated. Although the power of national governments over international investors may have decreased in recent years, new powers have been given to intergovernmental bodies, especially the World Trade Organization (WTO), which increasingly circumscribe consumers' influence over production decisions. WTO principles, for example, would prevent countries discriminating between timber imports on the basis of the environmental sustainability of their production methods. The WTO also recently accepted US objections to the EU ban on beef produced with growth-hormone implants. Voluntary codes of conduct and fair-trade labelling could be considered illegal under WTO rules if applied to government purchases, or if they are trade-diverting. These cases suggest that effective social and environmental protection will increasingly depend on reforming the rules set by these intergovernmental bodies, rather than individual company action alone.

Another concern already touched on is that the new forms of private independent monitoring may duplicate and weaken existing governmental and intergovernmental supervisory mechanisms. To date, there has been little formal comparison of the labour standards contained in voluntary codes with those contained in the legislation of the countries in which companies are operating or purchasing from subcontractors. Although most trade unions and NGOs insist that voluntary codes should contain as a minimum the seven core ILO conventions, surveys suggest that in practice, owing to hostility to trade unions, many companies refuse to incorporate standards on freedom of association or collective bargaining in their codes (International Centre for Human Rights and Democratic Development, 1997). This may actually mean that the content of voluntary codes is weaker than government legislation in some cases. In addition, both the legal obligations of companies signing up to codes of conduct, and how these relate to obligations under national legislation, are often unclear.

Moreover, although government enforcement mechanisms are notoriously weak in some countries, there is so far little evidence to suggest that commercial companies, or specialist units of NGOs or trade unions, will be able to carry out monitoring more effectively than governments (Forcese, 1997). This is not surprising when one takes into account the scale of the task. One US company sources from some 13 000 different suppliers, each of which uses an average of five subcontractors, making a total of 65 000 suppliers. It may well be that companies and NGOs alike eventually realize that working to improve existing government enforcement mechanisms, in partnership with other actors, is a more effective and financially viable strategy than promoting new forms of independent monitoring.

Another sensible strategy would be to press the ILO, which is the international body responsible for setting and monitoring labour standards, to engage more directly in the administration of independent monitoring systems, or at least to take on responsibility for standard setting, training and certification for any new bodies set up to carry out this role. Such forms of involvement would not be without precedent. In both the Bangladeshi garment industry and the football industry in Sialkot in Pakistan, the ILO has been involved in arranging the services of a professionally trained inspectorate in response to reports of abuses of child labour. However, the direct involvement of the ILO in monitoring codes of conduct is highly sensitive politically as governments of many developing countries still perceive them as protectionist devices. An alternative but complementary way of increasing the ILO's role may be by upgrading the content and monitoring mechanisms of the ILO Tripartite Declaration on Multinational Enterprises and Social Policy (1977).

THE CASE FOR INTERGOVERNMENTAL REGULATION

This analysis suggests that, with or without voluntary codes, there is still a strong case for developing binding intergovernmental regulation to protect workers and promote important development goals. This need was forcibly brought home to NGOs and campaigners with the advent of the proposed OECD Multilateral Agreement on Investment (MAI) on the international policy agenda. As pointed out by other contributors to this book, if implemented this agreement would prioritize the reduction of government controls on, and granting of rights to, international investors, without matching such measures with strengthened national or international standards for workers, communities, consumers or the environment, nor would investors' rights be made conditional on their acceptance of responsibilities in these areas.

The unbalanced nature of the proposed MAI clearly illustrates that the key question is no longer the desirability of the free market as opposed to regulation, (or more specifically about whether voluntary or statutory means are better means of regulating TNCs), but rather the desirable *content* of global economic rules, many of which are already being put into place. This in turn invokes the question of who should decide the rules and in what forum.

National or International Regulation?

Even where policy makers accept the need for stronger labour regulation, it is still hotly debated how far responsibility for this should rest at the national, regional or international level. In the case of labour regulation, because countries are at different levels of development, many aspects of statutory labour regulation should remain at the national level.

However, there is a strengthening international consensus that certain *core* or minimum labour standards representing fundamental workers' rights should be implemented in every country irrespective of their level of development, thus suggesting the need for an international approach (see Bob Hepple in Chapter 10 for discussion of core labour standards). Moreover, in an increasingly global economy, in which companies can relocate operations freely between countries, there are also social and legal arguments why national regulation needs to operate within an international framework. The social case for the international regulation of labour standards was identified in the preamble to the ILO Constitution written as long ago as 1919, which states that 'the failure of any nation to adopt humane conditions of labour is an obstacle in the way of other nations which desire to improve the conditions in their own countries'. From a legal perspective, each branch or subsidiary of a TNC is primarily subject to the laws of the country or region in which it is established, with no single authority able to exercise control over the whole network and its global operations, which leaves a democratic deficit in the governance of TNCs (see Chapter 7).

There appear to be three main approaches to developing multilaterally agreed intergovernmental regulation of minimum labour standards:

1. Non-binding aspirational guidelines or declarations may be adopted by governments in international fora, such as the ILO's Tripartite Declaration of Principles Concerning Multinational Enterprises and Social Policy, or the OECD Guidelines for Multinational Enterprises.
2. International conventions may be agreed which have the force of international law, such as ILO conventions (which essentially means that once ratified, countries are bound to implement them into national legislation), although there are no international sanctions to enforce these beyond the use of moral persuasion and public shaming.
3. Linkages may be established between intergovernmental multilateral trade and investment agreements, and compliance with certain minimum or core labour standards. Such linkages could involve a sanctions based approach involving the threat of the loss of certain benefits (not necessarily market access) to governments or companies which stem from membership of trade or investment agreements for failure to comply with core standards, or alternatively the use of trade preferences or aid as an incentive to improve compliance (Mayne and LeQuesne, 1998; Picciotto, 1998). They could operate at the regional or international level.

In addition, some NGOs have recently proposed the establishment of a new international Commission which could monitor TNC compliance with key international human rights conventions and other standards.

Intergovernmental Regulation: the Case for Positive Linkages

The first two approaches are discussed in Chapter 1, and the proposal for a Commission merits further debate. This section will focus on the third approach, which proposes establishing positive linkages between trade and investment agreements and labour regulation. Not surprisingly, this approach has faced significant governmental opposition partly because of legitimate fears about the possible negative economic and social effects of trade- or investment-based enforcement mechanisms. For this reason great care is required in designing such mechanisms (Oxfam, 1996; Mayne and LeQuesne, 1998).

Opponents also argue that this approach to international regulation is illegitimate because there is no discernible link between international trade and investment flows on the one hand, and employment opportunities and working conditions on the other. This is a less convincing argument. The determinants of employment and wage levels are indeed hotly contested, in particular the relative importance of national versus international factors. Nevertheless, while there is broad consensus that national factors are still more important than international factors in explaining national employment patterns, there is growing evidence that international trade and foreign direct investment *are* contributing to the increase of income inequality in both richer and poorer countries alike. For example, a recent report by UNCTAD has argued that in almost all developing countries which have undertaken rapid trade liberalization, wage inequality has increased, most often in the context of declining industrial employment of unskilled workers and large absolute falls in their real wages (UNCTAD, 1997). Wood argues that trade with developing countries reduced the demand for unskilled labour in developed countries by 20 per cent in the 30 years to 1990, with three quarters of this decline taking place in the 1980s. This claim is disputed by most trade optimists, but is actually supported by standard trade theory which predicts that free trade will lead to a widening gap between skilled and unskilled workers in developed countries (Wood, 1995).

The opponents of the link between trade and labour standards also reject the notion that free trade and capital flows will result in a relocation of capital to countries with the lowest wage costs thereby provoking a 'race to the bottom'. As Bob Hepple argues in Chapter 10, because productivity is much higher in richer countries, unit labour costs vary much less than nominal wage costs would suggest, thereby limiting the incentive for capital to transfer to cheap-labour sites. As mentioned above, this view is supported by evidence from the OECD which shows that low labour standards do not generate long-term competitive advantage (OECD, 1996). This ultimately relies on increasing productivity through investment in technology, skills and education. It is also true that wage costs are only one factor among others which affect companies' relocation decisions. Moreover, the extent to which they do so in order to avoid rising labour costs will be restricted by considerations such as the value of their fixed investments and their need to maintain market share in the country concerned.

Yet despite these considerations, some companies still can and do seek to achieve short-term competitive advantage by directly cutting labour costs. This can be achieved by relocation or subcontracting to cheap-labour sites, or by using the threat of relocation to restrict wage claims. Small and less scrupulous firms, especially those working in labour-intensive industries, are often attracted to economies with weak labour and environmental standards. However, even large multinationals take advantage of cheap-labour sites by sourcing from domestic subcontractors (Fitzgerald, 1998).

Additionally, it is important to note that the increasing ease with which companies can move technology across borders threatens to break irrevocably the traditional link between high productivity, high technology and high wages. As a result, it is now possible for large transnational companies to combine high productivity, high technology and *low* wages, thereby maintaining their incentive to move to cheap-labour sites (*Harvard Business Review*, 1993). For example, Mexico's productivity per worker has risen from one fifth to one third of the level in the USA between 1989 and 1993, in part as a consequence of increased foreign investment geared towards production for the US market. Meanwhile, the average wage gap has narrowed far more slowly, with the Mexican wage still at only one sixth of the US level (the *Economist*, 1994). For example, Ford's plant at Hermosillo in Mexico which, unlike its other Mexican plants, uses the latest technologies and production methods, has productivity levels comparable with the most modern US plants, with markedly lower wage costs (Carrillo, 1995).

Another indication of a race to the bottom is the growing number of governments which have sought to meet the challenge of intensified global competition by restricting workers' rights and promoting cheap-labour strategies, despite evidence that in the longer term this is economically inefficient and self-defeating. This can be seen in the growth of free trade zones, the legalization of flexible working practices in the formal sector and government measures to deregulate labour markets. These moves have been fostered by policy advice from institutions such as the IMF, which still advocates labour market deregulation as a means of achieving competitiveness, without specifying the need to protect basic workers' rights.

Political Feasibility

Given the continued resistance to stronger labour regulation by many governments and companies, it will take time and energetic efforts to convince policy makers of the need to include binding regulations in multilateral trade or investment agreements. On the other hand, recent developments may begin to convince policy makers of the need for new forms of social and environmental regulation at the international level. If untreated, the widespread unemployment and underemployment, erosion of rights and growing inequality associated with globalization may well contribute to the growing instability in global markets. This possibility has been exacerbated by the high and spreading social costs of the East Asian financial crisis, which was in part due to under-regulated international financial markets. Moreover, the strong and growing public opposition to the MAI has sent a strong message to policy makers that they need to rethink the closed and untransparent character of international trade and investment negotiations.

CONCLUSION

NGOs and trade unions need to improve their understanding of the role of, and relationship between, voluntary corporate codes of conduct and governmental regulation and ensure that this is reflected in their campaign strategies. In particular, they need to rebuild public campaigns aimed at developing multilaterally agreed intergovernmental regulation to oblige governments and international firms to adhere to certain minimum or core labour standards. Such campaigns could build on the growing consensus generated by the voluntary code of conduct campaigns about the need to regulate business practices. They could also enlist the support of those companies already implementing their own codes, and where necessary galvanize consumer pressure to help pressurize other less compliant firms.

REFERENCES

Bilmes, Linda, Wetzker, Konrad and Xhonneux, Pascal (1995) 'Value in Human Resources', *Financial Times*, 10 February.

Carrillo, J. (1995) 'Flexible Production in the Auto Sector: Industrial Reorganization at Ford-Mexico' *World Development*, vol. 23, 87–101.

Chetley, Andrew (1986) *The Politics of Baby Foods. Successful Challenges to an International Marketing Strategy*. Pinter, London.

De Haan, Arjan (1997) 'Urban Poverty and its Alleviation', *IDS Bulletin*, vol. 28(2), 1–8.

ECLA (Economic Commission for Latin America) (1997) *Reports to First Regional Conference in Follow-up to the World Summit for Social Development*, April.

The *Economist* (1994) *War of the Worlds: a Survey of the Global Economy*, 1 October.

Fitzgerald, E. V. K. (1998) *The Development Implications of the Multilateral Agreement on Investments*. Study commissioned by the Department for International Development, London.

Forcese, Craig (1997) *Human Rights and Corporate Codes of Conduct, Commerce with Conscience*. International Centre for Human Rights and Democratic Development, Montreal.

IBFAN (International Babyfood Action Network) (1997) *Breaking the Rules.* Available from www.gn.apc.org/ibfan.

ICFTU (International Confederation of Free Trade Unions) (1995) *Annual Survey of Violations of Trade Union Rights.* ICFTU, Geneva.

International Centre for Trade Union Rights (1997) *Nike Code of Conduct,* vol. 4, Issue 4.

ILO (International Labour Office) (1995) *World Employment Report.* ILO, Geneva.

ILO (1996) *World Employment Report.* ILO, Geneva.

ILO (1998) *World Employment Report.* ILO, Geneva.

Mayne, Ruth and LeQuesne, Caroline (forthcoming) 'Calls for a Social Trade', in Caroline Thomas and Anni Taylor (eds.) *Global Trade and Global Social Issues.* Routledge, London.

Oxfam (1996) *Reforming World Trade: the Social and Environmental Priorities,* by Caroline LeQuesne, Oxfam Insight. Oxfam-GB, Oxford.

OECD (1994) *OECD Jobs Study. Facts Analysis, Strategy.* OECD, Paris.

OECD (1996) *Trade, Employment and Labour Standards: a Study of Core Workers' Rights and International Trade.* OECD, Paris.

Patterson, Malcolm and West, Michael (1998) 'People Power: the Link Between Job Satisfaction and Productivity', *Centre Piece* (Centre for Economic Performance), vol. 3, 2–5.

Szreter, Simon (1999) 'A New Political Economy for New Labour. The Importance of Social Capital', *Renewal* vol. 7(1), 30–43.

UNCTAD (1997) *Trade and Development Report, Globalization, Distribution and Growth.* United Nations, Geneva.

Wood, Adrian (1995) 'How Trade Hurts Unskilled Workers', *Journal of Economic Perspectives* vol. 9, 57–80.

World Bank (1994) *Labour Markets in an Era of Adjustment.* Eds. S. Horton, R. Kanbur and D. Mazumdar, Development Studies. Economic Development Institute of the World Bank, Washington DC.

World Bank (1995) *World Development Report, Workers in an Integrating World.* Oxford University Press, Oxford.

Part IV
The Politics of Accountability

14 NGOs, Global Civil Society and Global Economic Regulation
Robert O'Brien

In a period of less than a year three events dramatically highlighted the necessity for change in both the form and content of global governance. The three events were the Asian financial crisis of 1997–98, the failure of President Clinton's attempt to secure fast-track negotiating authority from the US Congress in November 1997, and the postponement of the negotiations for the proposed OECD Multilateral Agreement on Investment (MAI) in April 1998. Each of these events illustrate the need for international regulation to be rooted in the democratic consent of national societies and the degree to which such regulation is likely to fail if it lacks a social element.

The East Asian financial crisis, which began in July 1997, swept through much of Asia and threatened other countries, demonstrated the dangers of unregulated financial flows on economies that had previously seemed dynamic and healthy (RIPE, 1998). Reinforcing the lessons of the Mexican crisis of 1994 it raised serious doubts about the benefits of short-term capital movements for developing countries. Moreover, the stability of the international financial system has once again been called into question by the mounting costs of 'casino capitalism' (Strange, 1989). This offers an opportunity for interested parties to question the content of global governance. Has the case for neo-liberal deregulation been fatally wounded?

Equally importantly, the form of governance is under scrutiny. The fallacy that agreements can be reached between states or between international organizations and states without reference to domestic societies has been exposed. Certainly, institutions such as the International Monetary Fund (IMF) and the World Bank have recently been in search of social partners to assist in the design and implementation of structural adjustment policies and loans. The contrasting fate of the Korean and Indonesian governments in the wake of financial crisis illustrates the importance of a vibrant domestic civil society for successful international economic regulation.

The failure of President Clinton to secure Congressional approval of fast-track authority in 1997 reveals the degree to which domestic opinion in the most influential of states is increasingly wary of international economic regulation. Fast-track is a mechanism which allows the President to negotiate international economic agreements and put them to Congress for approval or rejection as a single package (Destler, 1992: 71–6). In the absence of fast-track any amendments by Congress could transform the agreement beyond the consent of other parties to it. In practical terms fast-track authority is needed to secure legislative consent to trade agreements, although there is some debate as to whether it is necessary for, or could cover, other economic agreements such as the MAI. The rejection of fast-track highlighted domestic discontent with a series of international economic regulation measures such as the North American Free Trade Agreement (NAFTA), the World Trade Organization (WTO) and funding for the IMF. This opposition comes both from the far right, which is opposed to internationalism, and from the left, which is seeking greater social regulation (Rupert, 1995). The lesson for the architects of international regulation is that severe doubts exist about the wisdom of present policies even at the heart of the economic system. In some cases these doubts can be backed by sufficient political power to frustrate extension of neo-liberal regulation.

The MAI postponement was also seen by participants in the negotiations and observers of the process as having an important symbolic significance and as demonstrating the mobilization capabilities exercised by the NGO community. Through imaginative use of the Internet and other new information technology, NGOs have been able to bring the MAI to the attention of large numbers of people and politicize the negotiating process. The derailment of the MAI negotiations was seen as an indication that NGOs are now, officially, a force to be reckoned with (de Jonquières, 1998; Strom, 1998).

This chapter does not examine the MAI negotiations, but aims to step back from particular NGO campaigns and offer some thoughts on the relationship between NGOs, global civil society and global economic regulation. It draws on a recently completed research project which studied the interaction between three global economic institutions (the IMF, World Bank and the WTO, referred to collectively here as GEIs) and three social movements (involved with the environmental, women and labour).[1] The chapter will argue that NGOs are contributing to a new form of international organization called complex multilateralism. Although this is a time of considerable fluidity with possibilities for transformation in governance structures and rules, NGOs have a series of difficult problems that they also need to address.

The rest of the chapter unfolds in four parts: (a) an overview of the concept of global civil society and the practice of complex multilateralism;

(b) an explanation for why regulators listen to NGOs; (c) an examination of problems within the NGO community; (d) a consideration of the opportunity recent events and activities have offered for a change in governance structures and content.

GLOBAL CIVIL SOCIETY AND COMPLEX MULTILATERALISM

This section of the chapter sets the context of the NGOs' role in global governance by considering the broader social context within which NGOs operate and the ongoing transformation of global governance. Internationally active NGOs are part of a broader global civil society and they are increasingly taking on a role in what has been called 'complex multilateralism'.

Global Civil Society

The modern history of international organization has seen non-state actors play an important but fluctuating role. The early public international unions of the nineteenth century often relied upon interest groups within domestic civil society, such as labour unions in the case of the International Labour Office, for their creation and maintenance (Murphy, 1994: 72–3). NGOs of many varieties were particularly active in the creation of the League of Nations system after the First World War and the United Nations after the Second World War. However, initial activity was followed by a period of disengagement from 1935–44 and underachievement from 1950 to 1971 (Charnovitz, 1997). The importance of NGOs to governance has mirrored the degree of openness in the international system. In times of interstate tension, NGOs have lost their significance. In times of system change or creation, NGOs and other civil society actors have had an opportunity to play a significant role.

The term 'global civil society' has been coined relatively recently to capture a third upswing in the activity of non-state actors operating across borders. Traditionally, the field of international relations has focused upon the activity of states (Banks, 1988). In the 1970s there was an attempt to broaden the study of international relations beyond state activity. One trend was to characterize the international system as one of interdependence rather than, or in addition to, anarchy (Keohane and Nye, 1977). Within this interdependent system there were many levels of political and economic activity. Interstate relations were the most important arena, but they were increasingly challenged by other actors. NGOs, multinational enterprises, charitable foundations, religious organizations and labour unions were thought to play a role in the system (Keohane and Nye, 1972). In its more enthusiastic versions analysts dropped the notion of a state system of international relations in favour of a world society (Burton, 1972).

Although interdependence research was neglected with the renewal of the Cold War of the early 1980s, the 1990s has seen a resurgent interest in examining non-state actors (Peterson, 1992). In an edited volume dedicated to reopening this line of investigation Risse-Kappen (1995: 280) concluded that 'we cannot explain state behaviour in crucial issue-areas without taking cross-boundary activities of non-state actors into account.' This increased transitional activity has lead to a lively debate over the significance of what has variously been called global civil society (Lipschutz, 1992), global society (Shaw, 1994), world civic politics (Wapner, 1995) and transnational advocacy networks (Keck and Sikkink, 1998).

Although there is a temptation to equate global civil society with progressive, non-profit voluntary organizations (Lipschutz, 1992), this is a mistake. Firstly many actors in the public space between and across states are not very civil. They may actively use violence to accomplish their aims or offer violence to those who can pay for it. In the former category we may put the activity of transnational criminal organizations or terror groups (Strange, 1996). In the latter we may put the activity of an increasing number of individuals and groups offering security services.

The second reason for taking a less utopian view of global civil society is the presence and activity of neo-liberal forces in global civil society. Sklair's (1997) research into a transnational capitalist class highlights the role of TNC executives, globalizing bureaucrats, globalizing politicians and professionals, and consumerist elites in working to create a global system in their image. Previous studies have also pointed to the ease and effectiveness with which elite networks operate transnationally (Gill, 1990; Van der Pijl, 1984). The significance of this activity is that most of these groups espouse norms that conflict with those of the NGOs studied in this book. In addition, they tend to have far better access to key decision makers and members of the media.

A third reason for caution is the unevenness of global civil society. In many states the ability of citizens to participate in public debate protected by the rule of law remains restricted. The state can act to suppress civil society and remove certain voices from the global discussion. In other cases, people may wish to participate in debate, but do not have the resources to do so. Concerned civil society groups may not have access to information technology or media outlets to advance their views.

The combination of state repression and unequal resources may result in a skewed debate in the realm of global civil society.

NGOs are one aspect of a broader global civil society. While they increasingly have the means and incentive to operate transnationally, NGOs are not moving into an empty space. Transnational commercial interests and chauvinistic organizations also operate in the space beyond and between states. Thus, it is more useful to think of global civil society as an arena for conflict than as a progressive force in world politics.

Complex Multilateralism

'Complex multilateralism' is a term developed to capture today's form of global governance (O'Brien *et al.*, 1998). It refers to a cooperative form of international organization that falls between state-based and society-based models. Traditionally, scholars of international relations have viewed multilateralism as 'an institutional form that coordinates relations among three or more states on the basis of generalized principles of conduct' (Ruggie, 1993: 11). This state-based view of international organization has recently been challenged by proponents of a 'new multilateralism' which stress the needs and desires of social groups. The 'new' or emerging multilateralism is an attempt to 'reconstitute civil societies and political authorities on a global scale, building a system of global governance from the bottom up' (Cox, 1997: xxvii). This includes the work of NGOs and broader-based social movements. The new multilateralism offers a challenge to existing multilateralism not just because it entails institutional transformation, but because it represents a different set of interests.

Our study of GEIs and social movements suggests that we are witness to a transformation of the state-based multilateralism into one that increasingly includes social groups, but stops far short of a 'new' multilateralism (O'Brien *et al.*, 1998). The mobilization of various elements of civil society in response to increasing globalization has complicated multilateral governance by bringing new actors into the field. Multilateralism is more complicated because international organizations must take some account of a range of civil society actors. Securing the agreement of government officials is not enough to permit the smooth running of these organizations. Constituencies within and across states must be appeased or, at the very least, their opposition must be diluted and diverted. The form of multilateralism is changing by providing points of access for social actors.

Four characteristics of complex multilateralism have been identified. The first characteristic is varied institutional modification in response to civil society actors. While institutions are modifying their behaviour and structure this varies depending upon institutional culture, structure, the role of the executive head and vulnerability to civil society pressure. A second characteristic of this institutional form of international relations is that the major participants are divided by conflicting motivations and goals. The goal of the institutions and their supporters is to maintain existing policy direction and facilitate its smoother operation. The aim is to improve the implementation of policies and management of the institutions. In contrast, the goal of many civil society actors, and certainly social movements, is to change the policy direction of the institutions.

The clash of rival goals leads to a third characteristic, which is the ambiguous results of this form of organization to date. If accomplishments are defined in terms of the actors achieving their own goals, both institutions and social movements have enjoyed only limited success. Social movements have found that the institutions' generalized principles of conduct are subject to debate, but relatively immune from revision. The institutions have enjoyed slightly more success by being able to bring elements of social movements into a dialogue and institutionalizing some of their concerns, thereby reducing the level of antagonism directed at the institutions.

A fourth characteristic of complex multilateralism is its differential impact upon the role of the state depending upon the state's pre-existing position in the international system. In general, an increase in GEI-civil society activity undermines the state's claim to be the sole legitimate representative of the public interest within its territory. However, in the case of more powerful states, such as the United States, civil society activity has reinforced the importance of their domestic political process for global governance. For many developing countries the activity of civil society groups which are either Northern-based or seen as funded and inspired from the North challenges national governments as representatives of the interests of their populations and undermines their state.

The relevance of complex multilateralism for this book is that the campaigns and issues discussed in previous chapters are part of a larger transformation in the process of global governance. It is not just the MAI or company codes of conduct that are up for discussion, but the process of governance itself. NGOs and other social actors have a role to play in influencing this modified framework.

WHY DO REGULATORS LISTEN?

This section addresses the question of why international regulators creating or implementing policy would bother to listen to NGOs. Many of the most powerful international organizations (such as IMF, World Bank, WTO and UN Security Council) are responsible only to their member states. The shift to actively consulting elements of civil society is a major reformist step which sometimes goes against the intention of the founding principles of these organizations and the wishes of some of their members. The two leading explanations for this phenomenon are the expertise and power of NGOs.

Expertise

The first possibility is that regulators will listen to NGOs because they have expertise that the institutions do not have, but which would help with the implementation of their tasks. The World Bank's relationship with women's organizations is a good example. In the 1970s gender advocates pointed out to Bank officials that development policies were going wrong because they were gender-blind. This corresponded with a Bank review of failed policies and a desire to improve efficiency. Gradually, the Bank has taken steps to integrate gender concerns into its programmes in order to improve their success rates. For example, the Bank has increased the percentage of projects which have an explicitly gendered dimension and it has established institutional mechanisms such as the External Gender Consultative Group.

Crucially, gender expertise is brought into the Bank's work to the extent that it bolsters the 'business case for gender equity' (Goetz, 1998). Concerns about gender equality will be considered if it can be shown that to do so increases the financial viability of Bank projects or loans. Thus the rush to embrace micro-credit for women rests not on a concern with equality, but on its financial efficiency.

In the trade field, it is possible that the WTO will listen to NGOs when they have information about a case which falls outside the bounds of trade policy analysts. This is particularly true in the case of environmental issues where a specific NGO may have information about the environmental impacts of particular policies. However, NGO participation is at the discretion of the WTO and its members, and civil society groups do not yet have a right to make submissions to dispute-settlement panels, although proposals to this effect have been made.

The IMF is an institution that prides itself upon containing most of the expertise that is needed in the management of international financial stability. It is far less likely to listen to policy advice from outside groups than the World Bank or even the WTO. At the IMF, social groups must develop a particular form of expertise simply to engage in conversation with officials.

Expertise has enabled some NGOs to participate in the process of governance, but this is very limited. The expertise must mirror the immediate needs of the institution. Rather than listening to a broad critique, GEIs tend to pick and choose from the NGO table. Expertise must also be in a form with which the institution is comfortable. For example, the IMF might value an economic analysis of a particular country, but have no interest in a sociological study of the power relationships that might hinder or assist reform in the same country. This restricts the number and type of NGOs which have the opportunity to influence GEIs. However, if NGOs can combine together in a broad campaign, as they did in relation to the MAI, they may be able to have a more substantial impact.

Power

Although power is a term neglected by economists, it plays a significant role in the operation of economic institutions. GEIs are much more likely to modify their policy when confronted by the possibility that social actors may be able to damage their institutions. To paraphrase a point from a union publication, the force of the argument must be matched by the argument of force (Lipow, 1996: 72). This doesn't refer to force in the form of violence, but force in terms of being able to deploy resources so that others' objectives are frustrated and costs are inflicted. There are two arenas where this struggle is conducted. The first is in the funding centres of the developed world and the second is in the project centres of developing countries.

GEIs require the consent of the most powerful states to continue to operate or expand. The need to obtain a domestic political mandate for key decisions or international agreements has provided an important pressure point for NGOs. Agencies which require large amounts of funding such as the IMF and the World Bank are vulnerable to having their money reduced by national legislatures. The WTO must rely upon the support of national parliaments in order to agree to new trade-liberalization measures. A proposed new agreement such as the MAI would require ratification by national parliaments. This vulnerability has led to changes in the operation of GEIs and the possibility that their agendas can be modified. A few examples will illustrate the point.

The IMF established a Public Affairs Division to deal with civil society only in 1989 following street demonstrations during its 1988 meetings in Berlin. It remains sensitive to demands by the US Congress for transparency as a condition for replenishing its funds. As a result, the Fund has taken steps to provide more information about its activities and programmes. In the case of the World Bank and environmentalists, transnational campaigns against large-scale dam building, such as in India's Narmada Valley (Udall, 1995), forced the institution to change its behaviour and procedures. The blocking of projects on the ground combined with pressure in the US Congress and elsewhere on funding has led to the Bank bringing in innovations such as environmental assessments on large projects and the creation of an Inspection Panel to hear local complaints.

The WTO, in contrast to its GATT predecessor, now makes extensive provision for NGOs to attend its biennial meetings. In addition, the WTO Secretariat hosts workshops and has begun a process of consulting with NGOs over key issues. Although limited, this new engagement has much to do with the record of environmental groups causing difficulty for the GATT Uruguay Round agreements and the ability of social groups to derail the possibility of a new trade negotiating round in the year 2000.

The recent financial crisis in East Asia has forced both the World Bank and the IMF to modify their policies towards organized labour. The ability of organized labour potentially to destroy any austerity package in South Korea forced both institutions to consider the social dimensions of their projects, especially their effect on workers. Whereas previously the Bank viewed organized labour as an obstacle to poverty reduction (Deacon *et al.*, 1997: 69–70), the most recent structural adjustment loans to South Korea contain provisions which advise the government to provide social protection for workers (World Bank, 1998: 19–21).

International negotiations for new economic rules, whether they are for investment in the MAI or trade at the WTO, must obtain domestic support if governments are to live up to their agreements. NGOs have become important in this process because they have been able to use their ability to collect information about international negotiations and then mobilize constituencies against proposals. NGOs make negotiators aware of potential objections and then work in a national setting to block the political process of approval. The vulnerability of GEIs to pressure from NGOs and their partial opening to NGO expertise provides some opportunity for influencing policy and regulation. However, it also highlights the differences between NGOs and raises difficult questions about their operation and influence.

TROUBLE IN THE NGO FAMILY

While many people have turned to NGOs to re-establish social regulation in a global world, their activity is also deserving of critical analysis. This section highlights three faultlines in the NGO community. The most pressing problems are those of representatives, North-South relations and divisions between NGOs. These are not problems that can be 'solved', but are structural tensions that need constant attention.

Representativeness

On whose behalf do NGOs speak? The proliferation of NGOs and the limited ability of institutions to engage with them raises questions about who should be heard on which issues. Does a labour union which represents a small number of people in the formal sector in a LDC speak on behalf of 'workers'? Does a two-person university team conducting research on rural development speak on behalf of peasants? Do the professional NGO summit tourists reflect the views of the average people in their countries any more accurately than states reflect the will of the people within their territories?

Although institutions such as the IMF, World Bank and WTO seem to have a great deal of power and influence, their resources are usually stretched to the limit. Budgets and pressed personnel time prevent exhaustive consultation, even if there is the will. In addition, officials are often puzzled by the wide range of groups with conflicting messages that they face in civil society. There are many more NGOs than resources to engage with them. What are the mechanisms for consultation in such circumstances? In some cases there might be a GEI-NGO committee with a rotating membership, in others it is simply left to chance and the power of particular NGOs to make themselves heard above the general din of lobbying.

Some NGOs claim that they have no representative functions at all and should be listened to because they have sound policy advice (NGLS, 1996: 46–7, 64). This position raises a number of problems. For instance how does one determine which policy advisers should be given a platform? It seems likely that those in the most privileged position will make their way into the policy forums. Again, advice that is accepted has repercussions. To what degree do the advisors take into account the impact of their policies on other groups? What responsibility do they have for their actions? How are they held accountable?

There are cases when representativeness becomes important. For example, in the debate over whether core labour standards should be incorporated into the World Trade Organization, development groups often disagreed with organized labour. Labour organizations claimed that their internal organizational structures allowed them to speak on behalf of a considerable number of workers in the north and south. Development groups countered that organized labour neglected the interests of rural and informal workers. However, development NGOs can also have tenuous links to the groups whose interest they claim to advocate. Does a network of intellectuals represent the interest of the informal or peasant population? From a policy maker's perspective whose claims should carry greater weight? This again makes it important for NGOs to try to construct joint positions and actions, which may account for the success of some campaigns, such as the alliances around NAFTA and against the MAI, although divergent perspectives and differing constituencies can make this very difficult.

North-South Inequalities

A central element of many NGOs' legitimacy and justification for being consulted by regulators emerges from their claim to speak on behalf of weak or vulnerable groups in society. This claim covers the powerless, the poor, and future generations. However, one difficulty of operating within a global civil society is that the power relationships that NGOs seek to challenge may be reinforced by their crusading activity. This is particularly the case in relationships between NGOs in the North and the South. There are several elements to the problem.

The Question of Resources

Groups in the North tend to have greater financial resources and are able to pay for the use of the Internet, phone calls, faxes and the distribution of material. Similarly, they are more able to attend conferences and summits where vital issues are being discussed. In this way their voices are more likely to be heard than those in the South. An example of how these resources can generate inequalities is the role being played by the Internet. Amongst those connected to the Net, information moves at a faster pace. Those unconnected are left further behind. Some international institutions claim that they are increasing transparency by posting reports, press releases and studies on the Internet. For NGOs with access this is an improvement. Yet, many people in developing countries require hard, rather than electronic, copies and are left out of the subsequent debate. The appearance of increased transparency is misleading because it is limited to particular groups.

The Question of Location

GEIs are located in Washington and Geneva. Southern NGOs, along with some Southern states, are often unable to maintain a presence in these cities and do not easily come into contact with decision makers. Linked to the question of location is the fact that Northern groups are more likely to have both the expertise and access to pressure points in developed states to influence GEIs. Many are skilled in providing the material that GEIs want and many have access to governments in developed states. US environmentalists have been able to put pressure on GEIs through the funding and trade decisions of the US Congress. These reflect the concerns of *American* environmentalists first and foremost.

Not only is it more difficult for the Southern states to influence the international agenda, but the activity of some Southern NGOs may be limited by authoritarian states. This gives rise to a different set of concerns and interests on the part of civil society actors attempting to work in such conditions. The activity of Northern NGOs may be welcomed, but may also pose a risk to their Southern partners.

Conflicts of Interests

There may be genuine conflict of interests between groups from different parts of the world. The challenge here is to come to some form of accommodation without Northern groups exploiting their structural power. This calls for a degree of self-restraint that is not always found in civil society.

These are not arguments against transnational NGO activities, but they are issues that should be confronted. In order not to reproduce North/South power imbalances concrete steps need to be taken to take account of the views of counterparts in developing countries. For example, on the question of costs, it is possible to take advantage of clearing houses which can act as a point of information for Southern NGOs. Geneva is indeed expensive, but the International Centre for Trade and Sustainable Development has recently been created to facilitate the work of NGOs around the WTO. Some Northern-based NGOs such as Development GAP are designed to empower Southern NGOs and assist in Southern priorities influencing Northern agendas (www.ipc.apc.org/dgap). The issue of accountability and responsibility is increasingly being posed and addressed within the NGO community (Edwards and Hulme, 1995).

Policy Divisions Between NGOs

Our study of GEI-social movement activity found a number of policy divisions within the social movement community. Any broad-based social movement with transnational aspirations will have disagreements amongst its component parts concerning the strategy to be followed in trying to create a better world. Reformers will suggest tinkering with existing institutions in an attempt to temper their excesses, while more critical elements will suggest a vigorous policy of confrontation and the creation of alternative institutions or practices. Some NGOs will seek to influence regulation while others see regulation as an attempt to pre-empt widespread social transformation by locking in *status quo* approaches. Some groups will argue for engaging with the IMF, World Bank or WTO (or the Bank, but not the IMF) while others see such a strategy as becoming co-opted. Some environmentalists favour continuing to work with the WTO to have their concerns integrated into the institution, others have given up and suggest alternative mechanisms. The leadership of the International Confederation of Free Trade Unions is anxious to engage the IMF in moderating structural adjustment policies, whereas many sectoral organizations are more combative. One way to deal with such differences is for organizations which are broadly allied but have different priorities to agree a twin-track approach, some aiming to secure reforms or amendments while others concentrate on outright opposition.

In addition to splits between groups working in the same issue area one can see broader divisions between issue areas. For example, environmentalists and labour groups tend to want to see international organizations which have some enforcement powers whereas many development groups fear that enforcement mechanisms will be abused by wealthier states to the detriment of developing states. This issue is particularly sharp in the discussion of new issue areas at the WTO.

Our study found a repeated tension between organized labour and elements of other social movements. Organized labour tended to be more institutionalized, better resourced and more willing to enter into negotiations with GEIs than the more radical elements of other social movements. Organized labour often had the ear of some decision makers while others were banging on the door to get in. For example, the IMF was interested in talking to labour groups which could exercise some power in civil society, but was not concerned about interacting with women's groups. In turn, many members of NGOs saw organized labour as being too cooperative with GEIs and not sufficiently critical. There is a midway point in the opposition of a conservative labour movement and radical NGOs which is the practice of social unionism (Moody, 1997). Social unionism moves beyond issues of wages to broad social concerns and creates alliances with other sectors of civil society such as women's movements, environmentalists and community groups. Conflicts of interests will still remain between various groups, but it is more of a strategic and cooperative relationship.

CONCLUSION

The ending of the Cold War, the technological advances heralded by globalization, the uncertainty introduced by recent financial crises, and widespread social rebellion have created a unique opportunity for social actors to become involved in the process of global governance. The emergence and expansion of a global civil society which includes non-elite groups offers the possibility for transforming the governance mechanisms left over from an era of superpower confrontation. A system of complex multilateralism is gradually eroding the state-based form of international organization. This provides opportunities for NGOs to influence decisions that have a global impact.

NGOs are making a difference in the content and form of global economic governance. Broad-based campaigns seeking to inject a social element into economic constitutions, such as NAFTA, the WTO and the MAI, are having policy impacts. The environmental and labour side-accords to NAFTA have many faults, but they only exist because of the campaign bringing together environmentalists, church groups, women's groups and organized labour against neo-liberal regulation. The WTO has done little on the environment and less on labour issues, but the fact that they are on the agenda at all is because of NGO campaigns. Finally, NGO activity against the MAI can take some credit for stalling the investment agreement and allowing time for opposition to build within countries and governments. In these cases NGOs have been able to offer some amendments to neo-liberal governance, but are unable to have an alternative project put in place. The explanation for such limited success can partially be found in the nature of global civil society.

Global civil society is not an even development. Those with resources are far more able to take advantage of new methods of communication and interaction. In the division between profit-seeking and non-profit organizations, business holds the upper hand with privileged access to local, national and international decision makers. Within the non-profit sector, Northern reformist groups exercise a disproportionate amount of influence. Influence between issues also varies. Environmentalists have enjoyed more success than those advocating gender equality. In the wake of the Asian financial crisis organized labour is making a concerted effort to insert itself into the operations of key international institutions. Various NGOs compete for influence from funders and with key agencies. Clashes of interests divide the NGO community. These divisions and activities indicate that global civil society is neither a level playing field nor a utopian replacement for the democratic control of national institutions.

It is another arena for action which must be contested in order to achieve desired objectives.

NOTE

1. The project is entitled Global Economic Institutions and Global Social Movements, funded by the Economic and Social Research Council of Great Britain, Grant L120251027. Other members of the research team are Anne Marie Goetz of the Institute for Development Studies, Jan Aart Scholte of the Institute for Social Studies (the Hague) and Marc Williams from the University of Sussex. Thanks go to the editors of this volume for giving me the opportunity to think about these issues in light of the MAI experience.

REFERENCES

Banks, M. (1988) 'The Evolution of International Relations Theory' in Banks, M. (ed.) *Conflict in World Society*. Harvester, Brighton.

Burton, J. (1972) *World Society*. Cambridge University Press, Cambridge.

Charnowitz, S. (1997) 'Two Centuries of Participation: NGOs and International Governance', *Michigan Journal of International Law*, vol. 182, 183–286.

Cox, R. (ed.) (1997) *The New Realism: Perspectives on Multilateralism and World Order*. Macmillan / United Nations University Press, Basingstoke.

De Jonquières, Guy (1998) 'Network Guerrillas', *Financial Times*, 30 March.

Deacon, B., Hulse, M. and Stubbs, P. (1997) *Global Social Policy; International Organizations and the Future of Welfare*. Sage, London.

Destler, I. M. (1992) *American Trade Politics* (2nd ed.). International Institute for Economics, Washington DC.

Edwards, M. and Hulme, D. (1995) *Non-Governmental Organizations – Performance and Accountability: Beyond the Magic Bullet*. Earthscan, London.

Gill, S. (1990) *American Hegemony and the Trilateral Commission*. Cambridge University Press, Cambridge.

Goetz, A. M. (1988) 'The World Bank and Women's Movements' in R. O'Brien *et al. Complex Multilateralism*. Unpublished manuscript, 25–58.

Keck, M. and Sikkink, K. (1998) *Activists Beyond Borders: Advocacy Networks in International Politics*. Cornell University Press, Ithaca.

Keohane, R. and Nye, J. (1977) *Power and Interdependence: World Politics in Transition*. Little, Brown and Company, Boston.

Keohane, R. and Nye, J. (eds) (1972) *Transnational Relations and World Politics*. Harvard University Press, Cambridge, Mass.

Lipow, A. (1996) *Power and Counterpower: the Union Response to Global Capital*. Pluto Press, London.

Lipschutz, R. (1992) 'Reconstructing World Politics: the Emergence of Global Civil Society', *Millennium*, vol. 21, 389–420.

Moody, K. (1997) *Workers in a Lean World: Unions in the International Economy.* Verso, London.

Murphy, C. (1994) *International Organization and Industrial Change: Global Governance since 1850.* Polity Press, Cambridge.

NGLS (1996) 'The United Nations, NGOs and Global Governance', *Development Dossiers.* United Nations Non-Governmental Liaison Service, Geneva.

O'Brien, R., Goetz, A. M., Scholte, J. and Williams, M. (1998) *Complex Multilateralism: the Global Economic Institutions – Global Social Movement Nexus.* Unpublished manuscript.

Peterson, M. (1992) 'Transnational Activity, International Society and World Politics', *Millennium*, vol. 21, 371–89.

RIPE (1998) Special Issue on the Asian Financial Crisis, *Review of International Political Economy*, vol. 5(3) (Autumn).

Risse-Kappen, T. (1995) 'Structures of Governance and Transnational Relations: What Have We Learned?' in T. Risse-Kappen (ed.) *Bringing Transnational Relations Back In.* Cambridge University Press, Cambridge.

Ruggie, J. (1993) 'Multilateralism: the Anatomy of an Institution' in Ruggie, J. (ed.) *Multilateralism Matters: the Theory and Praxis of an Institutional Form.* Columbia University Press, New York.

Rupert, Mark (1995) '(Re) Politicizing the Global Economy: Liberal Common Sense and Ideological Struggle in the US NAFTA Debate.' *Review of International Political Economy*, vol. 2, 658–92.

Shaw, M. (1994) *Global Society and International Relations.* Polity Press, Cambridge.

Sklair, L. (1997) 'Social Movements for Global Capitalism: the Transnational Capitalist Class in Action', *Review of International Political Economy*, vol. 4(3), 514–38.

Strange, S. (1989) *Casino Capitalism.* Basil Blackwell, Oxford.

Strange, S. (1996) 'Organized Crime: the Mafias', in *The Retreat of the State.* Cambridge University Press, Cambridge.

Strom, N. (1998) 'Taking Stock of the NGO Activity on MAI', *ICDA Journal*, vol. 6(1), 60–4.

Udall, L. (1995) 'The International Narmada Campaign: a Case of Sustained Advocacy' in W. Fisher (ed.) *Toward Sustainable Development; Struggling over India's Narmada River.* M. E. Sharpe, New York.

Van der Pijl, Kees (1984) *The Making of an Atlantic Ruling Class.* Verso, London.

Wapner, P. (1995) 'Politics Beyond the State Environmental Activism and World Civic Politics, *World Politics*, vol. 47, 311–40.

World Bank (1998) 'Report and Recommendation of the President of the International Bank for Reconstruction and Development to the Executive Directors on a Proposed Structural Adjustment Loan in an Amount Equivalent to US$2.0 Billion to the Republic of Korea', 19 March.

Index